MASHUP
RELIGION

MASHUP RELIGION

POP MUSIC AND THEOLOGICAL INVENTION

JOHN S. M^CCLURE

BAYLOR UNIVERSITY PRESS

Cover Design by Jeremy Reiss.

Library of Congress Cataloging-in-Publication Data

McClure, John S., 1952–
  Mashup religion : pop music and theological invention / John S.
McClure.
256 p. cm.
  Includes bibliographical references and index.
  ISBN 978-1-60258-357-3 (pbk. : alk. paper)
  1. Popular music--Religious aspects. 2. Religion and culture. I. Title.
  ML3921.8.P67M33 2011
  261.5'78--dc22
                                        2010053038

Printed in the United States of America on acid-free paper with a
minimum of 30% pcw recycled content.

CONTENTS

PREFACE

I feel the need to establish a bit of street cred for what I have to say in this book. Why should you listen to an aging, twenty-four-year-veteran homiletics teacher talk with you about the relationships between popular music and theological invention? How is it that I became engaged with musical technologies and inventive practices such as songwriting, studio multitracking, digital sampling and sequencing, digital audio workstations, turntablism, and the analysis of fan cultures? Perhaps a brief overview of my musical past will be helpful.

I grew up in a musical family in rural East Tennessee, surrounded by bluegrass, blues, spirituals, and gospel music. My mother played piano, and my father played baritone horn and had a lovely singing voice. All five children could sing and harmonize by ear, and we all took up a broad assortment of musical instruments. I focused my energies on trombone, piano, guitar, and bass.

I cut my teeth playing popular music in junior high school garage bands performing the Beatles, Kinks, Byrds, and Motown in the late sixties. During my high school years in Birmingham, Alabama, I played in two very different bands, one modeled after the smooth vocals and acoustic instrumentation of Crosby, Stills, Nash and Young and the other leaving my ears ringing with the blues-inflected music of Cream, Jimi Hendrix, Duane Allman, and Dickey Betts. Just as important for this book, during my high school and early college years I worked off and on as in intern in a recording studio and wrote radio jingles and soundtracks for small films. This involved me in the ins and outs of songwriting for popular audiences, and introduced me to what would become a lifelong interest in technologies of sound recording, editing, mixing, and mastering. For a while I considered a career in studio engineering, an idea that has now become a hobby of home recording. Both songwriting and studio engineering will be important ideas in this book.

During my college years at the University of the South (Sewanee), I earned spending money playing in two bands. In one group I played trombone and guitar. We played the jazz-laced rock of Chicago and Blood, Sweat and Tears. In the other I played keyboard (mostly piano and Hammond organ) and electric guitar, dealing out lyrical, mournful southern rock for those haunted by Vietnam and waiting for their draft numbers to be called. When I graduated from college and went to the University of Glasgow in Scotland, I played in a folk band that toured the folk clubs and blue-collar pubs.

When I entered Fuller Theological Seminary in the mid-seventies, it marked the beginning of many years of seeking ways to integrate popular music with various forms of ministry. When I arrived at seminary, the Jesus Freak movement in California was giving way to the praise and worship movement under the influence of Calvary Chapel and Maranatha Music. I helped start a praise and worship band at Fuller, and wrote and produced a gospel album of my own music. After my middler year, I took an internship at Independent Presbyterian Church in Birmingham, Alabama, working with young adults. We started a summer "Christian Night Club" for young adults in the entertainment district on Morris Avenue.

When I was a doctoral student at Princeton Theological Seminary, the urban cowboy craze was taking hold nationwide, and I played in a country rock band in order to supplement my income. During this time, I continued to use my music to lead worship for special services on campus. I entered parish ministry in Birmingham in 1983, and, much to the consternation of some church members,

I joined a blues band called the Fabulous Torpedoes, playing lead guitar. This became a way to recruit younger members to the church. Several years later I took my first teaching job, at Louisville Presbyterian seminary, and played organ in a blues band on weekends. When our children began to be more time-consuming, I left club playing for a while and started recording artists in a little studio in our home. I initiated an informal recording ministry with young musicians in Louisville, recording many of the popular youth bands around town.

When my son, Ian, became interested in hip-hop, I followed him into the strange land of turntables, samplers, and MIDI sequencers, helping him produce four CDs as a teenager and through his college years. It was through his influence that I was introduced to another concept that is very important to this book: remixing. He would sit for hours crate-digging my old albums, looking for breaks and beats that he could sample, loop, and record behind his raps. I still own some very strange (now vintage) beat machines, lo-fi samplers, and MIDI sequencers from that era.

In the late 1990s, when the so-called emergent conversation began, I joined with a student songwriter and musician at Louisville Presbyterian Seminary, Chip Andrus, to form a band that played in bars, deliberately mixing together secular and sacred music along with spiritual and socially conscious lyrics. Upon graduation, Chip moved into our denomination's Office of Worship, teaching worship and music ministry across the Presbyterian Church (U.S.A.). By the time this group disbanded and Chip took a church in Arkansas, this band had mobilized a "congregation" of around a hundred music lovers and expatriates of various religious traditions.

During this time, my daughter, Leslie's, voice developed into a beautiful instrument. We began singing at open-microphone nights around Louisville as a father-daughter duo. Leslie became an accomplished singer in the bluegrass and Americana music scene in Nashville as a student at Belmont University. I am grateful that she has always included me on guitar and vocal harmonies and permitted me to record both of her CDs. Together we have performed music in worship at church and provided music for conferences here in Nashville and at our denomination's conference center at Montreat, North Carolina. We have also experimented with "song-sermons," in which we weave together music and speaking in the proclamation of the Word.

In the midst of all of this, I have been an avid student of all forms of popular music, blues, rock 'n' roll, soul, Motown, hip-hop, jazz, reggae, country, Americana, techno, DJ, and indie. I make regular pilgrimages to bluegrass and blues festivals. I have subscribed to fanzines and blogs, and have at least thirty bookmarked websites of favorite artists and journalists. These pastimes have provided an important education in the ways fan cultures function, which will contribute to chapter 5 of this book.

Four years ago, I was having a conversation with one of our ex–music industry students in Vanderbilt's Ph.D. program, David Perkins. Dave is a fine producer, musician, and songwriter who has played with Jerry Jeff Walker, Carole King, Ray Charles, and many others. At the time, he had decided to leave behind his music career and enter exclusively into the life of the mind. I found myself encouraging him to keep his musical interests alive. In that conversation, he turned the tables and asked me about my own music, and I rehearsed some of the hidden parts of my résumé above. Then he asked me, "So how do you integrate this musical interest with your teaching and writing?" I hemmed and hawed a bit, but in the end realized that I was now in my mid-fifties and had done little to integrate this large body of personal experience, research, and reading into my teaching and writing. I began to search for ways to change this.

It was about this same time that I signed on to help ethnomusicologist Greg Barz and educator Allison Pingree direct an interdisciplinary project for the Center for the Study of Religion and Culture at Vanderbilt entitled Music, Religion, and the South. This project gathered together scholars from all over Vanderbilt to study the intersection of music, religion, and southern regional identity. During that three-year project Allison Pingree and I taught a course on music and religious identity at Second Presbyterian Church in Nashville that became very important in conceptualizing this book. During that course I realized that musical fandoms are crucial aspects of the religious identity of many, if not all, members of local congregations. This teaching exercise directly informs the emphasis on ethnography and congregational study in chapter 5 of this book. I also have begun teaching, on rotation, a course on Popular Music and Religious Identity at Vanderbilt Divinity School. In that course, students learn to think theologically about the way that popular music is written, produced, and consumed. In many ways, this entire book grows directly out of that course.

Another important aspect of the Music, Religion, and the South project involved using my home recording studio to facilitate an ethnomusicology research project. I used my mobile recording rig to help Greg Barz record and document artists from all over Nashville in the performance of religious music.[1] This helped me connect with musicians from all over Nashville and taught me the importance of listening closely to what musicians have to say about their own practices and development. This ethnographic project has fed directly into the research for chapter 1 of this book, which focuses on interviews with songwriters.

As the capstone of this project, this team of scholars produced a full semester of events for the University and Nashville community entitled God in Music City.[2] The semester included a series of concerts and programs culminating in a capstone conference. Taken as a whole, this three-year project energized me for the study of popular culture, popular music, and the interfaces that potentially exist between cultural studies and homiletics.

The Listening to Listeners to Sermons Project

Another very meaningful trajectory leading into this book project was my work on the board of directors for the large empirical project Listening to Listeners to Sermons, funded by the Lilly Foundation.[3] The research team for this project interviewed 263 people in twenty-eight churches of various shapes, sizes, locations, denominations, and racial-ethnic composition across the midsection of the country. Although these researchers approached the data collected in this study from many directions, I became most interested in how some of the people interviewed placed preaching into relationship with broader cultural practices of spiritual listening, listening that might include music, talk show hosts, media preachers, writers, bloggers, and so on. I found myself asking, What goes into listening for

God? What skills does it require? Where else, besides Christian worship, are these skills being developed? What are the implications for theological communication?

For years I have been watching as friends, family, and others around me within the larger culture attach religious, and in some cases theological, significance to forms and aspects of popular music. I am also very aware of how my own identity, in all aspects, has been shaped by popular music and music fan cultures. This is also true in the lives of students in my classes. Popular music often plays a key role in shaping spiritually charged memories, fears, understandings of the human condition, and ideas about the nature of redemption and transcendence. Many of the listening skills required for discerning religious ideas are developed and honed within soundscapes provided by iPod playlists.

Theological Communication in the Middle

Although I have read widely in the field of cultural studies, this is not my natural habitat. I am, by vocation and profession, a homiletician. For this reason, I find myself always asking the homiletical question "What could this mean for the practice of preaching and for other forms of theological communication?" It has long seemed to me that practices of artistic invention within popular culture have implications for every form of theological communication: academic theological production, religious journalism, religious education, advocacy, and so on. It is rather remarkable that, after so many years and so much time spent enjoying and participating in the world of popular music, I have never formally interrogated popular music in a way that might yield sustained theoretical and practical conversation regarding its usefulness for theological invention and production. Perhaps it is my awareness that I am transitioning into the later portion of my career that prompts me to reach backward into my life and ask if I have "taken care of business." Are there dormant resources that I am not using? It could also be that my context in Nashville is, after all, the primary catalyst for engaging in conversation with popular music. I am forever telling people that moving to Nashville, one of the hubs of the song-making world, was perfect for someone with my interests. Vanderbilt Divinity School has many students who are either currently working within the music industry or leaving that industry and pursuing a religious vocation. In some ways, then, this book is my attempt to speak more of the idiom of my students, many of whom will know exactly what I am talking about at every stage of the song-making process.

Whatever the impetus for this book, it has been for me a tremendous adventure. It has provided a way of reappropriating my musical past, refocusing my musical present, and thinking ahead about new ways of teaching homiletics and theological communication among media-saturated students. I have also found that engagement with cultural studies meets headlong the emerging interests of my students at both Masters and Ph.D. levels. Suffice it to say that increasingly a full-bodied engagement with media and culture is necessary when considering theological communication today. Students are keenly interested to know how practices of theological communication can make use of cultural resources and function better in relation to mass media models for communicating religious ideas. It is with this new wave of interest among my students here in Nashville that I step forward and offer this conversation between song-making and theological invention as it grows out of my own experience and research.

ACKNOWLEDGMENTS

I must begin by thanking my musical family and all the musicians I've played with over the years in many different bands and musical ensembles. Your passion for music has been a constant source of inspiration and delight. I have been surrounded by song-makers my entire life, so it is only natural that I finally came around to writing something that pays homage to your guiding light(s).

I also want to thank Doug Knight and Volney Gay, codirectors of the Center for the Study of Religion and Culture at Vanderbilt University, for providing the generous three-year grant that made the Music, Religion, and the South project possible. In an age in which most significant grant funding is provided for the sciences, it was refreshing to be involved in a university center with a vision for the humanities, the social sciences, and the study of religion. I hope that as the financial climate improves, money will again be provided by the university for this kind of project. I also want to thank my codirectors for the Music, Religion, and the South project, Allison Pingree and Greg Barz, whose persistence and imagination never failed and who encouraged me to step out of the narrow confines of the Divinity School and engage the larger university as a scholar. I also wish to thank Vanderbilt Divinity School for bearing with me in this project, and for the generous sabbatical to turn my research into this book.

I wish to thank three students, all song-makers themselves, whose work with me has been inspirational over the past four years. First, David Perkins, who unknowingly has challenged me to bring my love of music to bear in my teaching and scholarship, and whose fully lived life, musical genius, and scholarly acumen have been both a model and an inspiration. Second, Jewly Hight, whose skill interviewing musicians and persistent generosity toward their life and work have shown me how to balance my often overbearing critical tendencies with a healthy dose of listening and appreciation. Finally, Sherry Cothran Woolsey, whose CD project memorializing the women of the Hebrew Bible, recorded in my studio as I worked on this book, became an actual laboratory for this entire writing project from start to finish. With students such as these in classroom and conversation, one cannot help but develop creatively as a scholar and teacher.

Many thanks to Carey Newman, my editor at Baylor University Press, for his pivotal insights regarding my work. Carey provided a much-needed creative assist, encouraging me to turn this work outward from my native field of homiletics toward the larger theological guild. He also provided excellent counsel on the development of the logic and flow of this book.

Finally, I once again must thank my wife, Annie, who puts up with countless hours of music blaring forth from my home studio, hosts musicians who tromp through the house with guitars, drum kits, keyboards, and other instruments at all hours of the day and night, and has learned to enjoy the life of musical fandom, going out regularly with me in Nashville to hear countless bands and songwriters and traveling to remote music festivals to sit at the feet of the masters. She has been a "rock 'n' roll widow" many nights, and endured many evenings of helping me carry amplifiers, microphone stands, and musical instruments to and from musical venues of all shapes and sizes. It is a blessing to be married to someone who participates in my musical obsessions.

INTRODUCTION

For many people in developed nations, the religious life takes place at the intersection between religious traditions, religious or quasi-religious ideologies, and popular culture. Religious resources, which in the past were the sole property of traditional communities of belief, are disseminated widely through popular media such as the Internet, radio, and television. For years, sociologists have been heralding this shift, showing how traditional religious resources now take their place alongside a huge range of resources minted within the networks and flows of popular culture.

In this context, lived religion resembles a mashup. In the world of popular music, a mashup is a song consisting entirely of parts of other songs. Usually the work of one musical artist is sampled and broken into bits. These bits are placed into juxtaposition with sampled bits of music created by several other artists. The result is a musical pastiche that, in the final analysis, becomes something very different from its original prototype. By analogy, people who "do religion" today tend to take ideas within particular religious traditions and mash them up using ideas gleaned from many other resources, some religious and some not. In the process, for better or worse, they invent new theological ideas and models.

In the context of mashup religion, theologians are losing their inventive edge to other forms of cultural production. Musicians and other popular artists are using new technologies in the service of artistic invention, and in some cases in the service of theological invention. Whereas some theologians use newer technologies to spruce up the presentation of traditional ideas, they do not use them to aid in the invention of new ideas. Theological lecturers and preachers use presentation software to project pictures and video clips to help them teach the same ideas they've taught for years using handouts and slide shows. Religious journalists and bloggers use the Internet to present and disseminate preconceived ideas. Most contemporary Christian and praise and worship musicians use recent music technologies to dress up conservative evangelical theologies in the rhythms and sounds of pop music. What goes missing are the ways recent technologies, and the inventive practices they foster, can help theologians in a variety of contexts (higher education, ministry, journalism, music, activism, etc.) in the actual invention of new and useful theological ideas.

Invention

Four contexts for the meaning of invention are important in this book. First, from the fields of rhetoric and composition theory, invention simply means *deciding what to say*. Practices of rhetorical invention have a long history. When writing speeches, students of rhetoric and composition are usually told to ask a set of key questions and engage a set of standard topics that will help them decide what to say. This is one important aspect of theological invention, and in this book I will suggest that the technologies and practices central to the production of pop music encourage new practices and new layers of rhetorical invention.

The second context in which invention is defined is patent law. For the patent lawyer, an invention is a *discovery*. From this perspective, theological invention is like a trek into the wilderness in search of something important and useful. Out of the relative chaos of ideas and possibilities, something new is discovered that must be recognized and secured. In this sense, theological invention is a pilgrimage into the unknown in search of something that will be potentially valuable to others in the current situation. In this book, I will argue that in today's religious context, this journey involves living into the relative security of one's traditions, but only as the beginning point in theological invention. Technologies of sampling, remixing, and mashup suggest that theologians should also travel into seemingly chaotic intertextual spaces, some religious and some not, in search of new theological ideas.

The field of music theory presents a third context in which to consider the word "invention." For the music theorist, invention involves the creation of a novel sound or musical form that is not primarily imitative in nature. Throughout the history of music this has involved the invention of new instruments, new ways to make music, new notation systems, new scales or note values, new genres, traditions, or modalities such as "folk," "rock," and so on.[1] Within this frame of reference, I will show how new technologies push musical invention beyond both imitating and styling on a particular tradition, into the realm of *stylistic morphing,* a concept that is highly suggestive for theological invention and production. New technologies enable musicians to manipulate and juxtapose sounds in ways that promote a range of new musical sounds and forms. For the theologian, this process encourages the manipulation and morphing of the ideas of others within new juxtapositions that are cross-disciplinary, cross-traditional, and cross-cultural.

Finally, for historians and social scientists, invention sometimes means the creation of a movement, tradition, or idea as a way to legitimate certain economic actions or political realities (cf. the invention of new public holidays, ceremonies, heroes, or symbols). In the realm of popular music, fan cultures often function in this way. Fans of various forms of popular music spend hours crowdsourcing the symbolic value of an artist's work,[2] locating it within and in relation to existing movements, or arguing that it is part of a new movement, and, in effect, inventing the value of a work in relation to a particular social or historical epoch. Again, this form of invention is very suggestive for theological production. We will consider some of the ways the symbolic value of theological ideas are invented by users of those ideas within the networks and flows of popular culture, including fandoms, social networking, Internet journalism, and other popular media. I will suggest ways theologians might benefit by both analyzing and contributing to inventing the value of various religious ideas within the marketplace of popular culture.

Why Song-Making?

Song-making has become a significant locus for the dissemination and democratization of religious and prophetic speech in the post-Enlightenment era. Historian of religion Leigh Eric Schmidt argues that during the Enlightenment the ear (by which he means not only the outer acoustical ear but the inner ear), through which one hears the voice of God, was relegated to the danger zone of irrationality—outside the bounds of universal reason. The idea of hearing the voice of God and acting upon divine Words in the interpersonal, social, and political arena was anathematized. The Enlightenment required of everyone a massive reeducation of the ear in which attunement to God's Word was educated out of the general public.[3]

The story of post-Enlightenment religious hearing loss is, of course, not new and has taken many forms.[4] As Schmidt points out, however, various communities of faith, such as Evangelicals and Pentecostals, kept the religious auditory function alive, funneling it into forms of "auditory piety" through which individuals who are appropriately sensitized listen via Scripture or other oracular means for the divine voice.[5] Spiritual hearing became an important disposition for those who would resist the deafening silence of a disenchanted Enlightenment world.[6] According to Schmidt, the "fragmentation and privatization of religious authority" has led to a democratization of oracular speaking/listening.[7] Auditory piety has migrated into the culture at large and is assumed by individuals who have found it increasingly important to develop forms of spiritual hearing. The democratization of oracular speaking/listening has encouraged a wide range of forms of religious and quasi-religious listening/discernment and proclamation, not the least of which occurs through various forms of popular music, whether song-makers mean for this to occur or not. Like it or not, people are listening, and listening with religiously attuned ears, and song-makers have responded, not only because this represents a significant market share of fans and consumers, but because many find this oracular function commensurate with their own sense of musical vocation.

Within the larger culture, therefore, popular music assumes a powerful religious communicating function, encouraging consubstantiality with particular modes of being in the world, and a variety of ultimate concerns, some positive and some negative. Those who make songs and those who consume songs are well attuned to potentially spiritual or religious sounds and messages communicated by popular music. This attunement is not simply thematic, but operates at the kinesthetic and auditory levels of sound and soundscape.

In 1975 James W. Carey articulated a cultural approach to communication in which he encouraged a shift from a transmissive model of communication to a ritual approach.[8] He found the purpose of communication "not in the transmission of intelligent information but in the construction and maintenance of an ordered, meaningful cultural world that can serve as a control and container for human action."[9] Carey's model of communication has been central to cultural studies, permitting an approach to cultural artifacts in which a larger cultural whole could be seen as implied by each cultural part. Anthropologists of religion Birgit Meyer and Jojada Verrips suggest that popular cultural artifacts and processes of meaning-making are part of a religious aesthetics of "sensational form."[10] Sensational forms such as songs are "vested with the capacity to render present divine power," "address and form people's bodies and senses in distinct ways," and create "religious communities that thrive on a shared aesthetic style."[11] Theologians may learn important things by investigating the sensational form of popular music and the ways popular musicians create communities gathered to a shared aesthetic style. At the very least, theologians may want to consider the sociological and theological significance of their artifacts' sensational forms and aesthetic styles.

Technologies of song-making can also take on larger religious meanings. Philosopher of culture Jeremy Stolow points out how popular music-making has become a "technology of enchantment."[12] Those who have access to those technologies and are experts at using them achieve special legitimation and authority. According to religion and culture scholar Dorothea E. Schulz, "religion always entails a range of materials and techniques to which we refer as *media* and relies on specialists holding authority in questions relating to the proper use of technologies of mediation."[13] Using these technologies represents a significantly mystified practice of creation *ex nihilo* that is, in sociologist Pierre Bourdieu's words, "consecrated," vested by many with unique ethical and religious significance.[14] Therefore, not only do the songs as material forms of media hold potential religious significance, but the specialized ability to use certain technologies for producing such media has acquired religious importance as well. For many, the song-maker is a kind of mediator or priest who uses new technologies of recording and mass media to produce meanings, worldviews, and the moral soundscapes for our lives. It is conceivable, then, that theologians can learn from these technologies and the ways they are influencing practices of composition, arrangement, production, and reception.

Perhaps most profoundly, the popular song exists at the intersection where human desire for transcendence meets consumer desire within a commodity culture. Those who create meaning at this intersection are often aware that they are connecting the desire for transcendence with purchasable commodities. Within theology, commodification of the message is often associated with selling out and with the loss of prophetic (artistic) distance, or what cultural theorist Walter Benjamin called "aura."[15] The popular song-maker, however, suggests a different take on art-turned-commodity—one that seeks to preserve, and in fact increase the work's artistic aura in and through its reproduction, commodification, and mass dissemination. Often, popular song-makers place songs within the flows of desire within consumer culture in order to *steer* consumer desire toward transcendent referents that need not be wholly co-opted by market forces. We will therefore consider what the song-maker, located at this intersection between consumer and religious desire, has to say to the theologian regarding the possibilities of co-opting or at least *steering* religious desires latent within consumer culture.

At a very pragmatic level, practices and technologies of popular song-making show us with great clarity a range of inventive practices that are becoming ubiquitous within the larger culture today.

Although there are similar technologies and practices at work within other forms of cultural production (filmmaking, graphic arts, amateur video production, etc.), I find that song-making offers the clearest and most widely known model. This book, therefore, uses popular song-making in a heuristic and analogical way. I will be concerned to show that popular song-makers have a lot to teach theologians about inventing artifacts that will both keep traditions alive (through sampling) and foster new ideas through creative juxtapositions across religious traditions, cultures, and traditional disciplinary lines. I believe that theologians within all arenas of theological invention, whether academic, journalistic, ministerial, artistic, or activist, have much to learn about invention from the technologies and practices of popular song-making.

I will argue that these practices directly reflect cultural and social shifts. Religious pluralism, multiculturalism, and postmodernity have led us into a situation in which more pragmatic and postsemiotic forms of communication are now necessary. My argument, therefore, is set against culturally and linguistically bound models of communication in which culture, language, grammar, and the correct appropriation of the internal structure of religious narratives are the keys to religious communication and knowledge. Instead, I believe that theologians must, like the musical DJ, learn pragmatic skills of identifying the key "breaks" and "beats" within a vast range of religiously attenuated ideas in order to effectively place them into a religious and ethical conversation ruled by the desire to mutually survive and flourish on this planet.

I have narrowed my conversation partner to popular song-making within the mainstream of studio-produced and electronic mediated popular music in order to focus attention on shared elements of composition and reception that exist between song-making in this particular context and theological production. This has meant setting to one side as secondary larger concerns regarding what philosopher of culture Theodor Adorno called the "culture industry" as an economic and social construct.[16] I will also avoid taking the time to engage in arguments regarding "high" and "low" (or mass) culture, popular music in performed versus presentational forms, folk versus mass-mediated popular music, and some of the laborious work of establishing popular culture and popular music as meaningful socio-logical and musicological constructs in the first place. I will defer to the excellent work of others in this regard.[17]

When I refer to "popular music" or the "popular song," I do not mean songs that are proven to be popular in the sense of best selling or widely disseminated. Instead, these terms refer broadly to music created with mass audiences and popular tastes or preferences in mind.[18] I also use these terms to indicate music that constitutes a common resource "of everyday life for ordinary people within a particular society."[19] In the North American context today, this includes a broad range of musical genres, including, but not limited to, pop, country, Americana, reggae, rock, R&B, blues, hip-hop, alternative, punk, gothic, trance, and heavy metal.

The reader who is aware of popular culture studies and popular music will immediately notice the particularly limited slice of the popular song-making spectrum that I will engage. It goes without saying that I might have learned a good deal more had I taken the time to engage the popular music scene more broadly. I do maintain, however, that the inventive aspects of popular song-making I engage can be found across popular musical genres, with very few exceptions.

Inventive Practices within Popular Song-Making

The chapters of this book will chart inventive practices within the popular song-making process, bringing song-making and theological invention into dialogue along the way. At each stage along the way I will engage a particular set of theoretical and theological themes.

In chapter 1, which focuses on the practice of songwriting, I make use of sociologist Pierre Bourdieu's idea of "habitus," or the "feel for the game,"[20] which "generate(s) and organizes practices."[21] At this stage, I will focus attention on the ways in which musical invention is a matter of learning to write in and out of a specific tradition of music. This encourages a set of similar tradition-bound practices as an initial stage of theological invention.

Chapter 2 focuses attention on the ways in which audio is layered within the context of the multitrack studio. "Tracking" (recording tracks for) a popular song involves certain defined codes or conventions of production, including "melody," "rhythm," "backing," and "fills." In this chapter, I revisit and revise my former work *The Four Codes of Preaching: Rhetorical Strategies*, which was based on multitrack sequencing.[22] I argue that theological invention is a matter of stylistically layering four central authorities (tracks): Scripture, culture, theology, and reason. I create a theological "loop browser" that organizes the range of current styles used to track these four authorities, showing how each style of tracking contributes to the invention of a particular form of memory (Scripture tracking), experience (culture tracking), worldview (theology tracking), and truth (reason/message tracking). I then show how awareness of these stylistic options opens the door for hybrid configurations that respond pragmatically to different communicative needs and aspirations in our religious situation today.

In chapter 3, digital sampling and remixing practices become more forcefully involved in song creation. At this stage of song-making the tradition-centered *hermeneutic* model undergirding the habitus of the songwriter, and the modest forms of hybridity involved in studio tracking and "loop browsing," morph into a more open-ended *intertextual* model of invention that thrives on the seemingly random juxtaposition of artistic elements. The writer, who worked hard developing good judgment within a tradition of writing, steps into a process of cut-and-paste sampling and random trial-and-error juxtaposition of sampled bits of sound in a broadly collaborative context. I argue that this collaborative artistic process suggests a form of *kairotic* (opportune, timely) theological invention focused on articulating the theologically possible within a highly pragmatic and post-semiotic model of theological communication.

Chapter 4, which follows the song into the stages of mixing and mastering, addresses embodied sound: the relative volume, tone, and energy of each track in relation to one another. How much of this or that? How will this aspect sound? Does pitch need correction? Is the tone correct? The question here for the theologian is one of soundscape and what semiotician Roland Barthes called the "grain of the voice."[23] What sonic impact or tone of voice needs to be invented for this theological production? How does one gauge a theological work's role in the larger soundscape in a religious community and within culture at large? At this stage we will turn the corner to a theology of listening, and the forms of prelistening that theologians must do as they compose, in order to invent an appropriate sound or tone for their productions. In this chapter I urge a deeper form of theological listening by theologians, listening attuned to the larger ethical and theological soundscape. Within this theology of listening the theologian seeks a tone or form of resonance, which becomes the shape that belief takes in theological invention.

In chapter 5, I look at the role of fandom in the reception of songs. This chapter engages the shifting nature of theological reception in a commodity culture. I argue that those on the receiving end of our theological inventions are themselves very much like mashup artists. They are constantly involved in cutting and pasting words, images, and ideas from multiple sources into personal and communal religious narratives in ways that help them construct and maintain their own religious identities. Scholarship regarding fan cultures can help us understand how religious consumers mash up religious ideas within communities of taste that inform religious identity. Recently, through blogs and social networks such as MySpace and Facebook, listeners are learning to promote and disseminate religious ideas while connecting with others of similar interest. In this process, mashups invented by consumers create the actual symbolic value of our theological productions. In this chapter, therefore, I examine issues posed by these configurations of community that are at once strongly individualist and yet increasingly democratic, participatory, and negotiative. I argue that theologians can play a key role in these communities, helping to invent the value of particular theological ideas, while adding depth, complexity, and steerage into the mix.

In chapter 6, I further explore fandom for theological meaning through textual analysis. In this chapter I outline a simple narrative form of analysis that can help theologians determine the theological worldviews around them within culture and religious community. I postulate that by learning to read the pop-cultural genres of religious communication, theologians will learn to invent messages that engage the textuality of cultural life more deeply. Theologically, in this chapter I take a more missiological turn, bringing confessional Christian theology into direct dialogue with song lyrics.

At the end of the day, I hope to identify several key shifts in the nature of invention in today's context, and demonstrate a range of practical possibilities that can inform the inventive practices of theologians operating in a wide range of contexts. When these are engaged, I believe theologians stand a better chance of inventing, positioning, and communicating ideas that will be received and integrated as valuable components within today's mashup religion.

1

THE SONGWRITER

INVENTION IN AND OUT OF A THEOLOGICAL TRADITION

When a poet's mind is perfectly equipped for its work, it is constantly amalgamating disparate experience; . . . experiences are always forming new wholes.

—T. S. Eliot, "The Metaphysical Poets," 1921

Any musicologist, neatly tracing the development of music, can tell us that rock 'n' roll did not come out of nowhere. But it sounded as if it did.

—Greil Marcus, *Mystery Train: Images of America in Rock 'n' Roll Music*

The first stage of the song-making process to investigate for the purposes of theological invention is song*writing*. Most songs begin with a fairly traditional songwriting process, in which the songwriter sits with guitar, keyboard, or some other instrument, with pen or word processor close at hand, and crafts music out of sound and lyrics.

Popular songwriters are today's poets for the common folk, writers who mirror for us our foibles and graces and help us to see ourselves more clearly. In reaction to the disenchantment with religion as a result of the Enlightenment, the Romantic literary movement elevated the artist to a stature not unlike that of prophet or holy fool. The Romantic poet was imagined as someone who suffered in self-imposed isolation and estrangement in order to give birth to images that would plumb the depths of reality on behalf of others. Within the bohemian tradition, a development paralleling the Romantic movement, the artist often embraced poverty and sometimes immorality and eccentricity of behavior and fashion.[1]

The mantle of the artist as prophetic mediator of truth in a post-Enlightenment world has been placed by many enthusiasts of popular culture onto the shoulders of the popular songwriter. This idea is easily stereotyped and commodified, as theologian of music Jeremy Begbie observes in his complaint about the typical CD cover picturing a singer-songwriter "a step apart from the ordinary, staring away from the camera in a misty wash."[2] On the whole, however, interviews with songwriters show them to be very aware of the power of this Romantic archetype and the need not to abuse the privileges it affords them within the larger culture. I speak here, of course, of *successful*, working songwriters, those who cannot exist in the misty wash of the isolated bohemian, but have actually experienced their music connecting deeply with a broader community of listeners and sense some responsibility toward that audience.

Unlike the high artists of the Romantic period, reverenced in the works of Schleiermacher, Schopenhauer, and Emerson, who may indeed spend an entire lifetime writing only for themselves and for other artists and critics, the popular songwriter is never dissociated from a public.[3] This public can only come into being and survive if the writer's lyrics and music are understandable and connected to the realities of everyday life. To use the language of sociologist Pierre Bourdieu, the popular songwriter does not have the "interest in disinterestedness" that characterizes the bohemian or Romantic artist.[4] It is true that belief in the authenticity of the popular songwriter is to some extent predicated on the artist communicating disinterest in success. This disinterest is usually expressed through the use of poetic elements (ambiguity, symbolism, irony, mythmaking, etc.) and prophetic distance or critique, which give voice to what music critic and theologian Bill Friskics-Warren calls an "urge for transcendence."[5] The urge for transcendence expressed by the popular songwriter, however, must connect with the same urge as it is expressed within the experiences of ordinary folk. The popular song must provide poetic and prophetic images that are nonesoteric, accessible, and, in fact, obvious.

Instead of presenting disinterested, isolated, and aloof individuals focused entirely on prophetic distance, interviews with songwriters yield a portrait of profoundly communal, connected, collaborative, and *tradition-bearing* writers who are beholden to those who have gone before and aware of those around them who are good at writing similar material. In the end, songwriters seem to be striving to develop what John Henry Newman once called the "illative sense," or good judgment within a tradition of ideas, experiences, and practices.[6]

Songwriters Write In and Out of Traditions

There is perhaps no more striking refutation of the stereotype of popular songwriters as individualistic, Romantic visionaries than the deep witness to tradition-building and collaboration that pervades all published interviews with songwriters. Writing within a tradition is deeply *hermeneutic* in nature, in the sense of hermeneutics promoted by German philosopher Hans-Georg Gadamer. Within Gadamer's aesthetic, a work of art is created and comprehended primarily within the horizon of meaning represented by a historical tradition.[7] This tradition establishes appropriateness in both the creation and reception of the work of art.[8] It would be nonsense to assume that one could write something out of thin air, with no mooring in a tradition of writing upon which to draw. How would one know what is appropriate to the genre? How would one know how to create or interpret the nuances of form, style, cadence, inflection, and substance? Within a hermeneutic framework, tradition and community bring a deeply heteronomous element to writing, keeping it responsive to others. All new, autonomous, and authentic words are improvisations on a living tradition and gain heteronomy by being beholden to traditions of communication long established and revered within the community itself. Prophetic speech never comes from outside the tradition or community. It is always a word that wells up from within. The sense that song-making is supported by, and in fact can be done *only* within, traditions of music-making is palpable among songwriters. Songwriters testify to two different but interrelated levels of tradition-building in their work. Both are of importance for the task of theological invention.

Covering the Work of Others

Popular songwriters are keenly aware that they do not exist in a vacuum apart from historical roots and influences. There is hardly a single interview with a songwriter that does not acknowledge debts owed to artists and traditions of music past and present. This is not simply a matter of name-dropping or fame by association. It is a matter of learning a language, style, phrasing, intonation, rhythm, and dynamics from others—many others, some known, some relatively unknown. As Smokey Robinson puts it, "I guess I've been influenced by everybody."[9] According to Sarah Chauncey, "One of the best ways to learn about writing songs is to listen to them. Listen and take note of what you like, what gives you goosebumps . . . then try to imitate it."[10]

One of the fundamentals of learning popular songwriting is covering other artists' material. Most songwriters can sing aloud hundreds of lyrics and turns of phrase used by other artists, and play on guitar or piano their own renditions of many songs. When speaking about Bob Dylan, Dave Alvin notes, "He sat down with all the folk records and the ballads and the blues, and he learned them all. And he can call any one of them up just about any time he wants. And that's one of the reasons he's such a great songwriter—he's totally immersed in all the songs that came before him."[11] Part of knowing songs within a tradition is being able to reperform them in one's own style.

Redoing a song makes it the songwriter's own song. As John Mellencamp puts it, "the way I look at it, anything that I've ever seen or heard, I own. It's not the Byrds' sound, it's my sound. That's what Picasso did, and that's what Dylan did."[12] Mellencamp is not advocating plagiarism. He is saying that a huge part of becoming a songwriter is listening to other people's music, past and present, performing that music until it becomes one's own, and then writing within and out of the ethos and imaginative worldview promoted by that music. K. A. Parker, a teaching songwriter, says that she often assigns her songwriting students the task of writing "a new lyric to an existing song, and then they have to sing the new lyric in front of the class."[13] She admits the importance to songwriting of a practice widely used by all popular musicians, listening to a song and writing the lyrics down by hand. According to Parker, "there's something that enters the bones when you write a lyric down yourself."[14]

Sammy Cahn provides similar advice for young writers, encouraging them to "write in the tracks of the great writers."[15] The goal is to "write with" great writers, entering as deeply as possible into the mindset and worldview of another songwriter in order to learn, through a practice that resembles tracing, what it means to be a songwriter oneself. Paul McCartney and John Lennon both strongly identified with and, in fact, imitated Buddy Holly in their early days of songwriting."[16] Imitating those in the tradition often means stepping into the actual personality and persona of a revered songwriter.

Songwriter Mark Simos asserts that songwriters either write *in* a tradition (blues, rock, country, etc.) or *out of* a tradition. Writing in a tradition means consciously trying to stay as faithful as possible to canons of style, ethos, phrasing, and attitude. Writing out of a tradition means working from models within a tradition, while "deliberately breaking conventions and forms," adding a "twist, and stretching boundaries."[17] In order to learn how to write "out of" a tradition, Simos encourages musicians to "make a map of your musical influences, and their influences in turn," claiming a "musical birthright." Then he encourages them to "learn a few hundred songs" within that tradition, and then "see what your inner ear spontaneously comes up with."[18] According to Canadian musician Warren Hill, "everything everyone does is derivative of something, something that they've heard, it's just how you piece it together in your own way."[19] One of the crucial elements within the habitus of songwriting is to be a fan of a particular tradition of music, and particular artists within that tradition. These artists are more than heroes; they are *prototypes* for the creative work of the writer of popular songs.

Living deeply into community through tradition and collaborative writing is an important part of the habitus of the songwriter and has much to contribute to those who are involved in creating theology at the intersection of overt religion and popular culture. Some black preaching traditions and rural revivalist and Pentecostal traditions are learned primarily through apprenticeship, but it is rare to find preachers or other religious communicators (educators, theologians, preachers, bloggers) working to "cover" and "riff on" the great works of exemplars within theological traditions. Theological education in the West is focused on complex systems of formal education dedicated to written curricula, syllabuses, or explicit teaching traditions; professional teachers, lecturers, or master theologians; systematic assessment mechanisms such as grade exams, national school exams, or university exams; a body of literature, pedogical texts, and teaching materials. Alongside or instead of formal education, however, emphasis could shift to passing on and acquiring theological skills and knowledge by watching and imitating theological thinkers within a tradition, through the reperformance of historical texts, or by making reference to existing recordings, performances, and other live events. In this model of education, students would spend time listening to sermon tapes, performances, presentations, or podcasts, or writing down and reperforming the words of religious communicators they emulate, catching hold of the way an idea sounds and works, grabbing words and sentences and playing with them in new ways. Students of theology would spend time imitating the riffs, cadences, or intonations of other scholars or preachers, making their ideas and turns of phrase their own. The goal is to begin to get the "feel" of a tradition of thought, to live into the rhetoric of that tradition. How do arguments work? What constitutes the repertoire of ideas and messages? What is the plot, and who are the characters of the theological story that is being told? What key words and phrases are important to learn and riff on, in order to be recognizably a part of that tradition? Again, this is not a matter of plagiarizing. It is a matter of locating oneself within a theological tradition and learning to cover the work of exemplars within those traditions, whose works represent key theological messages worth carrying forward in a new way.

Collaboration

A crucial aspect of writing in and out of a tradition is *collaboration* with other writers who write within that tradition. Whether Rodgers and Hammerstein, Lennon and McCartney, or two struggling song-writers sitting in a Nashville coffee shop scratching lyrics on a table-cloth, collaboration is an important aspect of the songwriter's work. A cursory glance at a CD cover or discography will reveal how often two or more writers have participated in composing a popular song.

It is difficult to know what is needed in collaboration. Sometimes collaboration is a matter of getting straight-shooting feedback from a trusted source. Smokey Robinson, speaking about his fifty-year rela-tionship with Berry Gordy, says, "We'd push each other and we still do to this day."[20] Glenn Frey of the Eagles makes it a matter of not trusting himself to ask the hard questions of his own writing. He needs to go to someone else he knows will speak hard words of criti-cism and provide direction.[21]

In other instances, collaboration is focused on complementary creative abilities. In speaking about what made the Lennon/McCart-ney songwriting team work, Lennon said, "Well, you could say that he provided a lightness, an optimism, while I would always go for the sadness, the dis-chords, a certain bluesy edge."[22] Alan Doyle of the band Great Big Sea sums up his relationship with cowriter Séan McCann: "He's really good at giving me hooks, and I'm good at giv-ing him words."[23] In some partnerships, different aspects of a song are contributed by different writers.

For others, collaboration is about having a good conversation partner (not necessarily a songwriter) to get the juices flowing for song ideas. As Tom Wilson puts it, "conversation is really No. 1 on the list as far as getting inspiration. . . . You catch onto some things that they say . . . and you've got great songs there."[24] Paying attention and remembering what was said is crucial. Most writers carry small writ-ing pads to jot down words, phrases, sentences, or ideas that occur in the give-and-take of ordinary conversations.

Although friendship is an important aspect of collaboration, it is not absolutely necessary. Collaboration is a discipline with a specific outcome in mind. Gary William Friedman emphasizes that collaboration is work and should be treated as such.[25] Partners in collaboration are striving to cowrite the best possible song, and this requires back-and-forth shifts in leadership as the song progresses. Friendship is sometimes helpful, but is not necessary for this process to achieve positive results.

Collaboration can potentially support the ways in which a song has integrity within a tradition of writing—through feedback focused on truth-telling, originality, and authenticity. Is the song too sentimental? Unfocused? Trivial? Stylized? At other times, collaboration helps the artist keep the song grounded in experiences that are central to a tradition of music-making. Is it too esoteric? Does it connect? Will it make sense? Does it have a hook that will draw people in? What does it need in order to exist in a particular tradition of songwriting? Does it connect to a shared world?

Religious communicators tend to avoid collaboration at all costs. Most assume that their scholarly essays, books, sermons, or blogs are intensely private matters that will lose originality if they are opened to the insights of others. Although we will have more to say about collaboration *across* traditions in chapter 3, the key to collaborating for the songwriter is to find someone *within* a tradition of writing who will provide critical feedback, complementarity, and reflective conversation.

At the heart of the habitus of the songwriter is a *tradition-based hospitality*, in which others, writing or listening within or out of a specific tradition, are welcomed into the cultivation of one's identity and vocational practice as a writer. Those who want to be involved in the invention of theology might cultivate similar forms of hospitality, seeing themselves as guests at the table of others within a tradition of thought and action who have gone before them and who bring potential gifts to them. At the same time, they will see themselves as hosts welcoming cowriting guests primarily within a tradition, who bring gifts to them through collaboration.

Learning to collaborate within a tradition of writing can be accomplished in many ways. Instead of sitting alone in the office, library cubicle, or pastor's study amidst a stack of books and Internet resources, the collaborative writer can take the process of theological brainstorming into conversation with others within a tradition of interpretation. This can be accomplished, in part, by fostering groups of others who are writing within a particular tradition. In these groups, practices of theological composition are deepened and grounded in traditions of interpretation and imagination. Writers can also seek out others within a tradition of writing (theologians, preachers, bloggers, educators) for mentoring or apprenticeship. Like the developing guitarist who takes a few lessons from a guitarist in a local band, writers can partner occasionally with those who have more experience at the game of writing. Similar to Smokey Robinson, writers can find someone who will give them the tough love they need—telling them when their prose is sentimental, abstract, didactic, oppositional, narcissistic, overstated, and so on. Or, taking a cue from Lennon and McCartney, writers can seek out collaborators who will complement their style—helping to provide the middle eight, hook, or melodies that will work within their tradition of writing.

Writing Matures the Writer in a Tradition

One noticeable thread throughout the interviews with songwriters digested for this chapter is that songwriters are keenly aware that their craft is cathartic, educative, and integrative in relation to their own lives. Writing in and out of a tradition of songwriting carries with it certain ways of externalizing and dealing with one's experiences and ideas. Songwriting, therefore, involves a constant reeducation and maturation of the whole person within certain traditions of thought and practice. Writing changes the artist, providing healing, perspective, vision, and qualities of good judgment. Most good songwriters are aware that songs are doing this to them, and how songs are doing it. Here are some key aspects of this awareness.

Externalization

Externalization is the process of getting outside one's experience in order to gain perspective. Bob Dylan asserts that externalization is one of the critical imperatives for good songwriting.[26] Even if songs bear within them no immediate confessional or self-disclosive aspect, songwriters are intensely aware of the relationship between their songs and their lives. Steve Goodman compared his songs to children; he was not proud of them all the time, but they are a part of him nonetheless.[27] Not every song is a gem, but all songs are important aspects of the artist's personal and vocational development, helping the artist see experiences more clearly. Holly Near says that she sings about her experience for her own education.[28] Or, as Dave Alvin says, songwriting "helps us explain the world to ourselves."[29] Through externalization the artist gains self-knowledge and insight into ordinary aspects of life.

Songwriters are aware of the problems that ensue when they make externalization of experience their primary reason for writing songs. Janis Ian argues that "cannibalizing your own feelings" can be unhealthy, leading to narcissistic and melodramatic portrayals of oneself as a victim whose creativity depends on suffering.[30] Joni Mitchell recalls being gently chastised by Kris Kristofferson after he read the lyrics to her album *Blue*; in displaying so much personal confession, he said, she seemed to have given away her entire self.[31]

What is worth noting, however, is that songwriters are aware that their own experience is inescapable and is reflected in their writing. They do not fool themselves into believing they can somehow set their experience aside, even when ultimately announcing a truth greater than themselves. The truth they announce arrives *through* externalization, as they gain and shift perspective on their experience of the world through poetry and music, a process that is significant for one's development as a writer.

Externalization is an important key to writing in a tradition of music-making. It connects the writer to the tradition's thematic repertoire and ways of expressing and handling questions that arise from experience. Although any experience is fair game, traditions of music typically focus on particular kinds of experience and narrow the range of thematic responses deemed adequate. (We will return to these experiences and themes in chapter 6.) For instance, within certain traditions of songwriting (blues, folk, gothic, for instance) what is often externalized is suffering. Peter La Farge, who lived a difficult life burdened with medical problems, observed that suffering often was a major impetus for his writing.[32] Bruce Cockburn says that his song "If I Had a Rocket Launcher" was one way to frame his experience after visiting a refugee camp and watching helicopters shoot down inno-cent people. The song did not express his ultimate or even best vision of what the situation required. But he felt the need to externalize his rage and desire for violent revenge.[33] The song gave expression to one way of dealing with feelings of helplessness and anger in the face of violence and injustice, and helped him to externalize a very difficult experience in his own life in order to make sense of it.

Within other traditions, (gothic, hip-hop, punk, etc.), experi-ences of violence, oppression, or addiction are externalized. Philippe Bourgois identifies in rap music, in particular, a way of transforming violent or addictive tendencies into a more reflective and critical practice.[34] As a reflective artifact, the song bounces like light off of the writer's everyday experience of the world and becomes one pos-sible perspective on that experience. This helps both writers and listeners gain insight into their experiences, and often leads to forms of poetic or prophetic insight and truth-telling.

Every aspect of a tradition of music conspires to focus the art-ist on externalizing particular aspects of experience in particular ways. Often a shift from one tradition of music to another, or col-laboration with artists from other traditions, is based on conscious or unconscious decisions about the relative adequacy of a tradition of writing to externalize experiences deemed important by the art-ist. Paul Simon, for instance, felt that American folk and pop music traditions were inadequate to express his experience with apartheid, and that the African continent was being largely ignored as a source of creativity. In 1986 he externalized these feelings and experiences through collaborative songwriting efforts that incorporated writers and musicians primarily from South Africa, some of whom were liv-ing in exile, resulting in the award-winning album *Graceland* (1986). In a similar way, African American rapper Nas and Jamaican reggae artist Damian Marley collaborated on a hip-hop/reggae project that arose from their experience of the shared African roots of both of their musical traditions, and their mutual concern for poverty and the lack of education on the African continent. In the project, *Dis-tant Relatives* (2010), they strove to externalize this experience and promote public awareness.

In ways similar to inventing songs, inventing theology involves externalizing events, situations, feelings, and struggles. Although much of formal education encourages theologians to put their experience on hold, the popular songwriter provides a warning that losing awareness of the role of experience in writing is a sure way to remain immature as a writer and theologian. Instead, they encourage forms of writing in which theologians implicitly ask such questions as How do I, within the framework of my religious experience, make sense of this idea, text, theologian, and so on? What can I honestly say about this religious idea? What do I experience as wrong in the world, and why? What is theologically alive to me? How do I find religious meaning and purpose by writing?

As time passes and we mature as theologians, it is not uncommon to find ourselves thinking, "I could never have said this ten years ago." Many of us have had the experience of pulling out an old essay, sermon, book, or blog, only to wonder how we could have missed so much the first time around. We are all aware, but not fully self-conscious, of the ways that our practices of theological invention are maturing us. One composition takes an experience of suffering and reframes it theologically. Another reflects theologically on injustice. Another reflects on addiction. As time passes, we frame things differently, and we become aware of new experiences that will affect what we have to say as theologians.

This maturation depends, in many ways, on operating within, or out of, a tradition. Specific experiences are more typically externalized (and not externalized) by virtue of being a Christian theologian within the Roman Catholic, Anglican, Reformed, Methodist, AME, Pentecostal, or Baptist traditions. One tradition will attend to the sacramental presence of God within the created universe. Another tradition will accentuate experiences of guilt and forgiveness. Another will lift up experiences of human limitation and grace. Or, if traditions are conceived ideologically, different experiences are lifted up by virtue of theological commitments to liberationist, feminist, evangelical, or existentialist traditions. One tradition will focus on experiences of oppression and liberation. Another will accentuate experiences of gender and identity. Another will focus on separation and reunion. Another will focus attention on estrangement and reconciliation.

Once one becomes aware of the traditions shaping the invention of theological messages, it is helpful to take the time to listen carefully to the way that human experiences are externalized and treated by exemplars within the tradition. Within a tradition of theological writing, which regions of experience are most important, and what are the tropes that are used to shape the rhetoric through which these experiences are expressed, organized, and redeemed? To teach this kind of writing, homileticians, theologians, and religionists need skills in helping students identify these tropes and regions of experience. Basic skills in rhetorical analysis would prove helpful for everyone involved.

Integration

Songwriters testify that songwriting helps them integrate the many creative aspects of their artistic personalities. The artist is a person of multiple creative personas, each of which is important for producing an excellent song. Billy Corgan of the band Smashing Pumpkins talks about how songwriting is like having five inner creative personalities trying to get along. Sometimes the emotional persona is in charge. At other times his technical self takes over. In the same way, the riffing guitarist is often at war with the vocalist. If the jam artist wins out, the song may end up with no melody. If the vocalist's desires take over, the song may lack musical depth and energy. If the technician seizes control, the song may feel overproduced. If the emotions take over, the song may become overly sentimental. His goal is to get these creative elements to join together in a common effort.[35] The creative process involves a conversation, and sometimes an argument, between different aspects of the creating self. The successful songwriter is aware of this conversation and this integrative process, and seeks a deeper integration of these internal creative voices.

This dynamic of integration is not an isolated individual phenomenon. It is largely responsive to the tension between autonomy and heteronomy in songwriting. This tension takes different shapes within different traditions of music. According to Bourdieu, the popular artist must pay attention to a heteronomous (connected, beholden to others) principle that keeps art connected to economic, social, personal, and political realities very differently than art created by the autonomous (disconnected, beholden to no one) artist. The autonomous, prophetic visionary who strikes hard-and-fast countercultural poses or itinerates as the lonely artist in the salons of the refined poetry-reading circuit must be kept in check within the realm of popular music-making, where artists must contend always with the realities of connecting with a large, multifaceted consuming audience. At the same time, as we have noted, popular songwriters are not free from the expectation that their works will demonstrate artistic and prophetic autonomy (authenticity, sincerity, originality, truth-telling). This autonomy, of course, remains worthless if it achieves little or no rhetorical connection to a broader audience. The popular artist, by definition, seeks a community beyond the cult of artists and critics, and writes in such a way as to connect with that larger audience.

Interviews with songwriters indicate that they are aware of the tension that exists between their autonomy as artists and their heteronomy as those who strive to connect with a real-world audience. They consider this tension to be resolved, however, by not opting for either side of the equation: either a frustrated life of critical autonomous distance spent railing against the status quo, or life lived as a soft-sell commercial success. Many songwriters seem convinced that this problem is managed best by integrating and managing aspects of one's creative personality that push and pull toward autonomy on the one hand, and toward heteronomy on the other. For instance, if the poet takes over, the song may become too ambiguous or flowery, shading into a kind of idiosyncratic autonomy. According to teacher of songwriting John Braheny, it is easy for the songwriter's poetry to become abstract or idiosyncratic, making it so that "we don't have a clue what the song is about."[36] If the prophetic voice is too strident, the song may sound moralistic and didactic. Song critic Richie Unterberger, assessing the catalogue of folk music entitled *The Best of Broadside, 1962–1988* (Smithsonian Folkways), observes that, aside from the work of Bob Dylan, Phil Ochs, Tom Paxton, Janis Ian, and Eric Andersen, "there are too many obscure strident singer/songwriters, . . . singing dry, didactic, unmelodic tunes with unimaginative plain arrangements."[37] On the other hand, if the empathic persona takes over, songs can overly accommodate to current cultural tastes and lose the ability to engage in truth-telling. Carole King warns against "chasing commercial reality" as a sure way to destroy one's unique voice as an artist.[38] If this empathic persona links arms with the artist's emotional persona, songwriting may sink into sentimentality or pandering.

Songwriters are aware that the songs they create emerge through the constant integration and reintegration of their creative personalities. Each song, in fact, signals a new integration and a new set of communicative competencies in relation to its audience. For most successful songwriters, the goal is not estrangement from oneself and others—a solipsistic or intentionally distanced life lived in poetic or prophetic alienation and dysfunction. Neither is it a life of writing according to the latest success formula. Rather, the goal is integration between aspects of the artistic self, which is always a task of negotiating between autonomy run amuck (self-indulgence) and heteronomy run amuck (pandering).

Similar to songwriting, theological invention involves the integration of a range of creative selves. These selves include vocational selves, such as the exegete, theologian, pastor, teacher, visionary, prophet, or counselor, as well as a host of other, more private selves, such as the humorist, parent, musician, puzzle solver, film lover, and so on. Over time, each of these selves can vie for control in the creative process. As time passes, some of these creative selves may drift into relative obscurity or get lost in the shuffle if the writer is not aware of the gifts they bring to the writer's table.

As in songwriting, it is possible to focus this integration around striking a balance between autonomy and heteronomy in theological invention. Deciding what to say will involve the integration of those creative selves that push toward autonomy (truth-telling, authenticity, sincerity, originality, distance, uniqueness) and those that push toward heteronomy (empathy, connection, relationship, marketability). For example, the autonomous writer may have a tendency to push the core of a tradition to extremes. When the formal theologian or exegete takes over, distance and abstraction may limit access to ideas invented to a relatively small elite. When the prophet or moralist takes over, theological invention can be pushed toward hyperbole, rigidity, and exclusivity.

The heteronomous writer, on the other hand, will tend to invent messages that are easy to grasp, palatable, sentimental, and immediately likable, with no thought for critical distance. For example, the "with-it" culturalist, film lover, and pop music critic may be tempted to reduce every theological idea to a movie scene or pop song lyric. Or the self-styled psychologist may invent only ideas that offer common sense, and often nontheological hints and helps for daily living.

It is not a matter of excluding these and other personas from the process of invention. Rather, what is needed is the ongoing integration and reintegration of these potentially creative selves through an investigation of their contributions to the tension between autonomy and heteronomy in theological invention, and to the resolution of this tension. In order to seek further integration of their creative selves in theological invention, writers can ask themselves a set of questions as to how various aspects of personal creativity (imagination, language skills, humor, enculturation, etc.) and vocational creativity (exegesis, theological knowledge, prophetic vision, pastoral insight, evangelical zeal, etc.) are engaged (or not engaged) in the inventive process. Is this creative persona overly distancing my ideas from the lives of those who are listening within this tradition? Is this persona overly pandering to those who expect only certain things from theological invention within this tradition? Which of our creative "selves" is being invited into the inventive process? Which are being left out? Why? Why not? Are autonomous elements, especially prophetic or evangelistic concerns, becoming strident or didactic? Are heteronomous aspects making us overly concerned with success or with marketing our ideas to listeners? How can we integrate all of our creative powers in the process of theological invention?

Empathy

For the writer of the popular song, the song is always about connection to a community of others within a particular tradition of music-making. Art is never for art's sake alone. Tom T. Hall reminds songwriters that their primary audience is ordinary people, not music critics.[39] According to John Hiatt, the popular songwriter *needs* to connect personally and artistically in order to legitimate one's work.[40] In other words, connection goes to the heart of what it means to be a *popular* songwriter.

Beyond self-legitimation, however, connection is motivated by a fundamental empathic element in the habitus of the songwriter. Empathy is built on what communication theorists call role-taking skills—ways of "getting into the shoes" of others.[41] These others, of course, are largely defined by the tradition of music-making in which the songwriter writes. The blues artist, for instance, typically gets into the shoes of those who have experienced poverty, infidelity, discrimination, addiction, or heartbreak. The gothic artist focuses more attention on those whose experience is defined by alienation, betrayal, and despair. The pop artist focuses on role-taking experiences of jealousy, desire, infatuation, and fun.

Songwriters testify that this kind of role-taking empathy develops over time. For songwriters in traditions such as folk or conscious hip-hop, this empathy often develops as an ethic of responsibility. Sara McLachlan observes that songwriting leaves her with a profound sense of responsibility for the feelings of others.[42] When Suzanne Vega encountered the harsh realities of child abuse and penned the song "Luka," she realized that she could no longer write in isolation; she had to use her talent to bring others' feelings to a larger audience.[43] Rapper Felipe Coronel, aka Immortal Technique, is a social activist and cofounder of the Grassroots Artists MovEment, which provides healthcare for underground hip-hop artists. His lyrics are often concerned with protesting the oppression of African Americans and Latinos.

For all popular songwriters, empathy develops through discovering and/or creating a community of shared feeling or commitment. Iggy Pop, for instance, wants his songs to put his inner self out in the public arena in order to see if anyone will identify with his ideas and emotions.[44] For Iggy and many other songwriters, the song is a lure cast into murky waters to seek out those of similar mind and emotion. Empathy can also be developed intentionally through a process of targeting a very specific group of people who share certain emotions and commitments, great care being taken in crafting a song for that group. Combining groups in order to connect more widely is often part of the agenda. Paul Simon is very intentional about the groups of people with whom he is seeking connection, and in his later work he seeks intentionally to combine divergent groups, a task he concedes is exceptionally difficult.[45] He has discovered that combining audiences potentially enriches his songwriting, but it also can confuse audiences who are unable to see the connections and integrations sought or perceived by the artist.

Songwriters testify to the artistic benefits of empathically connecting with others. Songs are not found within the recesses of the mind of the artist, but in connections the artist makes with other people's lives. Many songwriters believe that the best songs are actually *found* in making connection with others—the song is already out there among the people, waiting to be discovered. Irving Berlin, for instance, argued philosophically that "there are darned few good songs that have not been whistled or sung by the crowd."[46]

Beneath the obvious economic benefits of connecting to a large audience, therefore, the popular artist is intrinsically and vocationally an empathic communicator within a tradition of shared experiences. Empathic communication develops over time, and ultimately means sharing a world, to become, in the words of the great rhetorician Kenneth Burke, "consubstantial" with a listener or group of listeners.[47] Consubstantiality works against isolation and distance in art and makes it crucial that, when the song is finally heard, the audience not only gets it but also shares it.

Those involved in theological invention also have the potential to develop better empathic powers as they mature. Of course, this is not necessarily the case. For some, stereotypes harden, empathy dries up, judgment of others takes control, and one's connective powers become locked on a very narrow group of listeners. For most, however, relationships over time extend the range and depth of empathy. Old stereotypes give way to a new appreciation of the ways one's theological tradition can work to illuminate the lives of one's audience. For most preachers, for instance, it is possible to look back at old sermons and notice how one's understanding of the family, the elderly, children, and people of different races, ethnicity, gender, and sexual orientation have changed. Many preachers find that as they mature they can identify with a far broader range of listeners. They can also see tremendous evolution in the complexity of their understanding of economics, political realities, social problems, and cultural issues.

It is crucial to reflect on the shared world assumed by theological invention—ways in which messages are consubstantial or in solidarity with the lives of others. This will mean identifying and removing aspects of ideas that are idiosyncratic and not likely to connect with everyone. It can also include an assessment of the kinds of listeners assumed in one's messages, helping the writer identify stereotypical assumptions about family structure, lifestyle, social location, race, ethnicity, political affiliation, sports involvement, and so on. This can help the writer realize who is being included and who is being left out of the connecting process.

Songwriters offer a crucial insight into the development of empathy by highlighting its relationship to a tradition of music. Just as the blues artist invents songs that empathize with those who are suffering, or the gothic artist empathizes with those whose lives are marked by alienation, those who invent theology within a tradition will want to ask what core experiences call for empathy within a particular theological tradition. The conservative evangelical, for instance, may empathize with experiences of guilt, disobedience, and forgiveness. The Pentecostal may empathize with experiences of spiritual inhibition and awakening. The existentialist may empathize with experiences of finitude, depression, and courage. The liberationist may empathize with experiences of oppression and empowerment. Learning to invent ideas within a tradition always involves learning to empathize with those who share the real experiences raised up by a tradition for examination and expression.

Desire for the Song

For the songwriter, desire refers mostly to a life lived broadly for music and more specifically for "the song." Buffy Sainte-Marie asserts that in the final analysis she has "sold out everything" in her life that is not supportive of her music-making.[48] Van Dyke Parks asserts that music-making is the most important and constant element of daily life and that a day without it is literally "oblivion."[49] Successful songwriters are not primarily plumbers, painters, teachers, or business owners who happen to write music. They see themselves primarily as musicians, and music is what they live for. Songwriting brings tremendous pleasure, both in the search for the song and in the arrival and enjoyment of the song once it is completed. Jule Styne once painted a vivid picture of the perfect, joy-filled day as a day of sunshine and songwriting.[50] Cultivating this desire to create music is a crucial virtue for the songwriter.

Desire feeds the autonomous impulse in songwriting, the unsettling of one's life in pursuit of authentic, truth-telling lyrics and music. When describing their desire for the hook or the song, songwriters often describe their lives as disturbed, unsettled, lured onward by music. This hearkens back to the Romantic idea of the possession or madness of the artist. Many songwriters describe themselves as haunted by songs. They hear them at a distance and chase them in order to give them voice. John Stewart described the songwriter's life as one of perpetual desire to write the next good song.[51] Desire for the song is an essential quality of character that is necessary to rise above mediocrity and improve one's work. One good song prompts the desire for another good song, and there is always the hope that the next song will be more important to the listener than the previous one.

Although there is a strong future orientation to the songwriter's desire for the song, in most instances this desire is focused on producing songs that will stand the test of time. This is grounded, once again, in the debt songwriters feel to a tradition of music. In a scene in the documentary movie *It Might Get Loud*, guitarist and songwriter Jack White pauses to play a Son House record for the interviewer. He speaks of the song with almost religious undertones, communicating a deep desire that his writing and music would somehow do justice to the tradition of music represented by the blues master. Desire, for the successful popular songwriter, is almost always linked to this desire to reach more deeply into a tradition of writing, producing new sounds that will somehow live up to certain qualities represented by the tradition's great exemplars.

The songwriter's desire speaks to the need to identify theological invention as a central passion and joy in one's life, whether it takes the shape of a book, a song, a sermon, an essay, a blog, a Facebook entry, a tweet, a response in a classroom, or a contribution to a conversation. One can choose to be involved in theological invention at many levels of one's life, as a professional theologian or as a layperson seeking more insight into the deeper meanings of life. Regardless of what arena of life is involved, the desire to invent better theological ideas is crucial.

By accentuating the relationship between desire and traditions of invention, songwriters add something to our understanding of desire and theological invention. Just as the songwriter desires to reach more deeply into a tradition of musical invention and produce sounds that will somehow live up to qualities exemplified by the tradition's best inventive voices, the desire to engage in theological invention can follow a similar path. A tradition, whether ecclesial (Baptist, Methodist, Pentecostal, etc.) or ideological (liberationist, existentialist, process, conservative-evangelical, liberal, feminist), has the power to inspire writers to cover and riff on the work of its exemplars, write in community with its writers, externalize its experiences, integrate one's creative selves in light of its inner tensions, and empathize with its listeners. At the core of this is the deep desire to invent theology in and out of this tradition in a way that will be recognized as both consistent with, and showing respect for, the tradition, and yet building on it in new and creative ways. Always there is the desire that one's work receive some token of admiration and respect by those considered to be the great exemplars within the tradition itself. Such exemplars may be deceased—Augustine, Peter Abelard, Julian of Norwich, John Calvin, Martin Luther, John Wesley, Aimee Semple McPherson, Karl Barth, Paul Tillich, Simone de Beauvoir, or Jacques Derrida—or living, accessible exemplars such as preachers, teachers, authors, friends, or media personalities who self-identify with a particular theological tradition.

Persistence

Song-making requires two levels of persistence: vocational persistence and persistence in the mundane tasks of writing in the face of a variety of blocks and impediments. The songwriter must learn to persevere in the face of adversity and when energy and imagination are at low ebb. Persistence is a quality of character that fosters a range of practices leading to potential success.

For most successful songwriters, persistence is, once again, associated with exemplars within the tradition of popular songwriting. Songwriters are quick to tell stories about those who have preceded them in the art who have suffered through dry times and have persevered. A significant portion of songwriter lore is devoted to revering those who have continued to write in spite of the odds. For many, it took years to break into the industry. Once they experienced success, stories of dry spells endured and overcome abound.

As Willie Nelson puts it in his autobiography, "You can't tell a real songwriter he isn't any good, because he knows better, and he'll keep hacking his way through show-biz hell until he proves it."[52] To be a songwriter is to be a person with dogged determination, persistence, and desire to succeed. Songwriter and teacher of songwriting K. A. Parker asserts that "I'd rather work with people who are enthusiastic about their bad work than people who hate their brilliant work. . . . If you continue to write and learn, even though nobody buys your work or even likes your work—you'll probably get better."[53] Living with a self-critical or cynical attitude toward one's work leads nowhere. The virtue of persistently pursuing a good song, even when one's work is mediocre, helps one become better.

Randy Newman speaks of the ways that writer's block annihilates one's self-esteem as a writer, even to the point of making songwriters believe they are caught in an endless downward spiral and should give up writing forever.[54] During these times it is easy for one's imperfections as a writer to become a ball and chain. Joni Mitchell notes the importance of getting the internal editor/perfectionist out of the way when this occurs, remembering that both art and life are full of imperfections.[55] This may relieve some of the internal pressure.

It may also be helpful to set aside those personal and professional things that might be blocking the writing process. Peter Case advises writing down an inventory of things in one's life that might be blocking creativity: distractions, issues, relationships, worries, and fears.[56] No matter how one deals with writing blocks or thoughts of low self-esteem, most songwriters realize that dry times are a part of their vocation and that persevering through these difficulties is a fundamental virtue that must be developed in order to succeed and continue to flourish as a writer.

Just as important as vocational perseverance is persistence in writing the song at hand. Songwriters testify how easy it can be to give up on a particular song, yet how important it is to push on through. According to Mary Gauthier, "an awful lot of songwriting is about sitting down and, even if you don't want to, continuing to work on something until you get it, until it's right."[57] Sarah Chauncey advises her students to "finish your bad song, get it on tape, then fix the bad song."[58] Others, such as Paul Simon, advise a healthy dose of patience with oneself.[59] This does not mean giving up on the song. It means allowing the song to find its own timing, as much as possible. Dennis Lambert likens the songwriter to a sculptor who has to keep chiseling away till the hard stone finally begins to take shape.[60] Writing is a linear process. It goes from point A to point B, and there will likely be many curves and detours along the way. One will never arrive, however, if one does not persevere in the journey.

For the creative theologian, persistence speaks to the need for discipline, perseverance, patience, and consistent effort, as one with something to say theologically, in deciding what to say on a regular basis. Becoming a better inventor of theology means chiseling until the stones of one's words and powers of expression begin to give up well-formed messages, in whatever form. In this regard, theologians can learn to set aside debilitating perfectionism, recognizing that they are all limited. They can develop ways to shelve things in their lives that might be blocking practices of theological reflection and inventiveness—busywork, e-mail, relationship issues, deadlines, and so on—and clear the way for practices of invention.

The example of songwriters encourages theologians to develop a lore of persistence as a part of the habitus of theological invention. Most who have invented theological ideas of public or private significance will attest to the need for long-suffering persistence. Often, ideas that come too quickly are only half-baked. Many of the great works of theologians such as Augustine, Abelard, Calvin, Luther, Beauvoir, and Bonhoeffer were products of persistence through significant difficulties of life and belief. Sometimes the ideas of these exemplars immediately found a responsive audience; at other times they only found an audience later. In all cases, the theologians persisted in theological inventiveness, never giving up on the need for religion itself to persist and achieve significant voice in their day.

Attention

Songwriters speak over and over again about developing the ability to *attend* carefully to reality in all of its particularity and detail. Writing requires deep attention: awareness of what is immediately present to one's intellect, imagination, and senses. Chris Smither, speaking of the work of Dave Alvin, calls this form of attention "absolute directness."[61] According to Billy Bragg, "the songwriters I most appreciated were the ones who used their songs as a mirror for the world around them."[62] Paying attention involves mirroring the world: seeing the details, finding the universal in the particular.

When externalizing experiences that are shaped by a tradition, whether pain and suffering, violence, desire, or responsibility, it is common for the writer to reach for clichés, or stereotypes that bend toward abstraction or sentimentality. Attending to details helps one avoid capitulating to sentimentality or using emotional clichés designed to toy with the listener's feelings. As Craig Northey puts it, "life is really in the grey area, . . . extremes of emotion are always there; I think it's more interesting to write about your ironing."[63] Focusing on the details (such as ironing) helps songwriters avoid running to emotional excess to succeed with audiences. The reality and beauty of the song lies in what Willie Dixon called paying attention to the facts. Dixon said that his father once told him, "blues is facts, and the world don't want to know facts. . . . But if you can get the people to hear these blues, they can get a lot of wisdom out of it."[64] The task of the songwriter, then, is to bring forth the wisdom embedded within the facts, to see the facts in a new way. Seeing the facts means attending to what Randy Newman calls the "regular stuff,"[65] people going about their regular business, nature, animals, interactions, conversations, buildings, streets, and so on.

The primary practice involved in attending to the reality right in front of one's eyes is, more often than not, the practice of *lowering one's sights.* Pete Townshend argues for "reducing your expectations and putting a value on what you already have."[66] What one already has is not simply one's own internal experience. Randy Newman argues that songwriters are like short story writers or novelists who should attend to the ways truth emerges from the bits and pieces of people's lives.[67] Rupert Holmes likens songwriters to "harmless voyeurs" who are always observing people and asking, " 'What's their story?' "[68] The key to all great art is freeing truth from a particular moment within history, context, or situation. This cannot be accomplished without learning how to attend deeply and carefully to the actual details of a place and moment in time.

The theologian who desires a broad audience experiences a similar need to cultivate the deep forms of listening, seeing, and imagining the world that are required in order to faithfully communicate the realities of life in today's world. This often involves lowering one's sights in order to see the truth immediately at hand. Instead of spending hours scrolling through the ideas or anecdotes of others, writers can learn to notice what is immediately available. Rather than inventing ideas that push toward extremes (of emotion, antagonism, effusion), writers can learn how to identify religious truth in the "ironing," in the very particular bits and pieces of ordinary life.

Brad Wigger, Professor of Christian Education at Louisville Presbyterian Theological Seminary, teaches a course on attention and awareness, in which students learn to lower their sights and become aware of the religious truth available to them in the details of life. Leaving lofty theological ideas in the background, students focus attention on small patterns of behavior, types of words or phrases, colors, sounds, attitudes, styles, furnishings, habits, expressions of pain or joy, and so on. Beginning with simple attention to reality as it presents itself, students move from the givenness of these realities toward consideration of the larger scheme in which these realities exist, resulting ultimately in theological reflections that connect deeply with real, lived experience.

All relevant/real theological invention will require this kind of attention. Writers will need to be able to move from the details of life toward theological abstraction—as practical or lived theologians. The popular songwriter knows what many theological writers do not—that *applied* theology is not nearly as powerful or connective as *lived* theology.

Simplicity

Simplicity builds on attention. Songwriters place high value on simplicity or the ability to discover the complex in the simple. When asked who he considered a good songwriter and why, Daniel Johns replied, "Brian Wilson, definitely. He writes the most simple and beautiful melodies."[69] Kris Kristofferson, speaking of the first time he heard Mickey Newbury, says, "I heard these simple melodies with simple words that just broke your heart."[70] According to Patty Griffin, "When somebody can nail something with simplicity and it seems really honest and direct in its most simple form, that's the stuff that really gets to me."[71] Simplicity does not mean the loss of complexity. The most complex ideas and emotions are usually captured in simple, straightforward images, juxtaposition of images, or narratives. As Sylvia Tyson puts it, "Successful song lyrics put forth complex ideas in very simple language."[72]

The virtue of simplicity extends to economy with words, grammar, and form. According to Paul Westerberg, "it's either simple or its impossible. . . . I think the challenge of songwriting is simply to use the same few chords and make them fresh again."[73] When asked what he strives for in a song, Randy Newman replied, "A lot of it is the use of small words . . . you get the right one and it takes you to a good place."[74] Often, simplicity requires the willingness to become an active editor. Bruce Cockburn encourages writers to relentlessly cross out anything that is not absolutely necessary.[75]

The best songs are those that are able to express deep and complex thoughts and feelings as simply and elegantly as possible. The primary reason for this is *communication*. The writer of the popular song eschews esoteric art in favor of art that connects. This connection is made possible by a deep listening and the ability to identify and express truth in ways that are both beautiful and clear. As Tom Wilson so aptly puts it, "simplicity really rules. We are talking about communication, we're not talking about self-indulgence. . . . We're not dumbing it down . . . just making it simple . . . conversation."[76]

For the theologian, simplicity speaks to the need to seek the complexity of religious truth with simple, pure, illuminated clarity. Many trained leaders and scholars who have put in the time studying everyone from Augustine to Barth have learned vocabulary that is hard to leave behind. These complex ideas should not be lost; they must be translated into images and simple words that can be seen and felt.

Communicative Judgment

What, in the last analysis, have we learned from the popular songwriter that might be of some help in creating a habitus for theological invention? I propose that it is the importance of developing something as simple but elusive as *good inventive judgment*. Rather than relying on genius, instincts, divination, formulas for popularity, or their desire to speak tough prophetic words to a misguided generation, songwriters spend their time seeing if they can develop good judgment as writers, cultivating a life of self-awareness as those who must have the good judgment to choose "this" expression, not "that" expression, within a tradition of writing. As far as they are concerned, good judgment can and must be shaped out of the raw materials of their own ordinary lives as shaped by a tradition of writing, no matter how strange or ill-formed those lives might appear to many. Good judgment is an acquired habit of heart and mind that can be learned by practice and experience. It requires self-awareness, discipline, and community.

As we have noted, successful songwriters are profoundly aware that their work of composition is, in fact, composing their lives within a particular tradition of song-making. As they discover, frame, and reframe the reality around them, the best songwriters are always aware that this process is one of intensive self-education and maturation in judgment as songwriters operating in and out of traditions of music. They are aware that they are internalizing the rules of a genre and then connecting those rules to new situations and contexts. They are learning what is appropriate within a tradition of music in order to have the good judgment to improvise effectively on that tradition.

Good judgment is also an acquired habit forged through a lifetime of *practicing* one's craft. One does not learn to write by mechanically following the rules or hints and helps of the craft. One learns by putting on a tradition like a garment, writing in the tracks of masters of the craft, imitating excellence, and then passionately and persistently writing, being conscious of what one is doing and how it is best done when successful.

Keith D. Miller and Elizabeth Vander Lei have documented how during slave times African American folk preachers would repreach "sermons and portions of sermons, eliciting the verbal approval of their congregations while deleting material that fail[ed] to spark any interest."[77] In essence, these preachers and their audiences were collaboratively improvising within a tradition, assisting one another in deciding what, in fact, works and what does not, a process that helped the preachers learn how to preach within, and out of, a particular tradition. In a similar way, teaching theological inventiveness best resembles collaborative supervision or coaching, where the listener-teacher helps the inventor discover what is appropriate within a tradition in order to achieve better inventive judgment. In other words, good judgment is best learned in self-reflexive practice within a community shaped by tradition.

Emphasis on good judgment as central to the writer's habitus diverges significantly from the Romantic idea of unique, individualistic poetic genius, or the bohemian idea of the prophetic outsider, and requires a more positive view of the value of the writer's experience of maturation and learning, including the development of character within a tradition.[78] Significant value is placed on self-conscious maturation and on cultivating virtues such as a desire to faithfully represent a tradition, persistence in becoming effective, attention to the ways theological truth can be found in one's situation, and graceful simplicity in choosing the right words to say.

Theological invention within this frame of reference is profoundly *hermeneutical* and *communal*, sustained by shared traditions of engaging and interpreting texts and life. The writer is neither a diviner of sacred oracles nor a wandering town crier, heralding unpalatable truths. Rather, the writer is a theological interpreter of life who enters imaginatively into an ongoing spiritually charged theological tradition, recognizing and learning the prophetic and poetic wisdom of that tradition, and articulating that wisdom in situations, seeking out connection, feedback, challenge, support, insight, and argument.

While certainly not complete in and of themselves, these building blocks for sound judgment, as expressed within the habitus of the songwriter, commend themselves to the theologian in this generation. They have the effect of encouraging a life of passionate commitment to truth, in all of its authenticity and autonomy, while supporting a life of writing and composing that is grounded in the maturation of judgment, community, and the development of virtues of character.

In chapter 2 we find this habitus potentially broadened as the song-making process enters the studio and various styles of audio tracking are made available to the song-maker. At this point, the artist's good judgment begins to confront the reality that the products of good judgment are always produced, re-produced, and remixed once they start down the long and winding road that leads to reception. This move, if theological inventors are prepared to investigate it closely, will require belief that religious meaning can be found at and beyond the boundaries of traditions, in and through real relationships and sometimes random juxtapositions in history that loosen the hold that traditions have on the invention of religious truth. Here, what is prepared in good judgment, or along the pathway toward good judgment, with a particular audience in mind and particular results in the offing, is potentially deconstructed, reshaped, and connected to different traditions and publics. The song now leaves the narrow confines of the writer's pen and paper, and the small community of feedback grounded in a tradition, and moves into a new set of social locations and relationships, where it is "tracked," "remixed," and ultimately "mashed up." In this process, a new set of issues will confront the musician, and a new set of possibilities will be suggested for those engaged in theological invention.

2

MULTITRACK COMPOSITION AND LOOP BROWSING

STYLE AND THEOLOGICAL INVENTION

[M]ixing (and editing), as opposed to recording (and letting it be), is the dominant mode of recording today.

—Greg Milner, *Perfecting Sound Forever: An Aural History of Recorded Music*

The digital audio workstation (DAW) is a computer-based or free-standing electronic system designed especially to record, edit, and play back digital audio. Within the workface of a DAW, a studio engineer or artist can track audio (record audio on individual tracks) and manipulate and organize samples, regions of recorded audio, and MIDI-based audio. These sounds can be enhanced (morphed, time-stretched, tuned, trimmed, shaped, moved, compressed, phase-inverted, equalized, looped, and so on) through the use of a range of integrated tools or purchased plug-ins. Although DAWs come in a variety of very sophisticated and expensive models, many are now accessible and even packaged as a part of retail computer systems (especially GarageBand, Cubase, Logic, Acid, and Pro Tools). With this software, all the artist needs is an analog-to-digital converter (ADC) in order to get sounds into the computer or device, and a digital-to-analog converter (DAC) in order to get the sound out once it has been organized, processed, and mixed.

Most DAWs include an edit window or digital sequencer, which will be the focus of this chapter. In an earlier generation, keyboard synthesizers contained within themselves MIDI sequencers in which synthesized sounds could be arranged in sequences of a particular length, layered on top of each other, and then looped in order to be played and replayed at various intervals during a song. Solo performers in small venues could use these sequences to add bass, drums, and other orchestration to their music. With the advent of higher CPU speeds and more memory, these sequencers morphed into the edit windows within DAWs, in which recorded audio, MIDI notes, and samples could be arranged and integrated easily with synthesized sounds. Most DAWs now bundle sequencing (tracking and editing) software, sampling technology, audio recording tools, and audio mixing tools.[1]

By shifting attention from songwriting to the business of tracking audio within the DAW, this chapter follows as the song-maker moves from writing a coherent song within a tradition of music to layering tracks of audio that will enhance or re-create a song. For the popular song-maker, the practice of entering a recording studio and recording multiple tracks of audio is powerfully inventive, focused on deciding what sounds will ultimately be juxtaposed and layered to produce the song in its finished form. The song-making process involves many different layers of invention in the multitrack studio as different instruments and vocal parts are layered into the song. In chapter 3, we will focus on the way that these layers of tracks can be expanded to include the remixing and mashing up of beats and breaks across genres and traditions. In this chapter we will focus on more traditional forms of multitracking, in which tracks of audio are chosen largely as the result of stylistic qualities that have roots within traditions. We will see, however, how increased awareness of multiple traditions and styles anticipates the stylistic morphing that occurs within remix and mashup models of invention (chapter 3).

The edit window within a DAW affords the luxury of permitting the visual organization of tracks and the detailed editing of that

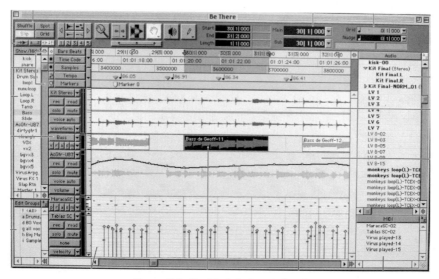

Figure 2.1. Pro Tools "edit window."

audio prior to performance or playback. It also allows us to fully visualize audio "transients" or waveforms as they are tracked and edited. The edit window of most DAWs is organized as in figure 2.1.[2] Stretching from top to bottom across the computer screen are layered tracks of audio inserted and organized according to their desired occurrence within the song. Each track contains bits and pieces of audio (recorded audio, samples, loops, MIDI sequences). In recording a band, there will typically be at least one track for each drum in a drum kit (snare, kick, hi-hat, tom, floor tom, overhead microphones for cymbals), along with tracks for vocals, bass, guitars, keyboards, and other instruments. As we will see in chapter 4, once these tracks have been inserted in the edit window and edited, the artist or studio engineer can make use of a mix window to adjust volume, stereo panning, equalization, and a variety of special effects in order to create the kind of sonic palette that is desired. Within any editing process, the engineer produces a number of submixes in which similar sounds are grouped together (drums, percussion, rhythm instruments, vocals, etc.) in order to allow for more precise placement in the final mix. These submixes are usually kept to a minimum to bring focus and clarity to the overall mix.

The edit page of a DAW inserts a significant prosthetic element into song-making. A powerful, computerized organizing device is appended to the hands, arms, and ears of the song-maker. Writing about photography and film production, Walter Benjamin observed that editing tools have shifted the way that perception is organized within so-called prosthetic arts (film and audio reproduction). Instead of moving from the whole to the parts, perception is reorganized from the parts to the whole.[3] Cultural theorist Lindsay Waters observes that in the digital age, "we have a method that proceeds in an experimental way, testing each element in isolation as it goes along. All the pop arts are put together this way, feelingly, bit by bit in a constant negotiation among humans and machines testing the capacities and powers and limits of all the players, human and non-human, adapting to the resistances of all."[4] In popular song-making, this part-to-whole editing process is a time-consuming and highly creative process of "feelingly" layering tracks of audio into a song. The way the tracks are chosen and arranged is always a commentary on the musical materials gathered in the studio, providing a frame within which the original pieces are set and set off from one another. Each sound, sequence of sounds, or track must be investigated for its own unique sonic character and possibilities and placed within the right sonic space and time. Different ways of juxtaposing and layering audio create very different end results. In this way, the arrangement and organization of layers of audio remain crucial to the invention of the song itself. It is not as if the song is conceptually complete, awaiting arrangement. Rather, the arranging and editing process is an inductive, part-to-whole practice of invention in and of itself. Deciding what to say (invention) is not complete until the artist, producer, and sound engineer have decided what to record on each track and how these parts will contribute to the larger whole.

Moving from left to right in the edit window, the basic organizing plot or linear arrangement for most popular songs is usually some variation of vocal verses and a chorus, instrumental passages (breaks, leads), and a bridge or "middle eight." These elements can be shifted around in any number of ways, but most popular music listeners expect at least some faint echo of this pattern as a way of ultimately organizing the way the parts cohere.

Arrangement at the level of plot or linear pattern is supplemented by arrangement at the level of layering, which is viewed from top to bottom on the edit window. Depending on the genre of music, layering a popular song includes four primary types of tracks: rhythm, melody, backing, and fills. Artists typically record initial tracks such as bass, drums, keyboards, and rhythm guitars, or whatever instrumental texture is required for the song's *rhythm* tracks or base. These are usually recorded while listening in headphones to a metronome aligned to a grid within the sequencer of the DAW. To this is layered (often simultaneously) a *melody* track (often vocal), which may be redone in a final version later. Next is layered in a set of *backing* tracks, which can be instruments such as brass, strings, electric guitars, and so on. The backing tracks often provide counterpoints to the song's melody, to make the song more memorable. To these are layered *fills*, which help with transitions, humanization (spontaneity), and the overall soundstage of the recording. In a song, layering is partly simultaneous. Tracks literally sit on top of one another. Layers of sound are also staggered, appearing and disappearing, as a particular track sounds forth in one sequence and then does not show up again for several measures.

Experimenting in the Studio

When the producer of a song decides what audio to record (track) within a particular submix (rhythm, melody, backing, fills), the choice is focused on a range of different content. Although the choice for a particular kind of content is sometimes made without any experimentation, loops of audio now play an increasingly central role in musical invention, allowing producers to experiment with the ways different sounds will affect a recording. Most DAWs include some form of "loop browser," which displays a filing system of recorded samples of audio (loops) that can be imported into different tracks and looped (repeated). The production of loop libraries is an enormous component of the recording business today. Recording engineers can purchase entire libraries of loops of nearly every instrument on the planet. At the same time, recording engineers can produce their own loops. Any sound can be recorded, sampled, looped, added to one's loop library, and filed for selection within one's loop browser.

Experimenting with these loops permits a producer or studio engineer to explore different styles of music and different instrumentation before committing to a particular way of tracking the song. Once an instrument and style are settled on, the producer will decide whether to invite a live musician to record a similar track of audio, or whether the digitally sampled loop will suffice. Looking at a loop browser within a DAW provides a good window into how these decisions are made.

Loops of sampled audio from instruments such as bass, guitars, pianos, organs, synths, and strings are usually organized according to at least two categories: *musical traditions*, such as rock/blues, electronic, world, urban, ska, and so on (see figure 2.2, column 1), and *styles of tracking*, such as acoustic, electric, clean, distorted, dry, processed, and grooving (see figure 2.2, column 2). Producers of music in a studio must decide which musical tradition and style of tracking will be appropriate for a particular song and when to track certain elements of that style into one of the four submixes.

In order to continue the song's legacy in or out of a particular tradition of music, and to aim the song at a particular audience, songmakers will usually choose styles that are mostly within that tradition. Sometimes, however, when it is deemed helpful for creating the song's overall experience, producers will include traditions of tracking that come from other genres of music. Experimenting with loops from different traditions (figure 2.2, column 1) will give the producer an idea of what another tradition of music might contribute to the song. If a producer decides to invite a Latin percussionist to record several tracks on a country-and-western song, the song's invention moves slightly in a new direction. Willie Nelson and many Tex-Mex musicians mix styles in this way. When the Rolling Stones recorded a children's choir for backing tracks on "You Can't Always Get What You Want" they gave the song a churchy, hymn-like quality. Kenny Chesney, inspired by Jimmy Buffett, incorporated Jamaican rhythms, marimbas, and steel drums into his country songs in order to support the "life's a beach" philosophy in the songs.

Choosing a musical tradition (figure 2.2, column 1) is not all that is involved in tracking. The producer must also choose a style of tracking (figure 2.2, column 2). If the Latin percussion instruments

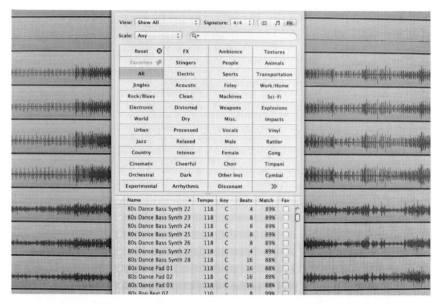

Figure 2.2. Apple Logic Pro Loop Browser. Column 1, under the word "reset" includes a broad range of musical traditions (rock/blues, electronic, world, etc.). Column 2 includes a broad range of tracking styles (electric, clean, distorted, dry, etc.).

are tracked in a distorted style, the choir is tracked with robotic filters added to the voices, or the marimbas are tracked out of phase and in an echo chamber, each song's invention will move in other directions. The style in which audio is tracked, therefore, is also powerfully inventive in the production of the overall meaning of the song.

Tracking and Theological Invention

From the early days of primary and secondary school education, students are trained to think of the invention and arrangement of papers, essays, and narratives as a distinctly linear, left-to-right process. From this perspective, inventive aspects of organization are focused on deciding what to say *next*. In the same way that songmakers learn variations of vocal verses, chorus, instrumental passages (breaks, leads), hooks, and bridges, writers learn meaningful patterns: deductive, inductive, narrative (plotted), cinematic (scenic), problem-solution, conditional (if-then), and so on.

Although this aspect of invention is certainly a concern for song-makers, invention at the level of top-to-bottom layering or tracking is far more important. Instead of focusing entirely on the question What will I say next?, song-makers focus on the question What will sound best with this? What needs to be tracked or layered in at this point in time in order to enhance and strengthen the song?

This layered aspect of theological invention will be the focus of the remainder of this chapter, for it is this element from the world of popular song-making that has the most to add to the invention of theology. How can we think about theological invention as a practice of deciding how to layer partly simultaneous, partly staggered tracks of theological content that function best with one another, in support of the overall invention and arrangement of this composition? What would this mean for theological invention as a whole?

I suggest that we can draw a direct analogy between song tracking and the layering of theological content within a theological composition. We might call this theological *tracking:* the sequencing and layering of levels of theological discourse. In many ways, theological tracking parallels the sequencing and layering of audio within the DAW.

The digital music sequence, as an identifiable linear (left-to-right) region of a song's tracks, provides an excellent way to think about the key blocks of organized material that must be decided on when composing theology. Sequences operate at the level of plot or linear arrangement. They are identifiable regions of theological material, organized roughly as blocks of thought with transitions in and out. Within each sequence, there are multiple layers of different kinds of content: stories, images, ideas, theology, references to Scripture, and so on. In theological compositions, whether lectures, sermons, songs, blogs, or conversational material invented on the fly, we can identify four basic layers of content (submixes of tracks) that roughly parallel melody, rhythm, backing, and fills in the popular song. These layers hinge on the four authorities (authors) for theological invention—Scripture, culture/experience, theology, and reason (idea/message). In other words, four submixes of tracks, which I will designate as Scripture tracks, culture tracks, theology tracks, and message tracks, can be used to organize all of the tracks within a theological composition. Theological invention and arrangement must occur at all four of these levels. For instance, in a popular song, although thirty-two rhythm tracks might be needed in order to get bass, guitar, drums, and keyboards recorded, these all constitute one submix or layer of audio, called the "rhythm tracks." Similarly, in a theological composition, although there may be fifteen direct or indirect references to Scripture, they all constitute one submix or layer, which we might call the "Scripture tracks."

The Four Layers (Submixes) of Theological Tracks

As in a popular song, there are four layers of tracks that typically go into theological composition.[5] Not all theological compositions will use all of these tracks, and they will not always be used consistently. These tracks do, however, constitute the primary layers or levels of theological invention. Each track is aimed at one of four dimensions of listening or reception. *Scripture tracks* are aimed at the listener's memory (anamnesis) of the ancient language and events that constitute the foundational core of a religious tradition. They include all references to these sacred texts or the world out of which they arise—that is, anything in a composition that speaks about the revelatory past referred to in the religious tradition's Scriptures. *Culture tracks* (we might think of fill tracks in music) speak to the way that a theologian and prospective audience understand religion at work in their daily lives within the larger culture. This includes illustrations and all references to contemporary human experience: anecdotes, stories, self-disclosure, and assumptions regarding manners, furniture, clothing, family life, newspapers, television, movies, and so on. *Theology tracks* (we might think of backing tracks) include any references to a theological tradition, whether ecclesial or ideological (theological world), and the way that the theologian orders and relates the various components of the Christian faith (theological worldview). Theology tracks include anything that identifies *which* religious story is being told and *how* it is being told. *Message tracks* (we might think of melody/vocal tracks) are aimed at the listener's lexicon of ideas, what the listener holds to be a significant religious meaning or truth. Message tracks in a theological composition include all thematic or idea words—anything that *explicitly* tells the audience what the composition is about, the message being communicated to one's audience at a particular moment in time. As in the melody track in the popular song, the way that the message track is layered controls the left-to-right, linear plotline or arrangement of the composition, controlling how the other layers are staggered and located within the composition.

We can group together the layers of tracks in a four-sequence theological composition (essay, sermon, blog entry) as in figure 2.3. Theological invention will take place at several of these levels within each sequence of thought. In other words, there are four authors or authorities for doing theology that can be given inventive power in theological composition. Theologians will therefore have to open the theological "loop browser," do some experimentation, and eventually select something to say at each of these levels. As we have indicated, these are largely stylistic decisions, which involve the theologian in choosing according to a ecclesial or ideological tradition, and a style of tracking.

Developing a Theological Loop Browser

Like the producer in the multitrack studio choosing whether to add Latin percussion, a children's choir, or marimbas to a song, theologians can choose to record each track making use of a range of possibilities. But theologians are not always as aware of the options available to them as the producer is. Sorting out these options, or creating a functional "loop browser" for theologians, is the focus of the remainder of this chapter. Emulating the way that software loops are organized into styles, we will attempt to provide a basic, first-level organizing grid for styles of theological tracking, focusing on the four submixes of theological composition: Scripture, culture, theology, and message.

I have two goals in doing this. First, I want to indicate the range of options for theological content and style that currently exist for theological invention. Second, and most importantly, I want to show how "browsing" traditions and rhetorical styles inserts into theological production forms of reflexivity and experimentation that begin

Layers or submixes of tracks	Sequence 1	Sequence 2	Sequence 3	Sequence 4
Theology Tracks				
Message Tracks				
Culture Tracks				
Scripture Tracks				

Figure 2.3. Edit window.

to break open tradition-bound and rhetorically consistent practices of theological invention and suggest hybrid forms of theological invention. This browsing creates a shift from *hermeneutical* forms of invention (invention in and out of a tradition and its typical rhetorical style) to *intertextual* forms of invention (invention across traditions and rhetorical styles).

The first element in the browser consists of sampled bits of material from a range of theological traditions, sects, and ideologies. It would take far too much time to describe the range of options available here and the kinds of theological "loops" one might sample from each tradition. Suffice it to say that the first column in our loop browser will be filled with bits of theological content from all the major world religions and sects, as well as bits of material from ideological traditions such as liberation theology, deconstructionist theology, process theology, conservative evangelical theology, and so on. As in the choice of a children's choir on the Rolling Stones' "You Can't Always Get What You Want" or marimbas on Kenny Chesney's and Jimmy Buffett's songs, a particular instrument or idea, recognizable for its relationship with a particular tradition of thought, is chosen in this column.

Given today's computer technology, theologians have immediate access to an array of content browsers, including multiple technologies for browsing the Internet and libraries the world over. It is also possible to store and file many ideas and quotations for easy retrieval. In today's context, therefore, theologians have instant access to a broad-based "loop library" of religious traditions and ideas from which to sample. The theological inventor does not need access to every aspect of a tradition in order to experiment with what a tradition might bring to the mix. It will be most important to include theological loops that are indicative of each tradition's core beliefs, themes, and styles of presentation. These will include sampled quotations, music, or video by major spokespersons from within each tradition or theological model, as well as samples of one's own unique perspective on these ideas and artifacts.

Most theologians know how to sample and experiment with theological content. What they are less aware of is the range of tracking styles available to them, and the ways that styles of tracking theology are crucial for theological invention. For this reason, I will focus in the remainder of this chapter on the second column of the loop browser: the typical variety of *tracking styles* for Scripture, message, theology, and experience in theological invention. I will treat these as rhetorical styles—ways of shaping language and thought—that shape theological invention in different ways. The song-maker must choose among different tracking styles such as acoustic, electric, clean, processed, reverberated, delayed, out of phase, and so on; I will suggest similar options for the theological composer. The categories of styles I will identify are based on the broad rhetorical analysis of theological compositions of various types (essays, sermons, tracts, blogs, websites, books, articles, etc.), mostly within the Christian tradition, and on the rhetorical styles scholars use within each category of tracking theology.[6] My categories, therefore, will be very broad, and are not meant to be exhaustive. Developing the categories for this theological loop browser is an open-ended process.

"Style" is not a trivial word. Process philosopher Alfred North Whitehead, in *The Aims of Education*, calls style the "fashioning of power."[7] According to religious educator Craig Dykstra, "one's style is the *patterned* manner in which a person draws together one's energies in order to have an effect on the world in which one lives. The *way* that one acts, in other words, results from the manner in which one's past experience, present situation, thoughts, feelings, beliefs, attitudes and values—one's powers—are structured into an organic whole."[8]

Depending on which of the four submixes of tracks is under consideration, the style of tracking is inventive of four elements of religious discourse. The style in which a theologian tracks Scripture is crucial for the invention of a form of religious memory, or *anamnesis*. The style used to track culture invents a form of religious *experience*. The style used to track theology invents a particular religious *world and worldview*. The style used to track messages invents an understanding of religious *truth*.

Tracking Scripture and the Invention of Religious Memory

The content of the Scripture tracks is any reference to a religion's sacred texts or Scriptures, or to the foundational events of a religion as articulated by those Scriptures. As we will see, this includes the words of the text itself, in the original language or in translation, the historical events, communities of belief, and sociocultural realities behind the text, the rhetorical and performative qualities of the texts, and the perceived theological and contextual claims of the text.

The style in which Scripture is tracked in a theological composition invents a form of religious *memory*, a way of recalling the meaning of ancient religious texts in today's world. Just as the clean, yet highly reverberated tracking of a children's choir invents the presence of a cathedral within a rock song, a style of scriptural tracking invents a way of remembering the ancient past in theological composition. There are several fundamental styles for accomplishing this.

Dynamic Equivalence

In the first style of tracking Scripture, the theologian simply translates past *words* (from the scriptural text) into present concepts or experiences. Hopefully, this is not done naively, that is, without the theologian having first considered the larger historical and theological context within which these words were crafted. The theologian with this rhetorical style, however, after studying the text, always returns to the obvious features of the scriptural text and looks for clear and obvious analogies between aspects of the text and contemporary theological ideas or human experience.

When working in this style, the theologian tracks what is supposedly "in" the text, its obvious features. The audience is led to believe that the theologian is making straightforward analogies between various aspects of the ancient text (characters, ideas, actions, places) and aspects of today's life or thought. The key to this style is the theologian's constant appeal to *the obvious features of the biblical text*. The listener hears mostly what the biblical text actually says (in translation), not about the text's context, theology, author, grammar, literary style, or tradition. If the text says, "When he [Jesus] went ashore, he saw a great crowd; and he had compassion for them and cured their sick" (Matt 14:14, NRSV), the congregation is likely to hear *these, or very similar, words* spoken. They get the sense that the theologian is inventing theology directly from "what the text says," its plain sense. Theological ideas appear to spring forth from a commonly accessible level of the text, whether it is what is happening in a story or an idea that is presented by the text.

Many theologians track the scriptural layer of theological composition in this way intentionally in order to make the ancient Scriptures seem practical, accessible, univocal, and clear to their audience. They are concerned that their audience be able to find in the ancient words a clear and simple reference point for thinking and living, and to remember these words through the straightforward imitation of what appears to be their obvious content. More complexity would take away from the simple, imitative quality of the religious life in relation to these words.

Most theologians use dynamic equivalence to some extent, even if it shows up only occasionally in their writing. No matter what theological model or understanding of scriptural authority undergirds this rhetorical style, the language that is tracked in the theologian's studio takes the hearer no further than the obvious features of the scriptural text: what the text in translation says took place, or what the text in translation actually says. The theologian wants the listener to believe that theological invention comes directly from imitating (finding equivalences for) what is "in the text," not what is behind or in front of the text.

When this style is chosen for tracking Scripture, memory is invented as a form of *mimesis*. Religious memory involves imitating ancient words and actions. If the words of the ancient text suggest an obvious idea or action, the audience remembers by striving to imitate this idea or action in the best way possible. If the text says that someone in the biblical narrative ate bitter herbs, fasted, or wore head coverings, the contemporary audience is to remember by doing likewise. If the text admonishes its recipients to forgive "seventy times seven," today's audience is to imitate as closely as is humanly possible.

Historical Continuity

Some theologians choose to make what is behind the text most important when tracking Scripture. This style indicates that theological invention is derived from something in the historical context of the passage, its grammar, the theology of the author, the tradition of similar texts in Scripture, or the impact of parallel texts. What is *in* the text (its obvious features, words in translation, etc.) remains important, but only as it connects to a *deeper* meaning that is *behind* the text. An audience expecting to hear from an educated person, and concerned with a deeper or special knowledge of ancient texts, will be listening for this style of scriptural tracking. Theologians who use this style may hint at the naiveté of simple dynamic equivalence, because it lacks an appropriate understanding of the historical distance between the ancient context and today. They will typically demonstrate some struggle to get at the meanings behind the text, since these are hidden from plain view and require a special interpreter (*hermeneut*) to be unearthed.

The theologian who tracks the scriptural layer of invention in this way must learn how to make the ancient historical and theological context integral and interesting as a key to theological invention. There are many rhetorical tropes that indicate this style of tracking. For instance, the author of the text may be raised up as the key to the inventive process ("Matthew is saying . . ."). At other times, the historical context will be given this authority ("for Matthew's Jewish audience . . ."). Another stylistic trope involves making a scriptural, oral, or liturgical tradition the cornerstone of theological invention ("like most of the ancient prophecies about the Messiah . . ."). In other instances, invention will spring forth from the way the text speaks about social realities such as Exodus, Exile, or Empire.

When the theologian chooses this style of tracking Scripture, memory is invented, not as a form of mimesis, but as a form of *alignment*. Instead of indicating that one's theological invention is in some way dynamically equivalent to ideas or actions that are obvious, based on the surface features of the text, the theologian invites the audience to be involved in a community of individuals striving to true up, or align, the ways that it lives or thinks in order to be in significant historical continuity with an ancient religious community. The audience is encouraged to discover similar theological, personal, social, and cultural issues today to those confronting the ancient religious community—suffering, oppression, war, cultural displacement, idolatry, interreligious conflict, and so on—and to place today's religious community into a relationship of historical continuity with its ancient past.

Literary Transposition

In music theory, "transposition" means changing a piece of music to a different key, while keeping the same structure. When the theologian tracks Scripture in the literary transposition style, the ancient scriptural text becomes the rhetorical model for theological invention. The theologian with this style of tracking works principally with what is "in front" of the ancient text: the text's literary and rhetorical qualities. The theologian transposes the literary or rhetorical shape or structure of the text into a new, updated key. In this style the theologian shows more interest in *how* a text functions than with *what* a text meant in its historical context. The theologian's work *does* rhetorically what the ancient text does or intends, but in a new key. Commonsense meanings within the text and historical continuities are pushed into the background, and the performative aspects of the language operating in front of the text become most important. Since language is formative of consciousness, the theologian seeks to promote, through language, the same strange and ancient forms of religious consciousness expressed by the ancient text (doxology, lament, parabolic reversal, etc.) A variety of literary, rhetorical, and reader-response approaches yields this same rhetorical result when tracking Scripture: the rhetoric layered into the theological composition accentuates what the text does (its literary impact) more than what it is about (its meaning) in its historical context.

There are several stylistic rhetorical tropes that often accompany this style. In some instances, the theologian will speak about the literary element (story, parable, psalm, poem, etc.) as a subject of theological invention rather than as an object. The literary element is not simply "about" something, it *does* something. The listener will hear rhetorical tropes such as "This story makes us . . ." or "These words are words of invitation that . . ." or "This is a hard word to hear, isn't it?" or "It is as if this whole parable conspires to . . ." At other times the theologian will imitate the tone and pattern of a particular kind of biblical literature. A doxological hymn yields a spirit of praise. A lament sends the theologian deep into a tone of despair. A parable is used as an opportunity to establish a pattern of hearer expectation, which is then dramatically reversed.

When the theologian chooses this style for tracking Scripture, memory is invented, not as a form of mimesis or continuity, but as a *performance*. As in ritual practices such as celebrating the Lord's Supper or Passover, memory involves us in a reperformance of the religious past in a way that makes it functionally present. Mimetic and historical elements are subsumed by dramatic, ritualistic, and performative attempts to capture the way that a past event would have sounded, felt, and had an impact on its original audience. Memory is bound up with particular forms of speech and how they work to shape consciousness and action.

Theological Transformation

Transformation is a style of tracking Scripture that is less text-centered than translation, transition, or transposition. At the risk of simplification, we can say that the transformation style is theology-centered. The ancient text exists to bear witness to certain theological *claims* made upon human life by the God of the text. These textual claims are pivotal for theological invention. Meanings in or behind the text and the rhetorical functioning of the text are subordinated to the potential transformative impact some pivotal aspect of the text can have on the audience. How the theologian understands these transformative claims (*theological* hermeneutic) is more important than the vicissitudes of textual meaning or rhetorical functioning (*scriptural* hermeneutic).

The theologian's understanding of those claims becomes central to the inventive task. For a liberation theologian, those claims will have to do with some aspect of divine justice. For an existentialist theologian, those claims will typically center in finitude, idolatry, and courage. For a conservative evangelical theologian, the claims of the text may center in the need for a personal relationship with Jesus Christ.

Theological transformation brings with it a stronger affective element than do the first three approaches. The Scripture bears witness to a living and evocative agent who wants to make a claim on, encounter, confront, shake, break into, or disrupt listeners' lives. For this reason, the theologian who tracks Scripture in this style will usually gravitate toward a pivotal moment in a scriptural text that focuses certain theological claims. The theologian will often ascribe a crucial turning point in theological invention to some aspect of a scriptural text.

When this style of tracking is used, memory is invented as *encounter*. The theologian's audience appropriates the past by encountering certain theological claims the ancient texts make upon their thinking and behavior. This encounter is framed as potentially transformative in nature—a pivotal text engendering pivotal claims on one's life. These claims are discovered in the text through the lenses of a particular theology.

Contextual Discovery

Whereas the transformationist theologian starts with theology or religious experience in approaching Scripture, the contextualist begins more broadly with common human experience and culture. In this style, the theologian will use issues, questions, events, hunches, suspicions, insights, or crises arising from contemporary experience as catalysts for the discovery of hidden or latent trajectories of meaning within the ancient text. Invention springs forth from the text as questions and issues present or latent within experience or culture spark new insights into the meaning of the text that were not seen before. The scriptural layer of invention hinges on what experiential issues or concerns are brought to the text.

The contextualist often has to move to a deep theological or historical dimension of the text in order to find a trajectory that correlates with the cultural or experiential issue at hand. This means going "beneath" the text, using a conceptual hermeneutic that appeals to a deep biblical principle such as "monotheism" or "justification" that rumbles beneath the particular text at hand. There is no longer an application to, or an analogy between, a scriptural idea and the theologian's context. Instead, there is a discovery of the implication of a scriptural idea for that context.

When the theologian chooses this style for tracking Scripture, memory is invented as a contextual *trajectory*. Contextual theologians discover a trajectory of meaning from the ancient text embedded in their own context. Scriptural events and ideas are not back there in history somewhere; they are occurring now, in the present moment, awaiting discovery as latent trajectories. Theological invention in this style has a heuristic flavor. This is because current issues within the culture, community, audience, or congregation appear to be so powerfully catalytic in relation to the scriptural text. Memory discovers trajectories of meaning from the past that are hidden from view, awaiting this particular moment in history and this particular situation to be drawn out into plain view. This hidden trajectory might not be unique. It might have been discovered before, but it is always developing further implications and meanings as it is interpreted in different epochs and situations. For instance, the deeper trajectories of meaning within biblical texts regarding slavery were not discovered until the modern Civil Rights Movement came along and brought out latent meanings for Pauline phrases such as "no longer slaves." Hidden trajectories of meaning regarding forgiveness in the New Testament were not fully discovered until issues of domestic violence and apartheid came into view.

Tracking Culture and the Invention of Religious Experience

The content of the culture track is every reference made to the broader culture in which the listeners live. This includes many different kinds of content: illustrations of all types (analogies, examples, metaphors), stories, anecdotes, clichés, appeals to cultural forms of authority, maxims, proverbs, opinions, assumptions regarding manners, morals, appearance, furniture, furnishings, clothing, design, references to the arts, literature, public and private ceremonies, sports, politics, customs, habits of eating and body care, modes of livelihood, social organization, and so on.

It is very important to become aware of one's typical compositional culture, the usual areas of culture and human experience to which one appeals in theological invention. This increases awareness of the potential for negative stereotyping and the creation of subtle messages that are contrary to one's theological commitments.[9] Even more important, theologians should be aware of the ways in which styles of tracking culture participate in the invention of forms of religious experience. These styles, in turn, work to invent forms of religious experience in theological composition.[10] There are several fundamental styles for tracking culture.

Identification Style

The identification style of tracking culture parallels the translation style of tracking Scripture. This time, however, it is the obvious features of the current *cultural text* instead of the scriptural text that are central to inventive style. The ideas one invents are actually *identified* with certain obvious features of the culture in which an assumed audience lives. Going behind or beneath these features is unnecessary. The theologian is not concerned with inventing theological ideas that require the discernment of profound religious aspects or deep elements of culture. Rather, the theologian uses certain obvious cultural types known to a particular audience through the mass media or the community's common experience. These become the source for illustrations, appeals to authority, clichés, and other cultural assumptions that authorize the theologian's inventive efforts.

The key to the identification style is to identify the invention of one's message with an aspect of the obvious features of the dominant culture in which the audience is embedded.

There are several typical rhetorical stratagems that identification stylists use. One stratagem is to clearly identify ideal categories (good and bad). The theologian invents the "good" and the "bad" with a particular ideal cultural-experiential *concept* in mind, such as "secularism," "humanism," "materialism," "dysfunctionality," "family," "community," "social justice," and so on. In a recent conflict between journalist and blogger Jim Wallis of Sojourners and Fox television political pundit Glenn Beck, both men engaged in theological invention that relied on the ideal category of "social justice." For Wallis, this was a good religious ideal amidst a sea of rampant individualism, whereas for Beck, "social justice" signified the evils of religion subsumed by socialism.

Another strategy is to identify certain heroes and villains within the dominant culture. Within the identification stylist's prototypical bad or good cultures there are certain well-known exemplars whose stories act as models. These are the ideal types that culturally represent or depict the theologian's ideal concepts. For many black theologians, for instance, stories of Martin Luther King Jr. or Rosa Parks become the source of theological invention. For liberation theologians, Nelson Mandela and Ernesto Cardenal are often used. At the same time, in every cultural context there are stories of villains, well-known people (George Wallace, Bull Connor, Hitler) or institutions (the "military-industrial complex") who exemplify values that are antithetical to the theologian's message.

Another strategy is to tell religious character stories. Some theologians who track experience in this style will tell stories in which a central character, living an ordinary life within the larger culture, becomes exemplary of ideal or correct moral or spiritual behavior. Well-known television preacher Joel Osteen, for instance, tells many Christian character stories in which heroes or heroines have persevered and succeeded in life within the dominant culture. On his Sojourners blog, Jim Wallis frequently tells stories of those who have decided for a less materialist and individualist lifestyle after encountering the meaning of particular biblical texts, or who have endured oppression or injustice yet risen above the odds with the help of a heroic community of compassion.

Another stratagem is to appeal directly to popular sources of cultural authority. Theologians who invent theology in the identification style will not hesitate to quote, or cite as references or examples, popular sources of cultural authority. Everyone, from talk show hosts to newspaper editorialists, can be appealed to as authorities for theological invention.

Those who use this style for tracking culture are inventing religious experience as *ideal* experience within the dominant culture. Religious experience can be located within the prevailing culture as an ideal, such as being a tireless advocate for social justice, being pro-life or pro-choice, being successful against all odds as a rugged individualist, being a patriot, and so on. Religious experience is directly identified with best ideals to be found within the culture at large, and no attempt is made to qualify or nuance these standards.

Dialectical Style

The word "dialectical" implies that the theologian's tracking of experience contains within it a critical antithesis or "no" to the obvious features of the audience's culture, before locating a new synthesis or cultural "yes." The dialectical style of tracking culture parallels the historical continuity style. The theologian goes behind or beneath the obvious features of culture and experience in search of deep cultural/experiential coordinates for theological invention. To a theologian employing this style, the obvious aspects of culture will not do. The theologian will try to discover hidden (critically discerned) *aspects* or *levels* of experience within the prevailing culture to fund the invention of theological meaning. Unlike the identificationist, who will tend to narrow the bad and the good to one or two well-known subcultures within the larger prevailing culture, the dialectical theologian of experience is aware of the gray areas of all cultural coordinates for religious meaning and works to convey the idea that one must search more carefully for the particular aspect of culture or experience from which to invent theological truth. Theologians cultivating this style will be drawn to many different arenas of culture, including unexpected or unpopular subcultures, as possible resources for theological invention.

There are several stratagems for tracking that are basic to this style. In the first, the dialectical stylist will carefully qualify any use of culture. Whenever the theologian says "yes" to a particular form of experience as religious experience, an accompanying "no" (qualification) must be articulated. Likewise, whenever the theologian wants to say "no" to a particular form of experience as religious experience, an accompanying "yes" will be noted. This stylistic feature indicates that surface features of culture and obvious forms of experience are inadequate and must be jettisoned for deeper, subtler, and more profound aspects or dimensions of experience.

Another stratagem involves the theologian in a kind of priestly or sacramental discernment, discovering deep aspects of religious experience within ordinary life. Instead of identifying heroes or ideal types, dialectical theologians of experience sometimes portray themselves as bystanders or narrators who hear or see something hidden behind an ordinary experience that funds their theological invention. The theologian's ordinary experience acts as a lens through which to see theological meaning embedded in human life. Compassion, for instance, may be seen in a kind word from a caring teacher, or in a small gesture of forgiveness or support. The lens of the theologian's experience becomes a telescope or microscope, searching for religious coordinates within ordinary experience, disclosing how the familiar sometimes bears the stamp of the religious truth. Good and evil are not found in ideal cultural types, heroes and villains, or exemplars of religious character. Instead, they are discovered embedded deeply within the ordinary experiences all around us, seen in a new way through eyes searching for the presence of theological meaning.

Another common stratagem is to look for theological meaning in a place where one's audience least expects to find it. The theologian seeks for ways to reverse assumptions about where theological meaning is located in human experience. For instance, a Christian might choose the experience of a Muslim to disclose religious meaning. A Jew might choose the experience of a Palestinian. A liberal might choose the experience of a fundamentalist. The goal of this practice is to say "no" to the stereotypical and obvious, while saying "yes" to a deep, shared aspect of experience that harbors within it the possibility of theological invention.

The theologian who tracks culture in this style invents religious experience as *profound* experience. Instead of religious experience being identified as an ideal form of experience within the dominant culture, it is hidden and only discoverable by going deeper, using critically trained eyes to locate a profound dimension of experience that is, indeed, religious in character. This experience is subtle, ambiguous, epiphanic, and sometimes unconscious—not easily accessed, except by critical and dialectical means. Religious experience is never free from qualification, and therefore cannot be obvious, on the surface, or culturally idiomatic. It only exists behind or beneath the surface.

Dualist Style

The dualist theologian of culture will use simile and analogy (likeness, similarity) in order to separate the dominant culture entirely from the invention of theological meaning—without, however, placing them into an oppositional relationship. This theologian is hesitant to track any identification or correspondence between what one decides to say (invents) theologically and lived experience within the broader culture. Theological invention is possible only in relation to other tracks of theological composition, especially the Scripture track and theology. Experiences within the prevailing culture are permitted to act as a supportive cast to invention, providing clarification, illustration, support, and deepening without actually bearing the freight of theological invention itself. Culture can be similar to or in some ways like religious meanings, but is never adequate for the discovery or adequate presentation of such meanings.

There are several common earmarks of the dualist style. First, dualists only speak of culture in relation to religious meaning by way of analogy. The dualist is not concerned to find cultural events or experiences that *are* theologically meaningful, either through identification or dialectical discovery. The dualist is satisfied to find events or experiences that are *like* the theological meanings that are invented at scriptural or theological levels of tracking. Often the language of similitude will be used: "This is like . . ." or "this is similar to . . ."

In some instances, the dualist will simply say "no" to culture as adequate to the invention of theological meaning by actually denying its adequacy of expression. In order to accomplish this, theologians use rhetorical cues such as "but how much more . . ." or "this is only an attempt to describe . . ." or "this can only begin to compare with . . ."

Anecdote is another common rhetorical device. Anecdote is the utilitarian use of human experience in communication in order to help the speaker make a point. Instead of finding an event or experience that portrays the message, or pursuing a close likeness, the theologian searches for an anecdotal story or image that will simply help make a point. An anecdote is *not an actual instance* of an experience of theological meaning. It is simply a paradigmatic illustration of a theological meaning already disclosed. In order to accentuate this anecdotal quality, many anecdotes are told in a way that insures that listeners know they are made up or imaginative: "Imagine with me . . ." or "Once upon a time . . ." At other times anecdotes are drawn from forms of experience that are far-flung or obviously different than the theological meaning illustrated. A comic strip is used to demonstrate qualities of leadership. An animal story is used to demonstrate the meaning of loyalty. For the dualist it is important that listeners not place any significant weight on culture or experience as a source for theological invention.

Theologians who use this style invent religious experience as *analogous* experience. Religious experience can never be wholly adequate to religious truths, but can be similar or analogous in significant ways. For example, even though divine love can never be found within our experience within culture, we can discover and promote rough analogies and similar experiences of love that are utilitarian—helpful in the task of roughly approximating the religious truths revealed in Scripture, doctrine, and tradition.

Separatist Style

The theologian who tracks culture in a separatist style sees theological meaning and the dominant culture as separate realities. Separatist stylists will commonly use oppositional rhetoric. They will invent theological ideas by opposing with vigor the immediate larger culture in which the audience is embedded, invoking clear cultural enemies, whether these are the liberals, secular humanists, fundamentalists, empire, or oppressors. Sometimes rhetorical cues such as "the world" or "in the world" will be woven throughout this track.

On the other hand, separatist stylists will celebrate, clearly and unambiguously, a minority or marginal culture and the values and characteristics of certain *countercultural* forms of experience. They will underscore, teach, and celebrate the unique characteristics of genuine religious experience, whether speaking in tongues, martyrdom, giving up all of one's possessions, or obeying particular creeds or doctrines. Sometimes they will use stories of saints, both present and past, to illustrate the gospel message. These stories will be similar to the hero stories of the identification style, except that the heroes and heroines will represent non–status quo forms of behavior within a specific countercultural religious community or tradition that exists as the result of very particular religious commitments.

This style of tracking culture is similar to the identificationist style except that theological truth springs forth only from what is considered to be a disenfranchised, non–status quo, countercultural type of religious experience. Good religious experiences are identified with a religious grammar, system, group, life world, or sect. Bad religious experiences are anything else.

Tracking Theology and the Invention of Theological World and Worldview

The theology track is similar to the backing track in the popular song. It provides a background framework for the rest of the tracks, establishing the larger narrative or mythos for the composition as well as the tone, mood, or atmosphere. Two things are invented by the theological track: theological *world* and the portrayal of a theological *worldview*.

Theological World

Theologian W. Paul Jones used the term "theological world" to define the mixture of ecclesial and ideological content that shapes a theologian's or community's religious narrative or myth.[11] A theological world includes several elements: the identification of what is wrong with us (suffering, brokenness, sin, oppression, despair etc.), where we are headed (enlightenment, redemption, eschatology, etc.), how we will get there (faith, hope, love, loss of self, etc.), and who or what will help us along the way (Christ, the Buddha, community, Scripture, priests, sacraments, etc.). We will say more about discovering, analyzing, and conveying a theological world in chapter 6.

Just as a song cannot be about every aspect of life, so a theological composition does not usually focus on every aspect of a theologian's theological world. Theologians must crop out certain theological elements and interpretations and focus on others as the key to what is said. This establishes the known theological world for a composition. The way a theologian frames the theological world for a composition will depend in large part on theological traditions represented (Christian, Jewish, Islamic, Buddhist, Hindu, etc.), denomination or sect (Baptist, Pentecostal, Roman Catholic, Orthodox, Reformed, Hasidic, Shia, Sufi, Mahayana, Hinayana, Vaishnavas, Saivas, etc.), and ideological/philosophical-theological perspective (liberationist, existentialist, conservative evangelical, process, feminist, restorationist, progressive, etc.).

Theological Worldview

If theological world is a matter of the theological content a theologian tracks, theological worldview is a function of the theologian's style of tracking that content. In effect, theological worldview is the religious mythos of the composition. Each theological idea is related to other theological ideas in particular ways. These relationships are a key to establishing the style of tracking. At the risk of oversimplifying, worldview is a function of whether, and in what ways, an idea is either negative or positive within a composition. This negative/positive or bad news/good news aspect is crucial in defining theological style. Essentially, there are five styles for tracking theological worldviews.

Tensive. In the tensive style, there is plenty of the negative and very little of the positive. Theologians will weight their ideas toward what is wrong in the larger theological narrative being told. Theological anthropology and the analysis or explication of the human condition will be dominant in the framing and invention of the message. Theological invention will be less concerned with resolving the human dilemma than with unraveling it and helping an audience to live honestly and courageously in the world as it is. Miraculous intervention or resolutions are played down. It is enough that the audience learns to appreciate and accept an irresolvable *tension* in human life and take responsibility for sharing to the best of their abilities in lessening its impact.

Oppositional. Similar to the theologian in the tensive style, the oppositional theologian will want to be realistic about negative elements in the framing of the message. Instead of simply accepting or acknowledging the reality of negativity, however, the oppositional theologian heroically *opposes* these elements. Theological invention will weight ideas theologically toward showing where the theological story is heading and how negativity is confronted or opposed by those ideas or individuals that courageously pursue that goal. This opposition does not end up in victory, however. Resolutions to the human dilemma are partial or promissory at best. Theological invention in this style often focuses on how to effectively challenge an audience to heroic thinking and action in the face of overwhelming odds.

Equilibrist. In this style, negative elements are brought into equilibrium by positive elements. Negativity is strong and burdensome, yet ultimately unable to present an overwhelming challenge to the achieving one's ultimate goal. To some extent, this is due to the fact that the positive elements have already proven equal to the task. There is, therefore, adequate help available to restore and maintain order. Theological invention focuses on how positive religious meanings have *already* resolved the essential problems at the core of the human dilemma. The theologian's task is to lead an audience toward this realization. No matter what else can be said, one's religion provides sufficient resources to satisfy human need. Problems of human lack or need are far less important for theological invention than the fact that significant religious help is available to provide answers. The audience is invited to recognize and embrace an already present and adequate set of religious resources.

Permutational. In this style, positive elements are given far more weight than the negative. To some extent, the negative is only a foil that sets off the wonders of the positive. Not only is the human dilemma resolved by the religious resources at hand, but a tremendous, qualitative gain or surplus can be discovered in the way that theological ideas are invented and communicated. In order to make theological invention permutational, superabundant and transformative religious powers may be given pivotal attention. Positive religious resources are powerful enough, not only to restore equilibrium, but to bring about an entirely new situation, one in which there is a qualitative gain over the old situation: a new order, a new reality.

Iconoclastic. In this style, the theologian invents by working a reversal on certain commonly held theological assumptions or ideas within an audience. What has typically or traditionally been negative becomes positive, or vice versa. Theological invention is designed to introduce contradiction and unexpected irresolution, where reconciliation and order are assumed; it is placed into the service of deconstruction, interruption, and change. The theologian's audience learns to expect and enjoy the introduction of contradictions or unexpected tensions where none previously existed. In this way of thinking, the deeper resources of a religion cannot be narrated in a consistent way at all, and remain elusive and surprising, able to change and bring about change at any time.

Tracking the Message and the Invention of Theological Truth

As noted, the message track corresponds to the melody track in the popular song. This melody is often the vocal track, and, in following it, the listener discovers the way the song is organized—typically into an intro, verse, chorus, verse, chorus, bridge, verse, chorus, ending format, or some variation thereof. In the message track the theologian invents a way to break the composition's larger idea into its component parts. There are many different ways that this can happen. Styles of message tracking are defined by the way that the theologian manages the arrival of meaning in the composition, how the key parts of the core idea invented by the writer are parceled out. Each style of tracking corresponds to the invention of a particular form of religious truth. There are two basic tracking styles, *connotative* and *denotative*, and two larger forms of truth that are invented by each style. Within each of these larger styles are two principal substyles, each of which again corresponds to the invention of a particular form of religious truth.

Connotative Styles

Connotative tracking is ruled by the principle of semantic motion. Meaning is constantly being detoured so that it arrives in bits and pieces. Religious meaning is not static but fluid, and it can only be approached by approximation. What the theologian is talking about is more ambiguous and unsettled. The composition relies on the hearer to do more work in sorting out what the theologian is saying.

The two typical connotative substyles are *artistic* and *conversational*. Both invent religious truth as *disclosive*. Truth is concealed and requires uncovering. Expectation is the basic condition of truth. It is anticipated as the object of desire and arrives within the field of that anticipation. Truth is similar to Heidegger's *aletheia*, "an unveiling which contains its own veiling, a truth which contains its own untruth."[12] We discover the truth by discovering its trace in the not yet true.

Artistic Substyle. Artistic tracking is ruled by the principle of semantic delay. The theologian delays the arrival of meaning, keeping the audience guessing while "semantic motion" happens in the hearer's mind through that delay. The message track is designed to keep people "on the hook." It provides a semantic "tick" but delays a "tock." Theological invention arrives as the result of a shared search for the fullness of what the theologian ultimately means. Semantic delay can be achieved at two different levels: *compositional delay* and *sequential delay*. Compositional delay is a delay in the arrival of the fullness of meaning that takes place over the course of the entire composition. Sequential delay is the delay of the arrival of meaning within a sequence of the composition.

Modern homiletics has been helpful in unpacking two popular artistic approaches today, *inductive* and *narrative* (plot) approaches. These approaches warrant examination by those engaged in other forms of theological invention and composition. Inductive approaches detour the arrival of meaning by taking the hearer through a series of experiences, each of which communicates a part of an overall idea. Narrative approaches delay the arrival of an idea with devices of plot, atmosphere, characterization, personification, or image. The narrative theologian often makes the message track resemble the plot of a detective movie or mystery novel: the audience has to wait until the end of the story to know "who dunnit."[13]

There are several basic stratagems for compositional and sequential delay within both inductive and narrative approaches. The first of these, which Eugene Lowry calls "upsetting equilibrium,"[14] involves the articulation of a central enigma. The enigma is a problem that energizes the composition's forward movement. Something is wrong that needs fixing, something is out of balance and needs restoration, something is missing and needs to be found, something is confusing and needs to be clarified, and so on. The artistic stylist will take plenty of time to deepen the enigma, acknowledging the depth and breadth, the apparent insolubility, of the composition's core dilemma.

Another stratagem is the setting of several snares, sending the audience on a "wild goose chase" after a "straw man." A snare is a false resolution, an impostor who masquerades as the answer to the enigma. Of course, the audience knows (or soon discovers) that this is only an artistic conceit.

A clue is a partial resolution, or a glimpse of what might be most significant in resolving the enigma at hand. In theological composition a clue finally places the audience on the right track. It points in the right direction and leads ultimately to a resolution that releases, to whatever extent is possible, the tension created. If the theologian wishes to provide a truly artistic resolution, the ending will avoid didacticism. This is sometimes accomplished by using a resolving image or story as a conclusion, instead of telling the audience directly how tension is resolved.

The artistic style invents religious truth as *epiphanic*. Truth is a showing forth of what is true, a manifestation or insight that occurs within the field of anticipation established by a delay. This form of truth resists conceptuality. It is invoked, not told or defined. It arrives in images, feelings, and intuitions rather than in concepts. Epiphanic truth embraces mystery and ambiguity and is only loosely held, remaining always open to revision by further insights or manifestations.

Conversational Substyle. The conversational substyle of tracking messages is ruled by the principle of semantic *reciprocity.* The conversational theological composition delays the arrival of meaning by following the relatively artless back-and-forth movement of an honest dialogue in pursuit of a shared meaning. Theological invention is the result of a roundtable conversation, in which discussion of a topic or idea moves around a table, encompassing several perspectives.

The conversational stylist is not simply a discussion referee, aiming the microphone at different speakers who then say their piece on a subject. Rather, the theologian is someone at the table who has an investment in the discussion and who brings resources and perspectives others may not bring. The theologian, however, unfolds his or her perspective in such a way that the audience receives it as part of a larger emergent meaning that all are discovering together. Invented ideas have the quality of generative hypotheses rather than delayed insights.

Conversational language is the language of listening. Several standard strategems are earmarks of conversational style. The first is to acknowledge potential misunderstandings. If the theologian knows about actual oppositions to ideas or of typical misunderstandings, it is important to acknowledge that these exist. This acknowledgment is similar to what homiletician David Buttrick calls a "contrapuntal," which "acknowledges, but does not reinforce, an opposition."[15] There is a variety of ways in which a theologian can acknowledge alternative perspectives on a meaning that is being pursued: by raising questions that acknowledge other points of view, by revising one's perspective midstream, or by briefly noting common misunderstandings.

Another common stratagem is to use language indicating that the theologian is following someone else's lead. In roundtable conversations, it is typical to permit topics to be set by others. It is not merely the theologian who is concerned with a topic and who is struggling to invent a hypothesis in relation to it. The language of following acknowledges that the theologian is following the hearer's lead in pursuing a topic of conversation.

Using the language of qualification is another common rhetorical stratagem. In a conversation, it is important to allow that other perspectives exist. This can be accomplished, in part, by qualifying one's own perspective as limited to a particular point of view. Words or phrases such as "perhaps," "maybe," "it seems that," "in my opinion," "I think that . . . ," "consider," "for many of us . . . ," "may," or "might" qualify what is being said and indicate that a conversation is more open-ended and inclusive. The language of qualification can also be helpful when attempting to paraphrase someone else's feelings or ideas. Because it is difficult to gain access to actual feelings, and even more difficult to avoid imputing feelings that do not exist, the use of qualifiers about what others at the table "may" or "might" think or experience will permit them room to identify or adjust as needed.

In a genuine conversation, ideas are in constant revision. The theologian working in this style, therefore, can use the language of revision to indicate that the ideas of others in the conversation are having an effect, leading the theologian to make revisions in light of new information. This information may come from Scripture or other sources brought to light by others in the conversation. In this way, others become empowered in the conversation. Revision sometimes involves some self-disclosure and may even take the form of self-correction.

Interruptions also occur frequently in conversations. In most cases, they occur in order to make sure that the voice of someone who may not have any other way to be heard is included. Conversational stylists may want to interrupt their message tracking from time to time to permit the melody line to be taken over by other voices.

Within conversations there are usually moments when the ideas of several parties begin to diverge or converge. Conversational stylists will be careful to track these divergences and convergences to show how theological invention involves a back-and-forth reciprocity between those who will not agree about everything but who can, in some instances, locate areas where shared meaning is possible.

The conversational stylist invents religious truth as *emergent*. Truth includes the probable and the plausible. It is a tentative agreement, momentary consensus, or unifying hypothesis, always open for further development as the conversation broadens and changes. Emergent truth is relational and often communal. It implies a community of the truth talking itself into the discovery of more truth.

Denotative Styles

Whereas connotative styles (artistic and conversational) are ruled by the principle of semantic motion, denotative styles are ruled by the principle of semantic *arrest*. The theologian quickly arrests the movement of possible meanings and locates invented truth as quickly as possible. Invented ideas are set forth without delay and with as little ambiguity as possible. There are two principal denotative substyles for tracking messages, *assertive* and *defensive*.

Denotative styles invent truth, not as disclosive, but as *conclusive*. Truth is concluded based on certain well-established paradigms of knowledge (assertive style) or what are considered to be facts or transcendent premises (defensive style). Conclusive truth is the further explication of the already true.

Assertive Substyle. Assertive tracking of a message is ruled by the principle of *clarity*. The assertive stylist is concerned above all else to be understood, by asserting ideas boldly, clearly, and memorably. There are several well-known devices that promote clarity. Introductions and conclusions are crucial in helping an audience have a clear path for listening. Likewise, reiterating ideas at the end of each sequence or composition provides further clarity about what has been covered. Along the way, assertive stylists will develop obvious transitions so that their audience does not get lost. The repetition of one's ideas at crucial intervals is also pivotal for clarity. Assertive stylists will repeat key ideas at regular intervals.

Clarity can be enhanced if ideas are organized according to standard patterns to which most people are accustomed. Books on public speaking will often list these patterns. Time patterns distribute ideas according to chronological time ("first," "second," "third," and so on), or discuss the way things are now and then go back to speak about how things were during earlier stages or periods. Spatial patterns organize ideas according to location ("On one side . . . ," "on the other side . . . ," and "in the middle . . .") or geography ("In Jerusalem . . ." and "in Ephesus . . ."). Faceting patterns divide ideas into facets and treat them like a diamond held up and turned slowly in order to examine all of its aspects (predicates; "Compassion is attractive," "Compassion creates problems of distribution," etc.). Problem-solution patterns examine problems and propose solutions.

Assertive stylists will explain how they deduce certain ideas. This indicates a close reliance on certain well-worn paradigms of thought (Catholic doctrine, Reformed creeds, feminist literature, etc.) that provide clear warrants for a certain way of thinking. Explaining an idea as it grows out of one or more traditions of thought ensures that the audience is clear about its meaning and significance and where it comes from. Assertive clarity relies on the audience having a clear understanding of the origins of message, in order to understand clearly what the theologian means by words, terms, and concepts.

Assertive stylists will also achieve clarity by comparing and con- trasting ideas with other similar or different ideas. This means going one step beyond acknowledging differing or opposing ideas (contra- puntal conversational style) to actually drawing favorable or unfa- vorable comparisons between an idea and other similar concepts in order to clarify the limits of possible interpretation of the message.

The assertive style invents truth as *paradigmatic* truth. The theo- logian treats certain paradigms of knowledge as storehouses of knowl- edge. These paradigms can be religious traditions, research models or bodies of literature, ideological frameworks, or well-established cul- tural or social hegemonies—any body of knowledge that is accepted by the theologian and his or her audience as already true and war- ranted. The role of the theologian is to further deduce the true from these already known paradigms of knowledge.

Defensive Substyle. Semantic clarity is not enough for the theo- logian with a defensive style. For this theologian, the tracking of the message is ruled by the principle of semantic *precision*. It is most important that hearers be given not only clear ideas, but ideas that are precise, correct, and singular in meaning. The defensive stylist takes denotation very seriously and sees all connotation as problem- atic. Theological ideas must be defended from dilution, ambiguity, and disregard. Message tracking is committed to this apologetic task.

For this reason, elements of argument, such as those employed by lawyers, are fundamental to this style. Several stratagems of persuasive communication are also typical in theological composition.

First, the defensive stylist goes one step beyond explaining ideas, inasmuch as they can be deduced from a certain paradigm of thought, to presenting objective, universally accepted definitions. For the defensive stylist, it is very important to discard second and third dictionary definitions (connotations) for all terms. Sometimes defensive theologians use word studies in other languages (Sanskrit, Hebrew, Greek, Aramaic, Arabic) to aid them in creating univocal definitions.

Defensive stylists are often oppositional. They articulate clear opponents and clear opposing ideas. Part of achieving precision and correctness is defusing opposing ideas. As any good debater knows, there are a variety of ways to establish the superiority of one's ideas. One way is to argue from necessity. Often a defensive stylist will argue that an idea is necessary in order to understand or make sense of a particular religious idea or reality. Without a particular idea it is impossible to proceed in one's thinking. Another way is to argue for correspondence. Defensive stylists will sometimes argue that their idea corresponds best with accepted experience and facts, accomplishing this by showing that the idea is in noncontradiction with the full range of Scripture and human experience. Another way to argue for one's ideas is to assert their viability. Defensive stylists often try to demonstrate that an idea provides the most viable explanation of certain existential or spiritual dimensions of human experience, or that it represents the most viable answer to major existential or spiritual questions.

Defensive style invents religious truth as *final* truth. The audience is not asked to decide on the relative adequacy of truths that are well warranted by certain paradigms of thought. Instead, they are asked to accept certain truths as "radicals" or "transcendentals" without which there could be no being or meaning at all.[16] Religious truths are both universal and absolute.

Consistency or Hybridity?

As already noted, most song-makers treat songs as artifacts that must be invented in or out of a particular tradition or genre of music. Both the content and style of tracking music represent a particular tradition of music. There may be occasional exceptions to the rule, such as putting a choir on a rock ballad, or Latin percussion on a country-and-western song, but these are elements that add flavor to a traditional form of music, not elements that suggest the emergence of a hybrid genre, or perhaps a new genre altogether.

In the next chapter, we will examine the ways that traditional artifacts are sampled, remixed, and ultimately mashed up, creating new, hybrid forms of music. Nonetheless, as we are beginning to notice, inventing hybrid or new musical forms is already inherent in multitracking itself, where it is possible to introduce other traditions or styles of tracking, if only at one or two levels of the mix.

This is also true in the invention of theology. The idea of browsing samples of theological traditions and styles of tracking those traditions demonstrates a new kind of reflexivity that is possible in the invention of religious ideas today. Making use of search engines and other technologies for browsing, the theologian browses for ideas within religious traditions that, when juxtaposed, will create theological intonations and ideas that have the potential to convey new forms of religious thought. At the same time, the theologian can select rhetorical styles from the loop browser in this chapter that will promote desired forms of religious memory, experience, truth, and worldview. In this way, the invention of new forms of theology can involve tracking and mixing theological content and styles that may not usually coexist.

Our now-complete *theological loop browser* suggests many options. Consider, for example, a theologian who tracks by mixing the following styles:

>Scripture tracking—historical continuity
>culture tracking—identificationist
>theological tracking—Christian/Southern Baptist/liberationist
>theological worldview—permutational
>message track—conversational

BROWSE TRADITION	BROWSE STYLE		INVENTION OF:
	SCRIPTURE TRACK		MEMORY AS:
Religion, sect, theology, etc.	Dynamic Equivalence		Mimesis
For instance:	Historical Continuity		Alignment
Christian, Southern Baptist, Evangelical, Liberationist	Literary Transposition		Performance
	Theological Transformation		Encounter
	Contextual Discovery		Trajectory
	CULTURE TRACK		RELIGIOUS EXPERIENCE AS:
	Identification		Ideal
	Dialectical		Profound
	Dualist		Analogical
	Separatist		Countercultural
◁ Theological World ▷	THEOLOGY TRACK: THEOLOGICAL WORLDVIEW AS:		
		Tensive	
		Oppositional	
		Equilibrist	
		Permutational	
		Iconoclastic	
	MESSAGE TRACK		RELIGIOUS TRUTH AS:
	Connotative		*Disclosive*
	1. Artistic		Epiphanic
	2. Conversational		Emergent
	Denotative		*Conclusive*
	1. Assertive		Paradigmatic
	2. Defensive		Final

Figure 2.4. The theological loop browser.

By becoming aware of all the options, it is possible to imagine new, seemingly inconsistent, yet entirely possible ways of inventing theology.

The use of organizational prostheses such as editing software and loop browsers in the song-making process introduces the tracking and layering of content, as well as issues of tracking style, into musical and theological invention. It also begins to suggest the ways that novel juxtapositions of content and styles of communication can nudge traditions of music-making and theology toward unexpected hybrid forms. In the next chapter, this interest in novel juxtapositions moves to the next level, as sampling, remixing, and mashup introduce the morphing of styles and content into practices of invention.

3

SAMPLING, REMIXING, AND MASHUP

INVENTING THE THEOLOGICALLY POSSIBLE

You should, like Bees, fly from Flower to Flower, extracting the Juices fittest to be turned into Honey. The severest Criticks allow such amiable Plundering. It is true, you may not equal the Merit of any of your Models; but you acquire a new, and become yourself an Original.

—John Lawson, *Lectures Concerning Oratory*

. . . the technique of reproduction detaches the reproduced object from the domain of tradition. . . . It substitutes a plurality of copies for a unique existence.

—Walter Benjamin, "The Work of Art in the Age of Mechanical Reproduction"

Sampling is the practice of converting analog audio (instruments, sounds, voices) into digital form. This audio can then be manipulated within hardware or software samplers (tuned, time-stretched, etc.) and inserted into recordings as loops (repeatable samples) or hits (single samples). Digital samples can also be spread out over the notes on a keyboard, which, in effect, converts a sampled sound into a polyphonic instrument. Complex sampling technologies can sample entire orchestras, drum kits, percussion sections, or choirs so that they can be played back on keyboards.

Remixing is the practice of taking an already recorded song and technologically changing it. There are multiple ways to do this. DJs and turntablists remix by placing two vinyl records on turntables and finding "breaks" or special moments on each recording that can be placed into musical conversation with one another. Sample-based remixes are more multifaceted and may involve sampling bits and pieces of several recordings and placing them into musical conversation.

Sampling and remixing are derived from multitrack studio practices of tracking artists, in which multiple artists add recorded tracks to a song in the studio, changing its sonic character. As we have seen, tracking an artist amounts to sampling an artist's musical expertise and remixing the songwriter's original song by placing it into musical conversation with the ideas of another artist. Digitally sampled audio is now taking its place alongside live studio musicians in the creation of popular music, placing a wider range of musical options at the artist's fingertips in the invention or song-creation process.

In today's world, the popular song is always written under the shadow of the recording studio and technologies of sampling and multitrack recording. The individual songwriter knows that once the written song enters the studio, either as the songwriter's own production or in the hands of another artist, it is subject to tremendous modification, if not complete remixing. And most songwriters know that in today's world it is entirely possible that they will one day hear cut-and-paste samples of small portions of their work within the songs of others.

Given the affordability and availability of home studio computer-based digital audio workstations (DAWs) such as GarageBand, Logic, Pro Tools, Acid, Cubase, Sonar, and a host of other multitrack recording systems, songwriters of all genres are making use of sampling and recording technologies in the initial stages of writing songs. There is also a host of writers whose initial stages of songwriting are almost entirely dominated by sampling and remixing, creating original songs as mashups or remixes of the work of others.

On one end of the spectrum, the traditionally written song of the individual artist is improved, reshaped, and modified by the work of others in the studio (musicians, technicians, arrangers, and producers) or by studio technologies (sampled drums, loops of instruments, etc.). The singer-songwriter hears his or her song, which he or she originally composed and sang on an acoustic guitar or piano, recomposed and remixed with drums, electric guitars, synthesizers, horns or other backing, fill, or lead instruments. At the other end of the spectrum are DJs and mashup artists, who create their songs on the spot by sampling and remixing the work of others. They sample snippets of everything from Bach to punk, weaving them into a sound palette held together by beats or loops or by rhythms contained in the remixed material.

DJ Shadow speaks passionately about "crate-digging," searching among thousands of old vinyl albums for breaks, beats, and sounds in the same way that an archaeologist might spend hours searching for ancient artifacts.[1] He uses these snippets of vinyl to cut-and-paste a brilliant pastiche musical composition. A similar process pervades all contemporary practices of composing in recording studios, where engineers flip through hundreds of samples, exploring sounds and beats that might take a song in a new direction, deepen its relationship to its own tradition of music, or relate it to another tradition. Even the modest home studio is likely to house several thousand samples of hundreds of instruments, loops, beats, and sounds, in eight-, sixteen-, and thirty-two-bar increments, all of which are used to get ideas or to embellish an already existing song.

The artist or producer brings into the studio live musicians (friends or professional studio musicians), who may spend hours exploring a range of musical possibilities, some of which will utterly transform the song at hand. It is also an increasingly popular practice to send a rough mix of a song to a contributing musician in a digital file or on compact disc and have the musician create a track in the privacy of another studio or home studio. These musicians may live across town, in other states, or in distant countries. The tracks are sent back to the artist or studio engineer, who then imports the digital file into the song. If it is decided that the track improves the song, the recording engineer mixes it into the final composition.

Practices of sampling and remixing are now ubiquitous in the composition of popular music and indicate that the playing field on which the song-maker strives to exercise good judgment has dramatically expanded, if not exploded. Multitracking, sampling, and remixing are all activities that suggest that songs are constructed increasingly at the intersection of multiple discourses and multiple traditions. The artist, in this perspective, shifts from a *hermeneutical* posture, in which he or she is influenced primarily by a particular tradition, into a more broadly *intertextual* posture, in which the artist allows his or her work (and artistic self) to be remixed at the intersection of multiple traditions and influences. At this point in the song-making process we shift from the artist as writer to the artist as producer, or, as we will see, the producer as artist.

Intertextuality

The Russian philosopher of language and literature Mikhail Bakhtin is considered an important contributor to the concept of intertextuality. Bakhtin argues that all writing contains within it "varying degrees of otherness, or varying degrees of 'our own-ness.'"[2] Writing is "always a free stylistic variation on another's discourse."[3] According to composition theorist Mary Minock, Bakhtin argues that there exist "extremely subtle and sometimes imperceptible transitions" between the "conscious intention to imitate and stylistic variation, or stylization."[4] She concludes that "Bakhtin's theory of dialogism enables us to disengage from our usual notions of originality in self-expression to espouse a more powerful notion of the writer who interacts and intervenes in dialogues of shared and appropriated language that are nonetheless original based on their situatedness in context."[5] Many composition theorists today embrace intertextual, multivocal space as the locus for creative writing.[6] Rhetoricians sometimes call this intertextual space *chora*, a word that brings to mind the juxtaposition of many voices, either as cacophony or chorus.[7] Essentially, intertextuality amounts to embracing the reality that all writing is a multitracking of the sampled ideas of others.

If all writing is intertextual, however, in what sense can we consider a composition original? According to theorists of intertextuality, originality in writing is a function of the composition's *kairos*, or the way that the ideas, utterances, and sounds of others are actualized in an opportune way in a particular situation or context at this unique moment in time.[8] Originality is a function of juxtaposing a particular set of samples at a particular moment in time, which involves adopting a particular position within intertextual space.[9] The DJ, as he or she reaches on the fly for another record from a crate and throws it onto a turntable, knows what it means to suddenly shift positions within intertextual space. The new audio juxtaposition produces a new set of possible sounds that could not have existed before. In this context, what is composed occurs *now*, at this critical juncture or season (*kairos*). It is the opportune (*eukairon*), or a seizing of an opportunity that could only present itself at this moment in time.[10] According to rhetorician Carolyn Miller, the notion of opportunity within the Latin meaning of *kairos* includes a spatial metaphor, "*porta*, entrance or passage through."[11] *Kairos* is "an opening" or "discursive void."[12] Rhetorician Lloyd Bitzer calls it an "exigency," or "imperfection marked by urgency . . . something waiting to be done."[13]

According to Miller, such openings "can be constructed as well as discovered."[14] They are a function of bringing seemingly disparate experiences, genres, and traditions into close enough proximity that intersections, parallels, common interests, and resonances begin to show themselves. Writers who embrace intertextuality seek new content and forms by entering into relationships with distinctly *other* voices, juxtaposing their ideas with a larger range of voices than may be available within a given tradition of writing. Rather than simply imitating these other voices, the writer engages them within a certain *kairos* or opportune moment in time in a way that generates a genuinely original product. Black feminist bell hooks calls this writing in a "multi-dimensional" voice.[15] Africana philosopher Paget Henry calls this "creolization," coining new words and phrases to meet emerging situations and developing forms of rhetorical invention that make possible original forms of writing and speech at the interface of differences.[16]

In this chapter, we will identify some of the key aspects of this shift toward intertextuality through sampling and remixing, and explore their relevance for both song-making and theological invention. We will observe some of the implications of these practices, when transposed from song-making to theological composition, for invention, or deciding what to say. We will encourage a shift toward pragmatic, postsemiotic invention, in which the invention of religious meaning across languages and cultures supersedes language and culture-bound invention.

From Imitation to Stylization

As we already observed in chapter 1, most songwriters place tremendous value on imitating the writing of others within a particular tradition of music. In an environment charged with issues of copyright infringement, writers are always concerned about stepping over the line between imitation and copying. On the other hand, imitating or trying on another artist's style of writing, mannerisms, phrasing, or gesture is a tried and proven pedagogy for nearly every song-maker. In the field of rhetoric, Mary Minock traces these practices into ancient rhetorical theory, in which "memorizations, oral readings, paraphrases, translations between Greek and Latin, transliterations between prose and verse, retellings and imitative competitions—were deployed for centuries with various pedagogical intentions."[17] She notes that "each repetition, even an 'exact' copy, if it is uttered in even a slightly different context, repeats, but also *alters*."[18] Practices of imitation and copying were taken up into homiletic pedagogy, coming to fruition in the eighteenth century, when preachers were encouraged to keep "commonplace books" in which they jotted down the words of other preachers' sermons—a form of "amiable Plundering" encouraged by Irish rhetorician John Lawson,[19] who advised preachers to take the words of others and "form them according to your own way of expressing, and not tye your self to the words of the Author."[20]

When one begins to shift from imitation to altering, one has moved ever so slightly into the world of stylization. Cultural theorists Aleida Assmann and Jan Assmann argue for two different approaches to imitation and stylization: the "logic of authenticity" and the "logic of textuality." The logic of authenticity "is based on the dichotomy original/fake, and binds up both terms in a relationship of antagonist tension and mutual exclusiveness; whenever one is present, the other one is logically absent."[21] Within this logic, imitation is usually considered as a bad practice, and writers are encouraged to discover their own originality.

The logic of textuality, on the other hand, "is based on the distinction original/copy. In this case the relationship is one of mutual implication: each term necessarily evokes and 'constructs' the other but neither is complete without the other; they are mutually constituted."[22] Assmann and Assmann go on to assert that "instead of an antagonistic tension we have an ontological difference—an asymmetry between the two terms—rather like a complete manifestation and its shadow. The shadow is not, however, merely an impoverished version of the initial term, but a *new* term that highlights the first and sets it off in more luminous colors."[23] It is the logic of textuality or "mutual constitution" between original and copy that undergirds both sampling and remixing. In this world, the copy is a commentary, or new translation of an original.[24]

Assmann and Assmann find in this shift of logic from authenticity to textuality a shift away from the Hebrew concern with having "no graven images" or reproductions of an original.[25] Philosopher Robert Hullot-Kentor goes further to identify a shift of thought that resembles Christian Eucharistic theology: "Copies are not dependent on the original as are manual reproductions and therefore they accent the original, regard it from various angles, and magnify what otherwise escapes the senses. . . . [The copy] brings the original into places where it could not otherwise be brought."[26] Difference is always at play in every copy, and copies create more desire for the original by interpreting, illuminating, and recontextualizing.

Stylistic Morphing

Sociologists Barry Sandywell and David Beer identify a significant shift in the role of stylization in the digital age, which they call "stylistic morphing."[27] According to Sandywell and Beer, the analog-to-digital converter (ADC), which takes analog information and converts it to digital information, became the technological turning point in a revolution in styling another's work. Sounds that are digitally copied can now be styled through processes of digital morphing: "The physical ontology of stylus-inscription-expression has been replaced by the purely virtual realm of morphed elements, transformation procedures, and digital re-processing programs. Today, 'orchestra' and 'orchestration' can be replaced by machine ensembles of virtual musical instruments (in effect by software program systems) that provide infinitely reproducible simulacra of 'real sounds' and 'real instruments.'"[28]

As we have already observed, once analog sounds are digitized, they can be nondestructively sliced, sampled, time-stretched, and manipulated within DAWs. Bits of sampled audio can be spread across a keyboard or touch pad and played according to different musical logics than those accompanying their traditional composition and performance. This means that sounds can be easily lifted from their moorings in traditional performances and inserted into alien contexts. For instance, orchestral passages or sections of church choral music can be sampled and inserted within a hip-hop song, or a section of hip-hop beats can be sampled and inserted into a traditional blues song, transgressing boundaries of origin, tradition, and style.

According to Sandywell and Beer, stylistic morphing potentially signals the end, or at least the *decreased importance*, of genres and traditions. They observe that the three most significant properties of a genre are transformed through stylistic digital morphing: (1) "identifiable formal elements (musical form, style, expressive typifications)," (2) "fixed group or ensemble of properties (e.g. the culturally valorized signifiers of classical, rhythm-and-blues, rock 'n' roll etc.)," and (3) "invariance (meaning frames as an anticipatory grid of cultural reception and performative expression)."[29] In the face of such a revolution, Sandywell and Beer posit that the "sampler has, in fact, morphed into the role of originator."[30]

Sampler as Originator

The push beyond a hermeneutic model of composition into intertextuality is often located historically in the DJ (turntablist) tradition. Director Doug Pray's award-winning movie *Scratch* chronicles the development of the DJ from the Bronx to the West Coast, highlighting the distinction between the DJ (turntablist) and the MC (rapper).[31] According to African American literature scholar Houston Baker, it was Kool DJ Herc, arriving in the Bronx from Jamaica in 1967, who "saw the possibilities of mixing his own formulas through remixing prerecorded sound."[32] Rejecting the music of the slick disco club DJ Herc and his entourage "decided to 'B,' to breakdance, to hip hop, to rhythms of a dismembered, sampled, and remixed sound meant for energetic audiences—in parks, in school auditoriums, at high school dances, on the corner (if you had the power from a lightpost . . . and a crowd)."[33] Whereas disco DJs "merely *blended* one disc into the next,"[34] Herc's followers appropriated the two-turntable technology of disco, placed discs on separate turntables, and sampled small "breaks" from each disc to the loud beat of a beat box, which became the hip-hop sound.[35] Baker concludes that the DJ became a "postmodern, ritual priest of sound rather than a passive spectator in an isolated DJ booth making robots turn."[36] To this was added the poetry of rap, which as "some commentators have suggested echoes African griots, black preachers, Apollo DJs, Birdland MCs, Muhammad Ali, black street corner males' signifying, oratory of the Nation of Islam, and get-down ghetto slang."[37] By the 1990s, "micro-computers, drum machines, electric keyboards and synthesizers [were] all involved in the audio."[38]

There is within scratching, remixing, and sampling both a traditionalist crate-digging, archiving aspect and a posttraditionalist resistance to any form of possessive, single-authorship ideology designed to protect the aura of original art. Walter Benjamin, in his well-known essay "The Work of Art in the Age of Mechanical Reproduction," argues that the aura of originality is lost when art is reproduced and disseminated in mass quantity. Within the logic of textuality, however, sampling small pieces of pop originals into a work of sonic pastiche promotes a certain pleasure in consuming multiple auras while resisting the individuality and autonomy of the original artist and artifact. When coupled with rap poetry, which Baker calls "an audible or 'sounding' space of opposition,"[39] resistance to the cult of originality is expanded into a critique of a culture of possession, injustice, and (copy)rights reserved only for artistic elites. Media theorist John Shiga calls this "the bravura of transgression," through which "participants in subcultures often frame their un-authorized copying or 'plundering' as resistance against dominant culture."[40]

By the time one gets to the full-blown mashup culture of 2010–2011, one has reached the logical postmodern extreme of the arts of sampling and remixing. Mashup culture is largely an online music scene in which practitioners use widely available audio-editing software (Logic Studio, GarageBand, Pro Tools, Cubase, Sonar, etc.) to sample and remix pop songs (either their own or the songs of others) in order to produce mashed-up versions. This culture includes virtual studios (see, for instance, http://www.indabamusic.com), online message boards, dance clubs, and a large market for remixes of all types.

According to John Shiga, several things are crucial to mashup remixing. First, remixers have developed "audile technique," or listening skills that help the mashup artist know what goes with what and how to put one sample together with another. Once reserved for the studio producer, this skill has migrated into the public domain and is now becoming fairly common. As Shiga puts it, "status and reputations within the mashup community hinge upon the capacity to hear affinities between seemingly disparate songs, artists, and genres, which requires pluralistic openness to music that has little or no value for professional DJs, music critics, or other individuals who act as intellectuals in popular music cultures."[41]

Second, mashup culture "is guided by a 'file-sharing' sensibility, a disposition toward sound as infinitely replicable."[42] Composition theorists Dànielle DeVoss and James Porter identify a new ethic among "copyleftists," which they assert is having a significant impact on composing: "Composing in the digital age is different—electronic copying-and-pasting, downloading, and file-sharing change the dynamic of writing. With the ubiquitous use of digital writing technologies, 'plagiarism' makes sense. It is a common practice, common in print culture too, and perhaps even a literacy skill. . . . Remixing is how individual writers and communities build common values; it is how composers achieve persuasive, creative, and parodic effects."[43] In order to avoid copyright infringement issues, online mashup artists often use pseudonymous identities. An increasing amount of purchasable copyright-free samples are now available, and, if copyleftist ideas continue to flourish, it is likely that this market will continue to grow.

Third, mashup artists, or those influenced by mashup culture, encourage others to remix their own work. This is reminiscent of Jay-Z's *The Black Album,* where the studio "encouraged authorized remixing by releasing vocal-only versions."[44] In other words, mashup artists not only wish to become "original samplers," they also want to promote further "originals" inspired by the sampling and remixing of their own work.

Sampling, Mashup Culture, and Theological Invention

Sampling and remixing imply significant cultural shifts in which theological invention is increasingly democratized, disseminated, and detraditioned (or cross-traditioned). What are the implications of these shifts for theological invention? What would a move from hermeneutical to intertextual practices of theological invention mean? Theological writing is always, of course, a remix of samples of the Scripture, theology, culture, and a repertoire of timely ideas within a religious tradition. We saw this when we discussed multitracking in the previous chapter. At this point, however, we want to consider the broader intertextual implications of sampling, remixing, and mashup for theological invention. What happens when we shift from the tradition-bearing writer to the sampler as originator of theology?

Several possibilities immediately emerge in relation to the idea of the theological sampler as originator. First of all, theological inventors might see themselves as DJs, rap poets, or turntablists either metaphorically or literally. In this model, the theologian becomes a remix artist. At a baseline level, this might involve inviting others to track in the theologian's studio. In *The Roundtable Pulpit,* for instance, I suggested a model of collaborative preaching in which a preacher cuts and pastes bits and pieces of a presermon roundtable conversation with laity into the sermon itself, in effect including sampled riffs, countermelodies, backing, rhythm tracks, fills, and beats from laity in the composition of a sermon. I encouraged the expansion of this practice to include a wide range of sampled voices from within and beyond the religious community and tradition, including those accessed through the Internet.[45] Social networking technologies such as Facebook groups or Twitter could also be used to receive input (samples of riffs, backing, fills, countermelodies, etc.) that could be helpful in remixing theological compositions. The goal is to hear from strangers whose lives have not been tapped as spiritual resources for one's theological invention.

In another model, the mashup leads the way. The theologian may take a single work by a known author, or a small cluster of such works, and mash them up by juxtaposing portions (breaks and beats) from these works with works from other traditions and genres of writing, theological and nontheological. For an example of this, see appendix 2.

Theologians could also release their "original" work to be tracked and remixed in the studios of others, seeking out other social locations in which to do brainstorming and invention and involving others in the process. This might mean going into "contested spaces," such as the streets where homeless live, as do Charles Campbell and Stanley Saunders,[46] or a women's shelter,[47] where those who will be particularly aware of poverty, oppression, or violence can be engaged in conversation. It might include sending out an interview team with audio or video recorders to interview people at random about an idea or issue, and incorporating samples of these interviews into one's work. No matter how one goes about getting others to provide input, the goal in this model is to push beyond the boundaries of a particular tradition. Similar to a mashup artist sampling hip-hop beats and adding them to a blues song, the theological inventor steps outside the comfort zone of the usual tradition to see what happens when ideas and aspects of that tradition are juxtaposed with elements from beyond those boundaries.

This model could take a turn toward performance by incorporating aspects of turntabling or mashup into the practice of theological performance itself—in effect making on-the-fly theological invention into a performance. This, of course, will require the development of the same kind of technical and technological virtuosity displayed by Kool DJ Herc and others within the DJ music scene. Much of this work could be accomplished before beginning a performance by using integrated audio and video technologies (Final Cut, Adobe, Soundtrack Pro, etc.), or incorporating a range of audio and video production resources, both online (YouTube, Facebook, MySpace, etc.) and self-created (iMovie, Easy CD Creator, GarageBand, Blogger, etc.). The performance could include sampled bits and pieces of the voices of others as a part of the performance itself.

In another model, the theologian crafts an original piece of inventive prose or performance, much as the songwriter crafts a song, and then releases it entirely to others for remixing. The theologian encourages active, *productive* remixing of the composition through the use of digital audio production software, real-time artistic networking technologies such as Indaba, social networking websites such as Facebook and Twitter, or blog commentary boxes, or through any process that permits scribbling, commentary, or feedback as a part of the composition itself. The theologian (teacher, scholar, preacher, musician, blogger) might post a portion of an original piece of work to an online remixing site such as Indaba, or to another social networking site, and invite the broader community of theological mixologists to cut, paste, add to, and reshape the piece, sharing their "jams" and "remixes" with one another online. Remixes, then, might be incorporated into the work, in part or as a whole, as commentary or core text, indicating ways that active listening and sampling can produce entirely new inventions of theological meaning. Of course, immediate remixing is possible as well, through the use of technologies such as Twitter. Performers of theology (preachers, teachers, etc.) might encourage real-time "tweeting" as a way to involve others in immediate, interactive remixing of the composition's message. These tweets could be saved and turned into textual or marginal commentary within the final theological product in order to indicate the role of other participants in theological invention.

The result in these examples is a multivocal composition in which the theologian becomes "sampler-originator." In either approach, the differences between audience and spectator, product and consumer, original and copy are transgressed, and theological inventions are styled and morphed into new creations.

Inventing the Possible

In chapter 1, we engaged the songwriter as one who goes in search of good judgment as the key to rhetorical invention. This judgment evolved, in chapter 2, into judgment in production, including decisions about what and how to track multiple layers of theological content—usually in a way that would enhance the song's relationship to a particular tradition of music-making. This traditional approach to songwriting and tracking mirrors the classical rhetorical category of *stasis*, or learning to ask the right questions of the reality at hand as the key to deciding what to say (invention).[48] As we have seen, however, when a song confronts the reality of sampling and remixing, the rhetorical categories of *chora* (the chaotic juxtaposition of voices available for *this* genesis) and *kairos* (writing in an opportune way at this particular time) move into the forefront. Philosopher of rhetoric Victor J. Vitanza calls this a shift from *stasis* to *metastasis.*[49] Vitanza argues that within the Western tradition "thinking has been done in terms of the ideal (Plato) or the actual (Aristotle) with the third term generally excluded or suppressed or unfavored."[50] This exclusion, he argues, is usually done in favor of stability (*stasis*). The term that is excluded is "the possible."[51] According to literary scholar J. Hillis Miller, writing the possible is not an act of "filling in the path between an origin and a predetermined goal," but is rather the process of "extrapolation reaching out into the void to create the goal."[52] The writer of the possible steps forth into the creative void, allowing otherness a more prominent role in deciding what to say by releasing one's writing into heretofore unexpected and unanticipated juxtapositions of substance, form, and style.

According to theorist of rhetorical invention Gregory Ulmer, one fundamental principle is needed for this kind of writing: "do not choose between the different meanings of key terms, but compose by using all the meanings (write the paradigm)."[53] This means inviting, at least in theory, all the meaningful juxtapositions that cluster to a term, concept, or theme into the writing process. Such an idea resonates with an older notion of truth in the work of German philosopher Jürgen Habermas, in which truth emerges in an unlimited conversation within an "ideal speech situation."[54] In his early work,

Habermas asserted that finding consensus within the lifeworld as a whole—entering into an unlimited conversation within an ideal speech situation in which all people participate—was the best pathway to truth.[55] Critics have argued, among other things, that this idea is unrealistic, unattainable, and avoids the reality and necessity of institutions to public communication.[56] Certainly gaining access to *all* of the world's thoughts about a particular idea at a particular time is impossible. The idea seems out of reach, for the most part, and doomed to significant limitations in practice.

Recent developments in artistic and social networking and search engine algorithms, however, have begun to place *more* of an unlimited conversation at the fingertips of the theologian/composer. For instance, search engines such as OneRiot, Collecta, Tweetmeme, Topsy, and Scoopier, which rely heavily on real-time conversations such as Twitter and blog sites, search immediately for what people around the world are saying *right now* about a particular word, topic, or idea.[57] Distinguishing themselves from the logic of search engines such as Google or Ask.com, which operate on older ask-and-answer, information-retrieval models of searching, these search engines strive to "organize experience into a keyhole glimpse of what the world is doing at this very moment."[58]

Both Ulmer and Vitanza use the hyperlinking "connectionism" of the computer as a metaphor for this *chorastic* and *kairotic* model of invention, asserting that nothing short of memory is implicated when composition shifts toward the discovery of the possible. According to Vitanza, "Opposed to the classical concept of memory as storing information in some specific locale from which it may be retrieved, connectionism designs memory as not stored at any specific locus (*topos*, lines of argument determined by negation) but in the myriad relationships among various loci. . . . It's worth repeating: not *in* loci but *among*."[59] According to Ulmer, "the change in thinking from linear indexical to network association—a shift often used to summarize the difference between alphabetic and electronic cognitive styles . . .—is happening at the level of technology itself."[60]

When one releases one's composition into the digital bit stream of studio sampling, sequencing, collaborative (re)composition, mixing, and remixing (perhaps even online remixing), or to information retrieved from real-time conversation-based Internet search engines, one opens composition up to the *possible* in no uncertain terms. In this situation, random juxtapositions within a particular creative place (*chora*) and time (*kairos*) pry memory away from *stasis* and into metastatic forms of memory (and knowledge) only accessed through positioned and opportune relationships *between* loci of meaning. An artist or theologian in this mode gains access to new worlds made possible by this adventure into open-ended collaboration.

Inventing the Theologically Possible

When one begins to reflect on this theologically, it is the God of the possible or, in the words of Richard Kearney, God who is "the possibility of the impossible,"[61] who enters the picture. Kearney urges a "poetics of the possible" within an understanding of "God as May-Be."[62] This poetics strives to articulate God as both "desire and promise,"[63] a God who "possibilizes our world from out of the future."[64] The sampling and sampled theologian will need to embrace a God whose creative *Logos* defies the *topoi* and commonplaces usually associated with human reasoning. This God encourages theologians to plumb the depths of seemingly chaotic experience for new juxtapositions and relationships that will signify religious truth, sampling anything and everything, styling and morphing human works in order to reveal something new. This God is also deeply relational, creating meaning through relationship, not through self-contained individuality—becoming ever new.[65]

Perhaps the most suggestive theological correlate for a release of one's thought and work to collaborative remixing and mashup in order to discover new possibilities can be found in the creative work of the divine Spirit, or what Jim Loder, following Martin Luther, calls the Spiritus Creator.[66] Loder identifies a form of knowing that he calls "convictional knowing," in which Spirit "transforms all transformations of the human spirit."[67] Observing a set of similarities between human creativity and the creating work of the divine Spirit, Loder posits an "analogy of the Spirit" between the human and divine Spirit in the work of creativity. The process of creativity, according to Loder, involves a grammar that moves from (1) *conflict*

through (2) *scanning* to (3) *transforming intuition*, followed by a (4) *release* or "dexathexis of energy from the aspects of conflict," and the placing of one's transforming intuition into conversation with others for (5) communal *verification*.[68]

At the center of this process, in the second stage (scanning) and third stage (transforming intuition), is something like the *chorastic/kairotic* emergence of new possibilities identified above. For the remixing/remixed/mashed-up theologian, within this human/divine Spirit analogy a "scanning" (sampling and remixing) takes place in which new redemptive insights are sought through opening the creative process to unknown possibilities. Insights emerge as the theologian is given from outside the situation intuitions born of seeing for the first time new relationships among the key elements of one's situation, relationships that have gone unrecognized or been deemed impossible. This scanning involves a kind of free fall into a creative void or *chora*, a fall (or falling apart) that is only fully possible by trusting the Spiritus Creator to hold, guide, and lead one through this *porta*, or aperture to the other side—a new integrating insight or truth.

For Loder, the unrecognized "inner teacher" (Spirit) is at work in this process, such that it seems that one's release into creative or inventive scanning is "undertaken by another initiative"[69] that is "working deeper than consciousness and well beyond it," bringing about an "inside-outside reversal."[70] This inventive process culminates in transformation, by which Loder means "the negation of a negation."[71] The "negation" Loder speaks of is at once the "existential" negation of our human finitude confronting its limited creative powers and the artist's experience of "negation" (void, exigency, *chora*) that exists as the locus for human creativity. This twofold negation is negated in the moment of transformation, in which the Spirit prompts new possibilities into consciousness.

At this point in the conversation between song-making and theological invention, the theologian is challenged to learn a creative process of active, intertextual scanning. Theologians are encouraged, through any number of methods, to open theological composition to often random, *chorastic/kairotic* juxtapositions with

other samples of thought, life, art, culture, Scripture, literature, conversation, and so on. This will require significant trust in the guidance of an inner teacher/Spirit to lead the theologian through that process toward new possibilities for theological invention.

Mashup as Postsemiotic Theological Invention

Sampling, remixing, and mashup suggest ways theologians can think of theological invention as grounded less in language and more in living speech, that is, in pragmatic, proxemic, interhuman witness to the transcendent. In chapter 2, we noted the restrictions placed upon theological invention by traditions and genres, stylistic conventions, and language systems that theologians use in order to negotiate a hearing for theology within a range of tradition- and genre-based expectations. This is largely due to the Whorfian hypothesis that controls much of theological invention today—the idea that categories, language, and culture *create* reality.[72] This hypothesis achieved its influence on theologians through the work of structural linguists such as Ferdinand de Saussure, cultural anthropologists such as Clifford Geertz, and ordinary-language philosophers such as Ludwig Wittgenstein and J. L. Austin.[73]

Language-driven ideas of theological invention have taken many different forms. Sometimes it is assumed, as noted in chapter 2 in relation to multitracking content and style, that the production of theological meaning is controlled by linguistic and cultural codes latent within historically conditioned styles of communication.[74] In another version, the dominant linguistic culture for theological invention shifts toward local interpretive communities.[75] We will explore this idea more in chapter 5 when we investigate the role of fan cultures and social networking in producing the social value of theological inventions. In another approach, theological invention issues forth from the way one (countercultural) culture resists the dominance of another (hegemonic) culture.[76] In strict "language-game" models, the strange acculturating power of Scripture, liturgy, or doctrine becomes dominant under the assumption that the framing and reframing of language will lead to a framing and reframing of reality.[77] In all of these models, the prevailing assumption is that language and culture

lead the way and exert a controlling influence in all things when it comes to the invention and communication of theological meaning and truth.

As I noted at the end of chapter 2, embedded within the multitrack approach there exists the hint of a pragmatic interest in the ways that theologians might track different layers of theology in inconsistent and hybrid ways in order to co-create theological meaning across seemingly distinct language games or cultures (the liberationist evangelical, for instance). In part, the possibility of this kind of hybridity issues from a postmodern hyperreflexivity. Theologians are now very aware of the styles of tracking that are assumed as normative within each theological tradition, and this awareness promotes the possibility of transgressing traditions and genres.

By learning, engaging, and categorizing the various styles of language that can be tracked as Scripture, culture, theology, and message (by exploring the theological "loop browser"—see chapter 2), it is possible for theologians, like musicians, to move over onto a small portion of the lived ground out of which each of these types of content and style has emerged. As a result of this modest empathic reflexivity, theologians begin to understand both the conditions that produce each content and style and the consequences, good and bad, projected by each style when added into a theological mix. In other words, they begin to understand the shape that desire for God takes for those who are attracted to and use each rhetorical style, that is, the promise, the hope, implicit in the performance of each loop or track.[78]

So it is that theological invention begins to flirt with a mashup mentality, wondering what would happen if seemingly inconsistent mixtures of styles should emerge, based on heretofore undreamt religiously motivated conditions or the need for different religious effects. What real-life conditions, for instance, would make for the appearance of a theologian combining an inerrantist/infallibilist dynamic equivalence way of tracking Scripture, a dialectical way of tracking culture, a liberationist theology world/tensive worldview, and a conversationalist way of tracking messages?

Reflexive awareness inserts a kind of playfulness into theological tracking that helps to open theologians to the possibility that traditions and styles of thinking can, in fact, exist in positive relationships with one another. As these relationships develop, traditions and styles are able to learn from one another. No longer caught up in the business of purifying theological invention within the range of options established by current codes and conventions for tracking theology, theologians cease to be consumed with the need for semantically and syntactically consistent sign usage (semiosis). They are able to see the dynamic ways in which theology can be remixed pragmatically, often in violation of code consistency, *as needed* in real-life situations of articulating religious meaning.

Mashup theologians, therefore, will be pragmatic to a fault, refusing to be ruled by a logic of authenticity that will help them become pure models of a pure originals. Instead, they embrace the logic of textuality and file-sharing, arguing that all words, traditions, and styles of speech are borrowed, plagiarized, and exchanged in an attempt to *communicate*—that is, to discover and share a lived religious world. Theological pragmatism of this sort invites theologians to drop the need to adopt a wholly consistent configuration of theological tracks. Instead, they will feel the strong urge to move the locus for theological invention toward the place where *lived theology* is most powerfully and actively emergent. This will mean two things. First, it will mean that theologians will increasingly wed theological reflection to ethnography. Sensing that most people, similar to DJs, are mashing up religion most of the time, creating inconsistent yet useful theologies in order to survive and flourish, theologians will increasingly take the time to study congregations and communities in which this is occurring. Theologians will study how theological invention is occurring in these places, and what forms of pragmatic theological logic and practice make this possible. Many of the newer studies in practical theology are proceeding with this in mind.[79]

In a second approach, theologians will strive to locate their own theological production in the give-and-take of real human beings striving to invent a language and messages adequate to their having come into proximity with one another and the transcendent at this time and place. In order to pursue the possibility of this kind of theological creativity and agency, theologians will relocate invention in the middle of intentional religious conversations in which individuals listen to one another, do the hard work of crossing over into one another's lifeworlds, and begin to see the hybrid possibilities for theological invention made possible through such engagement.

In either model, mashup religion is located in the fast-moving intersection of the company of strangers as they collaboratively listen for and utter religious meaning in hybrid categories and languages. Theologians, in this way of thinking, will see their work as listening into speech code–transgressing theological inventions that are adequate to lived religion. They will discover what DJs and mashup musicians know, that by crate-digging they can actually experience some of the conditions for another person's alien ways of speaking in another tradition or culture, and find ample means to generate a range of shared theological ideas, words, language, and meaning within and across strange or even estranged lifeworlds. In this situation, theologians, similar to DJs, will use words, phrases, doctrines, ideas, turns of phrase, and so on as juxtaposed breaks on the turntables of theological composition, as they invent new utterances, wordless gestures, hybrid linguistic constructions, and categories that create theological meaning in spite of seemingly incommensurate language games.

Instead of language and culture becoming more and more atomized and fragmented, therefore, theologians find themselves in a mashup situation in which they stand the great opportunity of beginning to treat language and culture as more contingent, fluid, malleable *things* alongside them in the world, things that can be stylistically morphed in the communication of theological meaning and truth. This, in itself, constitutes a certain exiting of tradition, language, and culture—paradoxically at precisely the moment in which ideas of tradition, language, and culture have become the most popular, powerful, and divisive terms in our midst.[80]

Mashup religion poses the following question: once we have exited language, shared beliefs, community and tradition, and scriptural grammars, arriving on the ever-present originary scene of spiritual and theological desire and representation without the formerly assumed tools of representation to guide us, how in the world is theological invention possible? Are we thrown back into the tongues of fire? Is this a call to spiritual enthusiasm: the world of the *Schwermer?* Perhaps.[81] At the very least, the cornerstone of theological invention in this situation is precisely that it begins *without representation at all.* It begins with encountering the real conditions for the God-speech and theological language spoken by one another, with the discovery of ethical proximity and requisite utterance (voice, sound) before witnessed transcendence. In other words, through a range of gestures, utterances, and speaking-across codes and conventions, theologians find that they can cross over onto the ground of another's desire for God. If this crossing-over process is reciprocated to some extent, theologians can begin to utter *together* something of the God witnessed through the lenses of these divergent religious desires.

Let me attempt to provide a couple of examples. In 2004, I gave a lecture at a worship conference for the United Church of Canada in which I observed (as many sociologists have done before) that there exists already in and around traditions of religion a huge body of religious persons who are extremely eclectic in their listening partners when it came to matters of spirituality and God. I suggested that a great many of these people are sitting in pews or kneeling in prayer in synagogues, mosques, and churches, barely hanging onto the ideas and styles of thinking espoused by religious traditions. Many of these persons represent a radical decentering of what constitutes religious authority, as well as an even more radical decentering of the boundaries separating secular–sacred, inside–outside, and center–margin. I suggested that with this growing segment of the population, those within religious traditions would need increasingly decentered forms of theological invention and communication, such as collaborative preaching or remixed or mashed-up theological practices.

The United Church of Canada placed these lectures up on their website for a year or so, and I began to get a little stream of e-mails, some chastening me for being a deconstructive atheist and others wondering whether or not I was potentially a closet mainstream Christian "emergent" church thinker. Not knowing a thing about the so-called emerging conversation, then dominated by "post-evangelicals," I decided that I should read into the emerging church literature in order to get some grasp of this movement. After finishing several key books, I decided that among some so-called emergents there exists, in fact, some bare-bones correspondence to mashup religion. To a great extent, emergents seemed to be exiting the tradition-driven, linguistic, and culturalist model of theological invention. They were doing this, however, without any explicit ethical or theological reflection on the problems and prospects of their interest in decentering communicative practices in the theological guild. From a perspective guided primarily by evangelistic (missional), doctrinal, and liturgical issues, they were beginning to explore proxemic, pragmatic, *agapic*, and desire-driven models of communication such as I am suggesting. They were doing this in very immediate and obvious ways, by moving across language and belief paradigms in what Brian McLaren calls a "generous orthodoxy,"[82] and taking the time to see if they could find, within the conditions giving rise to liberal, Orthodox, Roman Catholic, Pentecostal, and other traditions, useful elements for reinventing categories of thought about God today.

In my opinion, some post-evangelical thinkers in the "emerging conversation" ultimately recapitulate to a consistent usage model of theological invention, lining up reflexively under the semantics of the conservative evangelical movement and the new measures pragmatism of Finney.[83] Others are, however, engaging in an actual decentered model of inconsistent, hybridized communicative pragmatism reflective of the one emerging within popular culture at large. This is especially true in the way that they transgress codes, languages, and cultures in their appropriation of "vintage" religious traditions.[84]

Although they are not appropriating these other vintage traditions (yet) in any great depth, this naiveté is, perhaps, one of the *strengths* of this way of thinking about theological communication. McLaren, Kimball, and others intentionally seek out the simplest pragmatic conditions of life and the positive effects (future) sought by liberal, orthodox, and Catholic believers. These are given priority over the doctrinal warfare, or emphasizing the exclusivity of a tradition's language or ritual practices, as the way forward theologically. In the words of Peter Collins, they are rethinking orthodoxy as "a way of being in the world rather than a means of believing things about the world."[85] Those of us who are aware of the complexities of these traditions and languages will perhaps be perturbed by this reduction of our language games to their "use-value" on the street, but this is to miss the genius involved in assuming first of all the importance of having a real *relationship* with those who speak/

practice other traditions and styles of thought, seeking out the ways these traditions are actually spoken into human life and relationships. Often this means listening and talking together fruitfully in ways that stretch each party's language system *beyond* the breaking point. Some emergents, it seems, believe that piecing together (remixing, mashing up) a new street narrative of discernment and hope is more important than "getting it right."

The other example comes from my work with musicians in Nashville, as a part of the Center for the Study of Religion and Culture's Music, Religion, and the South project. One of the primary shocks for me, as a theologian grounded in a tradition (the Reformed and Presbyterian tradition) of religious thought, was the way that musicians in Nashville were relatively uninspired by the religious distinctions and categories imposed on their work by professional theologians. Although illuminating at times, these categories (liberal, conservative, praise and worship, contemporary Christian, etc.) were seen as unhelpful and potentially divisive. Time and time again, in interviews, conversations, and classroom settings, musicians and songwriters demonstrated more interest in getting onto the religious ground occupied by another person, and especially another musician or songwriter, in order to see what could be learned and appropriated. This never meant sacrificing one's own ideas. Rather, it meant that most of these musicians believed that the key to truly relevant and meaningful invention was the possibility of remixing another artist's ideas and allowing one's own ideas to be improvised, mashed up, or remixed by someone else. Holding a theological jam session was more important than getting all the notes and stylistic elements right by faithfully representing a particular tradition or genre. Figuring out how to make music together or create a great new song that would express more religious truth was more important than holding tightly to categories or frames of reference.

I will return to the issue of whether mashup religion means that "anything goes" in chapter 5, and suggest again the importance of traditions *within this larger framework* of mashup religion. What I want to emphasize here is the increasing cultural dominance of mashup religion, and its inventive importance. Increasingly, theologians, whether artists, musicians, preachers, bloggers, scholars, or educators,

are aware that traditions, languages, doctrines, homiletic constructions, religious cultures, and so on are not incommensurate, mutually
exclusive grids. Instead, languages are *things in the world* that human
beings shape and reshape in order to identify and deal *together* with
the conditions of life under which they live, as they perceive them,
and to identify, live into, and bring about certain (hopefully good and
true) desires and effects given that situation.

In spite of the joy any good theologian will find in a vibrant and
consistent usage of a particular semantic field, theologians do not
have to stop there, protecting and asserting one grid of meanings over
against another, or using elements of one grid to bring about a happy
"reframing" of another's rather inadequate grid. Rather, theologians
have the option of listening to multiple languages in order to gain
some access to the conditions of life endured by others, along with
the ways that they are using language to help them find their way to
God. Traditions, languages, and cultures, then, are properly partners,
not servants or masters: they are epiphenomena that provide hints,
clues, and traces of the ways in which we and others are navigating
the world.

If theological language is largely epiphenomenal in this way, what
is the purpose of invention of theological speech within mashup religion? Two things immediately come to mind—and these two things
stand at extremes from one another.[86] From there, we must begin to
imagine the middle.

At one extreme, mashup religion suggests that theological speech
bears testimony to a *certain kind of silence* in the world: the silence
of God. On one hand, this is experienced as the silence through
which God always escapes naming, or disappears when named (cf.
negative theologies, and some deconstructive theologies, especially
Altizer's work).[87] On the other hand, however, the silence of God is
the silence of *resurrection*, the silence of God *making room for speech*,
a welcoming silence, silence in which, in the words of Rachel Muers,
"*God* hears God's Word"[88] (emphasis added). Theological speaking
reminds us of the silence of God listening to God's Word in the
world, hearing into living speech all those who desire God. Theological speaking creates within human speech "the communicative
pattern that conforms to God's act of hearing."[89]

On the other extreme, mashup religion suggests that theological speech is the transgressive *breaking* of this certain kind of silence. Theological speaking is noisy, cacophonic, celebrative, ecstatic, glossalalic, overdetermined, shared speech, a voicing of what theologian of deconstruction Charles Winquist once called the "unrestricted desire to know."[90] Theological speaking indicates an infinite desire for God by breaking silence in extravagant utterance. In this sense, theological speaking always expresses a gap, or gaping, in God's silence—a breaking open of that silence toward the unknown *in the world* that implicates and deconstructs the known. This is the speaking of the Spirit through which our desire for God's Word emerges from and stands in (for) God's desire for (hearing of) God's Word.

Both of these aspects of theological speaking are, in their originary form, contra-semiotic. They are not nonsemiotic, or nonlinguistic; rather, they speak *across* language in a way that restores theological language its role as active utterance rather than as the further codification of the already said—as utterances identifying a certain kind of silence and breaking that silence. Theological invention within mashup religion is the breaking of a certain kind of silence, which signals simultaneously God's silent hearing of us in our desire for God and God's Word uttered among us as God's desire for us, in that very moment.

4

THE GRAIN OF THE VOICE

INVENTING THE SOUNDSCAPE OF RELIGIOUS DESIRE

The "grain" is the body in the voice as it sings, the hand as it writes, the limb as it performs.

—Roland Barthes, "The Grain of the Voice"

Touch is the most personal of the senses. Hearing and touch meet where the lower frequencies of audible sound pass over to tactile vibrations (at about 20 hertz). Hearing is a way of touching at a distance and the intimacy of the first sense is fused with sociability whenever people gather together to hear something special.

—R. Murray Schafer, *The Tuning of the World*

Our focus at this point shifts from inventive decisions focused on the selection and organization of sounds to decisions in the studio regarding the sound palette or voicing of a song. In song-making, this involves a shift away from decisions about what to track on a song and what instruments, sounds, and styles of tracks to include, toward the business of actually recording and mixing those sounds together into a sonic whole. When drawing parallels to theological composition, we will shift our attention to the way the words of a composition will sound and the final performance or presentation of theology, whether as the spoken word, multimedia, music, or some other form.

Decisions about the sonic palette of a song are usually made in relation to a particular desired soundscape or musical landscape into which the song fits. Studio mixing and mastering are focused on the invention of particular *qualities* of sound. At this level, we are confronted with studio engineers who fret, on the front end of recording, over the use of particular microphones, microphone placement strategies, the warmth of preamps, the relative transparency of ADCs, and the smoothness of compressors in the actual recording of the artist. On the back end, once the audio has been recorded and organized within the edit window of the DAW, the tracks are mixed in the DAW's mix window (see figure 4.1). During this mixing process, various audio plug-ins or hardware sound processors are inserted into each track in order to add dynamics such as compression, limiting, phase adjustments, equalization (treble, midrange, or bass), stereo panning (left, center, right), reverberation and delay, and a host of other sonic effects.

From microphone placement to the choice of mixing effects, the studio engineer is obsessed with certain qualities of sound. Within a more conservative aesthetic, the goal is *transparency*. The job of the studio engineer, from the placement of microphones to the final mix-down, is to get out of the way in order to foreground the (usually acoustic) artistry of the musician and instruments in real time. Transparency is not, however, a technology-free achievement. Certain microphones, preamps, compressors, and audio plug-ins are sold and purchased based upon their transparent qualities. These technologies are known to attract less attention to themselves and draw out certain qualities (woodiness, ambience, clarity) that signify to the listener that the audio is sonically pure. Engineers seeking transparency leave audio uncompressed or lightly compressed, use more distant microphone placement, and remove from one instrument frequencies that compete with another, more important instrument in the mix.

Within an alternative aesthetic, the goal is *color*. The studio engineer becomes more intrusive in the sonic process, and the listener becomes aware of the engineer's presence. In this approach, the

Figure 4.1. Pro Tools mix window.

listener's identification is not as much with the performing artist or beautifully sampled audio as with the more intrusive recording technology and the editor-producer of the sonic material. At the extreme of this aesthetic, the audience is invited to identify with the recording or editing device itself. In this model, reverb, delay, compression, dramatic stereo panning, subsonic bass, doubling, robotic vocal processors, and other special effects are added in large doses.

At the far end of this mixing process is the mastering portion of the production chain. The mastering engineer takes the final mix and strengthens the overall sonic palette. This can involve widening the stereo field, adding depth, presence, smoothness, volume, volume normalization, and equalization, and matching the sound of one song to others on a CD, even those recorded with different instruments or in other recording studios. Again, each part of the larger whole is analyzed, edited, and reintegrated.

The Microphone: Personality, Touch, Intimacy, and Distance

Although not all sounds are recorded by microphones (synthesized sounds, direct recorded sounds, etc.), it is the microphone, above all else, that stands as the symbol for the production of a particular sonic palette. When a studio engineer reaches for a particular microphone, it is with a very particular quality of sound in mind. Some microphones sound bright, others are smooth. Some have a noticeable boost in either the low, midrange, or high-frequency range. Some sound wooden, some metallic. Some are unidirectional, picking up only what is in front of them. Others are multidirectional, capturing the sound of an entire room. Some are designed to handle loud sound pressure levels (SPLs), and others are designed only for softer levels of sound volume. Condenser microphones require phantom power in order to operate, while dynamic and ribbon microphones are unpowered. All microphones have diaphragms of various types, some large and some very small. Most microphones are solid state, but an increasing number of tube microphones are now available that are designed to warm and saturate the sound. Some microphones are purchased entirely to capture the voice. Others are purchased to capture guitars, stringed instruments, drums, brass, choral music, orchestration, or ambient sounds. Most studio engineers know exactly what kind of sound each microphone in the microphone cabinet will produce, and reach for a microphone with that particular voicing in mind.

Once a microphone is chosen, the engineer must choose which preamp best fits the desired sound. Sometimes tube preamps are chosen to add further warmth or a particular color or texture to a sound. Sometimes a preamp is chosen because it either extends or narrows the dynamic range of the microphone, or will transparently reproduce the sound captured by the microphone. Ribbon microphones require special preamps with enough headroom to produce an adequate signal. A huge range of vintage preamps is currently on the market in order to help recreate analog-quality sounds within the digital domain.

Finally, on the front end of the recording process, the engineer must decide whether to add equalization, compression, gating, "de-essing," or effects as the sound is recorded. Some instruments require equalization (low, midrange, high frequencies). Compressors are used when there is tremendous variation in volume. A compressor is an audio circuit that acts much like having a very quick hand on the volume control. It pumps up the volume when the audio is quiet, and brings down the peaks when the audio is loud. The goal is a more uniform, consistent audio signal and maximum overall volume. Some sounds are "gated." A gating device removes audio when volume goes below a defined threshold. This effectually removes room noise or other competing noise that is below a certain level. In some instances, a "de-esser" is used to soften the loud "sss" sounds when recording vocalists. Sometimes effects such as delay or reverb are added as well, usually after a dry (unprocessed) signal of the sound has been recorded.

Many of the metaphors used by studio engineers and recording artists for this sound-capturing process are designed to describe a particular sonic *personality*: warm, muted, excited, low, high, subtle, soft, loud, strong, weak, focused, and so on. Cultural theorist David Buxton argues that the microphone was, in fact, the key element in the transition from operatic and music hall singers of the nineteenth century to vocal styles within popular music. According to Buxton, "the microphone . . . heightened the nuances of 'personality' in each singer, rather than the rigorous technical perfection of the operatic tradition."[2] Much like the mirror, which psychoanalyst Jacques Lacan associates closely with a child's first self-awareness of being a distinct personality, the microphone is a powerful self-referring tool, accentuating and drawing out elements of personality at close range.[3] Although many artists, when first recording their voice, exclaim, "It doesn't sound like me," in fact the microphone is drawing out and reflecting back any number of sonic qualities that are, in fact, "me." This "me," however, is a "me" without the ear's reception of the vibrations of the internal, resonant sounding board of the body. It is the completely externalized, and thus social, "me." To a great extent, microphone, preamp, equalization, and dynamic processor choices by engineers and artists are designed to either move this self-referential aspect closer in toward the body and its resonant qualities—emphasizing closeness and intimacy—or to add distance, highlighting the voice's social resonance within a larger space.

More than personality, the microphone and other sound-capturing devices are extensions of human *touch*. Cultural theorist Andra McCartney recalls attending a college dance at which "some of the most expressive dancers that night were the deaf students. They took their shoes off and felt the music through the soles of their feet, reaching up to animate their whole bodies in motion."[4] She goes on to assert that "sound is the language of vibration, and we hear this vibration with more than our ears."[5] The particular way that a sound touches us is "heightened by technology: when microphones amplify and record sounds, they not only involve the ears, but also every other part of the body."[6]

Contemporary soundscape art makes particular use of the microphone as "a listening instrument"[7] to capture audible, sometimes barely audible, sounds. The goal of soundscape artists is to magnify the availability to the ear of every aspect of human life. McCartney points out that some soundscape artists are now involved in "sound-walking," using microphones to accompany them on everyday excursions, recording the range of sounds they encounter each day. Soundscape recording has become a common practice in talk radio interviews such as those frequently aired on public radio, in which interviewers use microphones not only to capture interviewees, but to capture the sonic setting in which the interview takes place. The fact that very low-volume sounds can be captured and amplified magnifies the sense that the microphone is an instrument for increasing or, in fact, producing intimacy or distance. Distant things can be made close up through the use of this technology,[8] and this closeness is magnified by compression techniques in the studio.

Similar to film, the microphone increases in the listener what Walter Benjamin called the urge "to get hold of an object at very close range by way of its likeness, its reproduction."[9] Media scholars Hans Ulrich Gumbrecht and Michael Marrinan identify in this an "elementary dialectic . . . of the sacred."[10] Sacred objects are not only objects at a distance from our everyday lives; by establishing that distance they also attract and intensify a desire to touch. If it is the Word that is sacred, therefore, the closeness afforded by the microphone has the distinct possibility of creating the desire to touch or become intimate with that Word.

The Grain of the Voice

Whether the human voice or the voice of a particular instrument, what the mixing and mastering engineer is seeking, through the use of specific microphones and other sound-capturing devices is a particular sonic texture or grain. French semiotician Roland Barthes, in his famous essay "The Grain of the Voice," identifies a difference between the technically well-performed "pheno-song" and the aesthetically "voluptuous" "geno-song." According to Barthes, the pheno-song contains "all the features which belong to the structure of the language being sung, the rules of the genre, the coded form of the melisma, the composer's idiolect, the style of the interpretation: in short, everything in the performance which is in the service of communication, representation, expression, everything which it is customary to talk about, which forms the tissue of cultural values (the matter of acknowledged tastes, of fashions, of critical commentaries)."[11] The geno-song, on the other hand, is "the space where significations germinate 'from within language and in its very materiality'; it forms a signifying play having nothing to do with communication, representation (of feelings), expression; it is that apex (or that depth) of production where the melody really works at the language—not at what it says, but the voluptuousness of its sounds-signifiers, of its letters—where melody explores how the language works and identifies with that work."[12] Barthes goes on to assert that the whole of traditional musical pedagogy conspires to teach the pheno-song and not the geno-song. According to Barthes, the pheno-song is grounded in "the lungs" and the "breath," the "myth of respiration" and "the mastery, the correct discipline of breathing."[13] The focus of such music is diction and correct articulation of the language and genre of the song, in order to make it "expressive, dramatic, sentimentally clear."[14] The geno-song, on the other hand, is grounded in the grain of the voice, which, according to Barthes, finds its locus "in the throat, place where the phonic metal hardens and is segmented, in the mask that *signifiance* explodes. . . . The tongue, the glottis, the teeth, the mucous membranes, the nose."[15] The focus of such music is on this body making these sounds, on a unique instrument creating sounds on their way to becoming communicable language. Barthes later calls this "the body in a state of music,"[16] or what cultural philosopher David Székely calls "the body inscribed in music. Music written on the body."[17] Popular culture theorist Peter Antelyes, speaking about the music of Bessie Smith, uses the intense closeness of the microphone as a metaphor to describe the graininess of her singing: "Bessie didn't need a microphone because she was a microphone, or rather, she had swallowed it; and she would fill you up with her own 'muscle.'"[18] The geno-song "fills you up with the muscle" of the song's voicing, its sheer material beauty or voluptuousness, accentuating the shaping and uttering of sounds apart from their being communicable language in service to codes and conventions of proper speech and communication.

It is this grain that emerges as central to the sonic palette of remixed and mashed-up music. This is due in large part to the increasing importance of crate-digging: listening to and experiencing the desires that exist as the precondition for all invention. For a DJ, the decision to choose and remix any great sampled break from a crated vinyl album is focused on its sonic interiority—the voluptuousness of its signifiers. Before the meaning and history of these signifiers is known, the interiority of their sounds is intuited and sampled. In remix and mashup, the interiority of the signifiers (sounds, words) is just as important as the signified words or meanings that are ultimately produced.

It would not be going too far to say that the mashup studio engineer's focus on the final mix, from microphone selection to choice of samples or tracks to mastering, is entirely a matter of searching out the grain of the voice, the voluptuousness of sounds and signifiers— which amounts to capturing the *desire* that resonates beneath those sounds and signifier. It is this grain that attaches sounds to a *particular body* on the way to sound, not to a cultural value, critical taste, or linguistic meaning. Finding the grain means finding how *this* body in *this* place at *this* time, in all of its materiality, gave (and now regives) voice, speaks, or *works beneath and at the language of music.*

Cultural philosopher Mladen Dolar calls this "voiceless voice."[19] According to Dolar, the grain of the voice, beginning with breathed sound, "points toward meaning."[20] Graininess is similar to the voice (and voicing) of John the Baptist, the "voice of one crying in the wilderness," which is "the condition of revelation of the Word," but not the Word itself.[21] This parallels Roland Barthes' understanding of the grain of the voice as a "voluptuousness" that "explores how the language works."[22] It is not the language itself, but an exploration of the underpinnings of that language—the sonic interiority of the *logos*. This sonic interiority is best thought of as a form of *eros* or desire. Dolar, considering Augustine's theology of the voice, notes that the sensuous beauty of the voice is "beyond the word (*logos*)," and while it "raises our souls to God" it also "makes God ambiguous."[23] The grain of the voice initiates a desire to transcend ordinary experience, while directing attention to forms of transcendence that are not necessarily bound to specific religious traditions.

Soundscape

Personality, touch, intimacy, distance, and grain are ultimately sought by studio engineers in sounds that are mixed and mastered in a particular way in order to become part of a larger soundscape of music within the larger culture. Philosophers and sociologists are increasingly aware of our auditory experience of the world within a technological society. Philosopher George Steiner speaks of living in a pervasive "sound-capsule" that shapes all of our lives.[24] In other words, the sonic palette of the song that emerges from the recording studio meets head-on the larger soundscape that exists at large within popular culture. In large part, this soundscape is made up of music that accompanies us when we work, read, eat, relax, and travel. But this soundscape also includes other forms of media: television, Internet, podcasts, and so on, as well as the sounds of city and rural life, including automobiles, machinery, airplanes, street vendors, crying children, cheering fans, and so on. In particular, the artist or studio engineer is involved in discerning where, within this soundscape, the song fits and how it will function in relation to a particular *musical* aspect of the larger soundscape.

Often, when determining soundscape, the studio engineer will use a "reference CD" or recording as a basic sound palette to emulate. From time to time, the engineer will switch from "mix A" (the song in process) to "mix B" (the reference CD) to see if the overall sound is matching the desired sound (and soundscape). Does the bass track have the same punch? Are the drums sitting in roughly the same place in the mix? Is the vocal at about the same volume level relative to the rest of the mix? Is the equalization (treble and bass) similar for all tracks?

Discerning a song's relationship to a particular soundscape requires a different kind of listening than the "audile technique" required in order to piece together bits of sampled sounds (see chapter 3). It requires attention to what aesthetic philosopher Gernot Böhme calls "acoustic atmospheres" within an "ecological aesthetic."[25] Böhme argues that soundscape has more to do with being able to hear the "musicality of the world itself."[26] According to Böhme, "the feeling of 'home' is strongly mediated by the *soundscape* of a region, and the characteristic experience of a lifestyle, of a city's or a countryside's atmosphere, is fundamentally determined in each instance by the acoustic space."[27] Discerning soundscapes, therefore, involves sonic travel—the ability to experience and appreciate a variety of different sonic homes and the roles that music plays in the ecological aesthetic of these soundscapes. Does a particular form of music contribute to the relative loudness of the soundscape? Its texture? Its density? Its whispering or undercurrent sounds? Its expressions of distance or marginality? Its yearnings for intimacy and closeness?

The voicing of a studio recording, therefore, has a great deal to do with the artist's and studio engineer's ability to hear and connect to potential soundscapes for the song: the sonic landscapes in which the final musical artifact is to live. Mixing and mastering are, in the last analysis, about "the maintenance and the structuring of acoustic space."[28] The way that something is mixed and mastered, and the eventual sonic palette is sought, connects directly to supporting, maintaining, filling up, and filling out a particular soundscape. Aesthetic philosopher Gabor Csepregi asserts the importance of categories of *echo* and *resonance* to describe this sonic fitting process.[29] These terms indicate whether sounds "either correspond to or contradict our auditory habits."[30] Do they echo or find resonance in relation to a larger soundscape? The goal is a sonic palette that works to create a "community of consonance."[31]

As ethnographer Charles Hirschkind points out, however, sound-scapes can also be embattled domains. Hirschkind observed how fundamentalist sermons broadcast on loudspeakers and made widely available for listening in automobiles and on boom boxes throughout major Egyptian cities became a significant form of counterspeech. They did battle with the soundscape of political modernization supported by the "state's complete monopoly on all television and radio broadcasting in postcolonial Egypt, and strict censorship policies that severely limit unofficial viewpoints in the press."[32] Hirschkind points out that it is precisely the grain of the voice, and the voicing of these sermons, that turned them into significant voices of difference and dissent within the larger soundscape of Egyptian urban life. Approaches to soundscape, therefore, are not always based on fit, but may also be based on ideologies of subversion or transformation.

Tone of Voice and the Invention of Religious Desire

Barthes was correct in connecting the geno-voice to the voluptuousness of the musical signifier. Desire for the body and reality of the signifier is at the heart of what the geno-voice expresses, and this is true in the expression of theological messages as well. The grain of the voice invents the *tone* or tone of voice established by a theological composition. This tone of voice is pervasive and invents the shape that religious desire takes in a composition. Although the musician, poet, and prophet (and some preachers) understand this connection best, the voice is always there in the invention and communication of religious desire.[33] This desire takes many shapes, defined by many tones of voice—persuasive, collegial, moralistic, wise, insightful, responsible, anxious, troubled, longing, hopeful, and so on—and contributes to the construction of a soundscape of religious desire that a theologian and audience inhabit and rely on.

The tone or grain of the work is pre- or extraverbal. It expresses an *intention*: life lived within this religious soundscape, prior to, or in spite of, the content of one's words. It says such things tacitly as

"Welcome to the intimate, exclusive soundscape of the wise mentor who desires for you to learn what she knows," or "Welcome to the loud, nagging soundscape of the angry parent who desires a more obedient child," or "Welcome to the inviting, interpersonal soundscape of persuasion and the desire for your conversion."

As the sound of religious desire searching for language, the voicing of theology lies at a deeper, more interior level than words or ideas can express. As theologian Burton Cooper puts it, "Our love of God, our trust in God, our felt need of God, our loyalty to God, in other words our emotional relatedness to God, lie at a more fundamental level than our ideas about God."[34] Even without the words, the grain of the voice expresses a very particular religious intention, creating a soundscape that shapes the form of religious desire that exists between communicator and audience. The final sound of a theological performance, therefore, is a profound expression of religious interiority and intentionality, giving voice to the shape of the God-shaped hole between performer and audience as it reaches toward adequate words. When an audience hears the final mix, they tune in to the *tone* of the work and hear beyond words the sonic shape that desire for God can take within the larger soundscape of their lives.

The Grain of Theology

The theologian who sits metaphorically at the mixing and mastering console sits at the juncture between the graininess of the theological composition's voice or voicing and a variety of soundscapes: of classrooms, institutions, the Internet, liturgies, and a range of cultural and religious contexts. It is not typical for the theologian in the North American context to ask how the *tone of voice* of one's compositions is designed to fit, augment, woo, persuade, counteract, or transform a religious, cultural, or institutional soundscape. More often theologians think first about how words or ideas meet the larger community or culture, or how one can give voice to pheno-performances appropriate for the tastes and expectations of an audience (and former professors). Although they may be aware of it, and perhaps worried about it, it is not likely that many theologians spend time intentionally considering the grain, the actual microphonics of the words they body forth, the thickness of the sound one produces when speaking, its corporeality, sensuality, and musicality, and how it is shaped as the sound religious desire can or should have within the larger soundscape. Is openness, distance, closeness, or softness required? How transparent or natural does the theologian wish to sound either in intonation, emotion, or expression? How much color (distortion, modulation, reverberation, compression, echo, etc.) is required? Should the theologian's sound be "emo" (moodier), compressed (louder and closer), excited (more energetic), uncompressed (more subtle), "lo-fi," or "hi-fi"?[35] Should the tone be argumentative? Declarative? Slightly poetic? Meditative? Reminiscent? Solemn? Lighthearted?[36] What mix of sounds, noises, spoken or sung words, prerecorded music, video, microphones, and loudspeakers is required to actualize the desired mix? What is the soundscape of religion into which the theologian is inventing theology? Fundamentalists? Cultured despisers of religion? Skeptics? Seekers? Post-evangelical? Mainstream? And beyond this, what are the cultural currents that have become the dominant religious soundscape for listeners? Is the theologian aware of what other voices audiences are listening to on a regular basis as a part of their religious or spiritual soundscape: television, podcasts, music, Internet, and local thought leaders? How will the various performances of these theological ideas "sound" in relation to all of these voices? Will it fit? Will it subvert? Will it transform? Finally, and most important, into what soundscape, expressing what religious desire(s), will the theologian invite the audience? In other words, what is the A/B reference for this composition or presentation?

Many theologians will consider attention to technologies for producing voice a waste of time. The theologian within mashup religion, however, will show genuine interest and make a point of using technologies that will support the tone of religious desire he or she seeks to convey. Depending on the desired sonic palette, are the needed technologies available? What is needed in order to achieve the sonic mix desired? This is a question both of particular kinds of microphones and sound systems and of overall acoustics and acoustic space. Acoustic intimacy requires closeness to a microphone and perhaps the use of an audio compressor. Intimacy also requires a very different set of acoustical treatments (deadening and closing-in sound) than acoustical distance (broadening and expanding sound). At the same time, both closeness and distance can be embraced in a room affording two or three seconds of reverberation. Audio can be compressed and projected at higher volume to create both intimacy and distance.

Does the sound system need to accommodate electronic music and multimedia? If this is the case, many public speaking–oriented audio systems will be virtually useless, unable to handle the range of frequencies and volumes involved. Bi-amped or tri-amped music sound systems will be required, often including sub-woofers in order to project bass and sub-bass frequencies.

Equalization is another significant issue. If the theologian's voice needs to be warmer, or less abrasive, it is possible with today's technologies to roll off (turn down) abrasive high or high–midrange frequencies, producing a more pleasant sound. Low frequencies can also be added as a way of warming a voice. The opposite is also true. Poor diction can be ameliorated in part by enhancing higher frequencies or adding air to the middle of a mix by decreasing midrange frequencies slightly.

It is unfair and unwise to isolate the production of tone of voice to the final mixing and mastering stage of the popular song, or to technologies of live performance. As we have seen, decisions about one's voice, in the choice of microphones, preamps, compressors, and other recording tools, precede actual tracking. The same is true for the voicing of the interiority of one's theological inventions. Decisions concerning voice and soundscape must begin early in the process and continue through the tracking, layering, mixing, remixing, mashing up, and final mixing and mastering. In mashup religion, reflecting on how to voice religious desire is of increasing importance.

5

FAN CULTURES
GETTING THEOLOGICAL INVENTIONS
INTO THE DJ'S CRATE

The fan's relation to cultural texts operates in the domain of affect or mood. . . . Affect is not the same as either emotions or desires. Affect is closely tied to what we often describe as the feeling of life.

—Lawrence Grossberg, "Is There a Fan in the House? The Affective Sensibility of Fandom"

We use our power as consumers to engage in symbolic sojourns that transcend a consumerist culture.

—Roger C. Aden, *Popular Stories and Promised Lands: Fan Cultures and Symbolic Pilgrimages*

No artist can predict, let alone control, what an audience will make of his images; yet no rock 'n' roller can exist without a relationship with an audience, whether it is the imaginary audience one begins with, or the all-too-real confusion of the audience one wins.

—Greil Marcus, *Mystery Train: Images of America in Rock 'n' Roll Music*

When the song leaves the studio, it meets headlong the world of fans and fandom. According to musicologist Antoine Hennion, "pop songs do not create their public, they discover it."[1] A song is not fully made until it is *received* and appreciated by a fan—someone who identifies with the music and integrates it into his or her life. This amounts to a shift from what sociologist Pierre Bourdieu calls the "material production" of the work of art to the "symbolic production" of the work of art within the field of "spectators capable of knowing and recognizing" works of art as such.[2] The symbolic production of a work of art is the work done by fans of creating its value as art within a particular fan culture, or within the larger marketplace of fan cultures.

To continue our analogy to popular music-making, at this point in the process the *fan* becomes the DJ or mashup artist, adding a range of religiously attenuated artifacts to crates and placing breaks and beats into their remixes of religion. As we have seen, for DJs and mashup artists, crate-digging, or the archaeological business of connecting with the best truths (breaks or beats) within traditions of music, is important. DJs and mashup artists are not abandoning traditions as resources, or they would have little of value to mash up. The same is true for those who, as fans of religion, are remixing religion today. Traditions and traditional resources remain crucial, and being the best crate-digger, or one who is able to search out the best breaks within available resources to remix, is of increasing importance. In this context, it is important for theologians operating in and out of traditions to rethink the kinds of theological breaks and beats they are providing as resources. They must also begin to think strategically about placing their ideas in the place where crate-digging is currently occurring within popular culture—in fan cultures mediated by the Internet, online social networks, and pilgrimages to concerts and conferences.

In this chapter, therefore, we shift to investigate how songs and theological compositions are received and remixed by audiences who produce their value. Then we will consider how the ethnographic analysis of those audiences can help theologians learn the actual shape that religious desire takes within popular culture, and respond to it appropriately. If theologians are to invent theology at the intersection of a range of religious desires, it is important to learn what these desires in fact are and how they are mediated. When this is accomplished, theologians can discover how the resources of the traditions they are remixing and mashing up may, in fact, be of some importance in conversation with an audience.

Popular Music and Religious Identity

In the late 1950s, a dramatic shift emerged in the way popular music was consumed. Prior to that time, popular music was fairly homogeneous, and its distribution, although often locally controlled, was fairly centralized. Most popular music radio stations in the early days of radio played pretty much the same thing. By and large, entire families, communities, and the nation consumed similar programming. Since then, popular music has diversified, and the forms of production and distribution have decentralized to the point of almost complete fragmentation. In the late fifties and on through the sixties and seventies, with the emergence of rock 'n' roll, soul, Motown, funk, and rock music, radio stations began to fragment along lines of age, class, and race. This fragmentation accompanied, and indeed sponsored, the fragmentation of the identities of listeners. As developmental psychologists tell us, the teenage years are key years in the development of personal identity,[3] and since pop music was primarily targeted toward this age group, music and identity were wrapped all together into one package. Increasingly, what you listened to you became. One expressed one's identity in terms of the musical fan culture(s) in which one participated.[4] One's friends, or primary community of identity, were also those who listened to similar forms of music.

By the 1990s, it was clear to sociologists that music subcultures and music scenes were fulfilling a quasi-religious, or what sociologist Matt Hills calls "neoreligious," function in the lives of many people of all ages.[5] Popular music fans seek out communities of other fans (both actual and virtual) and attach themselves to a band, artist, or genre in a way that resembles the devotional practices of religious persons who attach themselves to religious leaders, traditions, and places of worship.

Religion and media scholar Steve Buhrman, summarizing the work of sociologist Peter Berger, concludes that, as a result of secularization, "traditional processes of religious socialisation have become reconfigured" so that the average individual is more likely to approach traditional communities "as a cultural resource (rather) than as an authoritative context to receive 'completed truth.'"[6] Burhman goes on to assert that "while this has contributed to a certain anxiety and self-consciousness about the religious process, it has not, as many modern theorists supposed, eliminated the religious impulse."[7] Citing the work of sociologist David Lyon,[8] Buhrman suggests that "on the contrary this increased pressure 'to choose' actually enlivens the personality to the questions and concerns that are the basis for the religious quest. The result has been a proliferation of eclectic and pluralistic religiosities."[9] It is in this context that popular music begins to play an important religious or quasi-religious role. Media, religion, and culture scholar Stewart Hoover has identified a pattern of "the consumption of mediated communication in relation to religion and spirituality" and the clear emergence of an "*audience for religion* (or spirituality)."[10] According to Hoover, "the media context" has become "a potentially legitimate source of religious and spiritual resources in ways that are unprecedented."[11] With respect to the world of popular music, Buhrman points to the work of religion and arts scholar Robin Sylvan, who charted the emergence of a so-called organic religiosity in the San Francisco music scene. Sylvan writes, "On many important levels . . . the music functions in the same way as a religion, and the musical subculture functions in the same way as a religious community. . . . It is clear that powerful religious phenomena are occurring . . . and that these phenomena are having a life-changing impact."[12] Buhrman concludes that "the focus of religious energies shifts from hierarchical institutions and local territorial communities to deregulated networks at the intersection of media and the whole of cultural life."[13]

This shift in focus, however, is not complete or absolute. Organized religion remains in view, as a resource and potential partner in one's spiritual pilgrimage. According to Hoover, "audience preferences and practices bring . . . historically legitimate symbols into a context where their particular claims are understood to stand along-side other interpretations and other symbols."[14] In this context, as theologian Vincent Miller points out, fans become "bricoleurs" or religious "builders" who cut-and-paste together a unified religious worldview and practice.[15]

Apart from their lives at work and the daily tasks of domestic life, fan cultures are where most of the people live most of the time. Fan cultures are the seedbed of everyday theology. Practices and skills of listening for God are trained and honed to a large extent by participation in media culture, and audiences for religion bring those practices and skills to religious institutions with them when they come. These are not highly trained skills grounded in the prolonged study of one's tradition in relation to all others. Instead, listeners for God within mashup religion, like DJs, are bricoleurs who have learned how to cut-and-paste words, images, and ideas from songs, sermons, lectures, podcasts, videos, blogs, and other mediated sources into their own life narratives in order to construct a meaningful religious worldview.

Miller points out, however, that what often goes begging in this situation is the "complexity of the building blocks."[16] With the recent development of fan cultures around Orthodox traditions, Celtic spirituality, and Taizé, pop-cultural bricoleurs are garnering more interest in the resources housed within traditional religious institutions and communities. Increasingly, local congregations and divinity schools are used as nodes of complexity within the network flows of mediated popular culture. Similar to used-record shops filled with vinyl albums, these institutions have become places where fans of religion, like DJs searching for breaks and beats, can engage more deeply with historical traditions and practices in order to add depth and complexity to their remixes.

There are two levels, then, at which fan cultures are important to mashup religion. In the first instance, fan cultures are quasi-religious communities in and of themselves, shaping religious desires and imagination. In the second instance, these fan cultures are seedbeds for the discovery of religiously attenuated breaks or beats that can be mashed up by audiences who act as religious DJs, crate-digging and remixing the best bits and pieces of several fan cultures.

Fan Cultures and "Mattering Maps"

Cultural studies scholar Lawrence Grossberg, mirroring our ideas regarding the relationship between tone of voice and religious desire in chapter 4, has shown how being a fan of a particular kind of music not only helps construct one's identity, it also constructs the deeper emotion and spiritual feel or "affect" of one's life.[17] According to Grossberg, when you are listening to my music, you are not only putting on a social and cultural badge of identity, you are listening to the way my life feels, or, in musical terms, the way my life sounds or resonates at the deepest levels.[18] You are listening to "the soundtrack of my life," to paraphrase the name of a popular Swedish rock band.[19]

Researchers of fandom also point out that although there may be primary genres of music or artists that express this life-affect, it is likely that each of us has several key fandoms at work in our lives, some musical, some not, which give expression to a range of emotional and spiritual elements. Grossberg calls our fandoms "mattering maps."[20] Being a fan of an artist, song, or genre is a way of expressing what matters to us, and if we take a close look at all the things we are a fan of in our lives, (music, cars, athletic teams, preachers, films, religious traditions, etc.), we begin to discover patterns of things that matter to us most. Determining what matters is crucial to the task of determining what theologian Paul Tillich calls the "ultimate concern" or object of religious desire in a person's life.[21]

Fandoms and Religious Pilgrimage

Further developing the ways in which fandom creates and determines our mattering maps, communications scholar Roger Aden makes use of the ideas of cultural anthropologist Victor Turner to help us see our fandoms as ongoing pilgrimages in our lives.[22] According to Aden, being a fan involves a person in an ongoing *symbolic* (as opposed to material or geographic) pilgrimage toward a particular promised land. In a postmodern world, in which larger metanarratives of promised lands supplied by the Enlightenment, American Dream, Christian eschatology, or social (Marxist) revolution have come unseated, popular culture supplies a huge range of smaller promised lands and invites fans on a variety of pilgrimages toward them. According to

Aden, these pilgrimages are "communicative experience(s) in which we are . . . able to move symbolically, in a variety of ways, to communities that provide an alternative to historical habitus."[23] This journey is paradoxical, according to Aden. "We use our power as consumers to engage in symbolic sojourns that transcend a consumerist culture."[24] In fact, one of the key reasons for engaging in this (consumerist) pilgrimage is to join an alternative community of fans that transcends, and to some extent critiques, our usual day-to-day lives.

It is possible to recognize in this aspect of fan cultures some similarities to the nomadic, migratory, prophetic function of Judeo-Christian allegiance to the Word in the wilderness, but without geography or a sense of place. Instead of alternative prophetic *places*, we find pilgrimages to alternative cultural *spaces*—fan-spaces. A real community is constituted by involvement in a fandom, if by community we mean a largely placeless *symbolic* gathering, or gathering to a personality and set of artifacts. As fans, we know that other fans are on similar journeys with us, even if we do not interact with them in person. Although fandom may, indeed, involve geographic, bodily pilgrimages to concerts, festivals, fan conferences, or conventions, or cyber-pilgrimages to online fanzines or blogs, many fandoms are participated in primarily through what media theorist Leah Vande Berg calls "living room pilgrimages,"[25] or what we might call "iPod" pilgrimages. We pull on the headphones, turn on the car stereo, or flip on the TV, and off we go on a pilgrimage, right in the midst of our mundane day-to-day experience.

According to Aden, fan pilgrimages involve four distinct aspects.[26] Each aspect corresponds to a particular religious desire expressed by a fan culture. First, *the desire to leave*. Pilgrimages give expression to a religious desire to leave or find release from ordinary existence. When someone travels (via iPod or attending a concert or festival) into a popular fan culture, he or she leaves home in order to participate in an alternative community. Theologically, this category of pilgrimage corresponds to the human condition. It asks the theological question What is wrong, missing, or simply desired that makes someone want to leave and go on this type of pilgrimage on a regular basis? The country music video fan may desire to return to an elusive or idyllic rural past. The fan of conscious hip-hop may desire answers to systemic racism. The gothic music fan may feel victimized by powers beyond one's control. In all three instances, the fan desires to leaves one reality behind, and sets forth on a journey away from something, into the music.

Second, *the desire to transcend*. While on these pilgrimages, fans desire to transcend ordinary life. They journey toward some aspect of a promised land and, through various rituals and practices, gain new insights. Music critic and theologian Bill Friskics-Warren argues that all music-making and consumption come from a deep urge to transcend our ordinary experience.[27] When we hook this musical urge up with certain lyrical forms and messages, we find that this transcendence can take on a spiritual and theological bearing and tone. Friskics-Warren writes, "Pop acts are constantly pointing beyond themselves, whether it is to a better future, to some higher ideal, or to some vision of deliverance. The Beatles' 'Help!,' the Rolling Stones' '(I Can't Get No) Satisfaction,' Bob Dylan's 'Like a Rolling Stone,' Al Green's 'Take Me to the River,' Afrika Bambaataa's 'Looking for the Perfect Beat,' and U2's 'I Still Haven't Found What I'm Looking For' are but a half-dozen of the hundreds of pop recordings that convey a longing for something beyond the everyday."[28] Committed fans of a particular song identify with some form of transcendence—a way beyond ordinary experience. It is up to the song to take them there.

Third, *the desire to return different*. The fan takes the headphones off, turns off the TV or computer, or arrives home from the concert, conference, or festival with a slightly transformed perspective. For a short time, fans have seen themselves and the world around them from within another artist's or community's frame of reference. Perhaps the country music video fan has tapped into memories of small town or rural life that provide a sense of rootedness in a constantly shifting world. The fan of conscious hip-hop may have learned new forms of social critique. The gothic music fan may have vented anger or frustration and felt empowered. Over time, involvement in a fandom adds something to the fan's life—a sense of a past, perspective on the present, empowerment, insight, community, hope, beauty, enjoyment. Fans desire to return with different eyes, to see their ordinary lives, to some extent, through the eyes of their fan culture(s).

Finally, *the desire for critique*. For better or worse, fans desire to gain critical perspective on their ordinary experience, and their experience as fans, by participating in fan culture. Over the course of time fans learn a particular critique of their own lives, or what they perceive to be the dominant cultural experience. The Toby Keith fan, for instance, may learn to critique a society perceived as weak and overly tolerant. The Johnny Cash fan may learn to critique a society that forgets the outcast and imprisoned. The U2 fan may learn to critique a market economy devoid of empathy and compassion.

According to Aden, as fans we also learn to be critical of our fan culture itself. As cultures designed to legitimate the work of a would-be artist as "art," fan cultures tend to be organized critically and hierarchically. Popular music fans are ardent critics of the music. Some fans have amassed more symbolic capital as critics than others, through closer exposure to artists or through accumulating more knowledge about influences, production, lyrics, and performances.[29] Fans always need to know more (thus the proliferation of fanzines, blogs, Facebook postings, etc.), and some fans have special knowledge or access to celebrities or performers.[30] Media theorist John Tulloch refers to "executive fans" or "fans who are executives of the fan club and its magazines."[31] Increasingly, with the advent of the blogosphere and more democratic technologies for the dissemination of fan information, this executive function is loaded onto those who are able to produce the most dynamic and provocative commentary on a song, artist, or genre. Fans, therefore, are involved directly in the production of the critical *meaning* and *value* of the work of popular musicians.

Traditions, Fan Cultures, and Mashup Religion

Theologians today are speaking to many people who are, or could be, fans—who have already added them, or are considering adding them, as theologians to their mattering maps. One does not need to capitulate to cross celebrity-fan dynamics to understand this process. Fandom does not necessarily mean worshipping a theologian (though this is sometimes the case)—but it does mean involvement in a community organized around theological performances and participation that helps one transcend and critique ordinary experience in some way. This occurs whenever someone makes a daily pilgrimage to a website with theological content; makes a weekly pilgrimage to a church, synagogue, or mosque; attends a lecture; downloads a podcast; or links to the blog of a religious journalist. This amounts to inserting the experience of various theologians and religious traditions into the collection of fan cultures that indicate what, in fact, matters to an individual or audience. In a world of mashup religion, in-depth participation in a religious tradition is waning, but traditions and theologians operating in and out of traditions are often included in the mattering map of religious desires that inform people's lives.

Musicologist Andrew Goodwin argues that sampling and remixing are still wedded to earlier forms of aesthetics, in which, through sampling, "pop *recuperates* its history rather than denying it."[32] In other words, when artists sample traditions of music, sampling is placed into the service of hermeneutics, or the retrieval of traditions, at the same time that it also serves open-ended intertextuality. By analogy, audiences within mashup religion collect crates full of theological information (breaks and beats) from a variety of fan cultures, religious and nonreligious, and are always ready to engage in their own theological production by pulling a bit of information out, throwing it on the turntable in juxtaposition with another bit of information, and seeing what invention issues forth. This practice functions as both retrieval and intertextual dialogue across traditions or remixes of traditional religious information.

Recently, the way that these breaks and beats are discovered has changed dramatically as music, ideas, blogs, lectures, academic papers, and other religious materials are sorted and sifted through social networks such as MySpace and Facebook. In these forums, fans of religion are learning to promote and disseminate fan identities while connecting with others of similar interest. In the process, they produce the value of religious materials by presenting them as crate-worthy—worthy of fandom. In different ways, Facebook and MySpace promote and provide forums for the critique of communities of taste that resemble fan cultures. These social networks are at once fiercely individualist, preserving the assertion of individual tastes, and yet increasingly democratic, participatory, and negotiative, promoting ongoing conversations about (and voyeuristic participation in) the tastes of others.

Media theorist Nick Couldry points out that in an older media environment there were two worlds, "'media world' (everything associated with the media process) and 'ordinary world' (everything outside it)."[33] These constituted "sacred" and "profane" realms within culture respectively. Couldry posits that those "outside" the "media world" endured a kind of "hidden injury" socially. Lack of media power translated into lack of social and class power.[34]

Social networking sites such as Facebook and MySpace exist at the interface between the media world and ordinary world and add what Couldry calls the "glamour of mediation" to ordinary life.[35] They herald what media theorist Mark Deuze calls "life lived in media," as opposed to life "affected by media."[36] Online social networks empower participants by allowing them to partake, if only in small ways, in the sacredness of mediated living. Millions of people now spend time daily in this mediated space associating themselves with other mediated personalities, artifacts, and events (celebrities, news blogs, critics, intellectuals, music, movements, etc.).[37] In these networks, fan-worthy religious information is quickly disseminated and is often stored (crated) for retrieval later.

In fan cultures and online social networks, therefore, the consumer becomes the producer or inventor of symbolic value within the cultural marketplace. This is true for both artistic and theological value. This production has become fast-paced, and even immediate, as Twitter and Twitter-based search engines such as OneRiot and Collecta demonstrate. Sociologist Nicole Cohen points out that the consumer production of symbolic value for artifacts, products, celebrities, events, and other aspects of cultural life amounts to a form of "unpaid labour."[38] Mark Deuze calls this "crowdsourcing,"[39] which is performed by "producer-consumers" who are involved in an ongoing form of self-surveillance regarding what is popular, sanctioned, and consecrated (as important person, art, event, idea, etc.) within the cultural landscape.[40] This consumer "work" saves marketing firms thousands of hours of research.[41] By tapping into Facebook's data, for instance, market analysts can instantly determine what has user-value within the marketplace. Cohen points out that in this process "the audience 'works' by learning to desire, generating demand for and consuming mass-marketed goods and services,"[42] and, I would add, generating desire and demand for certain religious ideas and perspectives.

Scholars such as Pete Ward and Tom Beaudoin suggest that in this situation the religious traditions and representative theologians should enter entirely into the network flows of popular consumer culture, placing themselves squarely into the middle of the consumer desire that prompts and encourages iPod pilgrimages and consumption-based identities.[43] Ward, for instance, argues for seeing the Christian church as a "personal lifestyle choice alongside many others," and for allowing worship to "become part of the culture industry."[44] Although I agree that much of the research points in the direction of a relative parity between organized church and other forms of religiosity, and that religious traditions should enter the flows of popular culture, I believe that to invite a folding of traditions into popular culture entirely is to miss precisely the importance of these traditions *to* the consumer of religion. Traditions are already, in fact, being consumed, with aspects patched regularly into the mattering maps that construct the identities of many. The key concern should be to discover why and how this is being done, and what kind of fandom one's remix or mashup of a tradition might represent in the mix. In other words, why would your remixed theological artifact or idea find its way into the crate of audiences who are remixing religion today?

My own ethnographic research (see p. 138 below) points in the direction already identified by Vincent Miller.[45] It appears that at least one reason religious traditions show up on these mattering maps is the desire for some religious depth, complexity, and steerage.[46] Set adrift in the great sea of popular culture options for religiosity, the would-be faithful consume breaks and beats from various religious traditions, searching for deeper historical and theological moorings, better theological arguments, conversation partners in discernment, more complex forms of religious education, and some kind of steerage through the wreckage and debris of ultimate concerns that turn out to be not as ultimate as expected.

I would also argue that congregations and other religious institutions potentially respond to a deep religious desire for a religious *home* within the vast ocean of mediated living. Media and communications scholar Roger Silverstone argues that the Internet's openness and open-endedness encourage the constant opportunity to encounter the other and otherness. Because of this, the Internet as a social network has some potential to foster an "ethic of hospitality."[47] He concludes, however, that what is missing from this ethic is the reality of a real, embodied *host* (welcoming, securing presence) and *home* (safe place of welcome). According to Silverstone, the Internet "is not, securely or consistently, a home, and individual sites, the home pages, are just as likely, perhaps even more likely, to reject the unbidden visitor as unwelcome as many of the more established broadcast media channels."[48] He goes on to conclude that "the requirements for media hospitality in a globalizing world are still premised on the continuing importance of . . . some meaningful exercise of individual and institutional responsibility."[49]

Within the codes of biblical hospitality, the host is responsible for the welfare of the household of faith and for creating a safe home. Theologian Amos Yong, for instance, shows how New Testament rules of hospitality included testing the stranger. This meant determining a stranger's name (is this who he or she really is?) and intentions (does this person intend evil?).[50] Parents who police their children's Internet use for potential predatory acts know well the meaning of hosting in this sense. According to Christine Pohl, "Boundaries are an important part of making a place physically and psychologically safe."[51] And, as Hans Boersma asserts, "Hospitality is an art that is impossible to practice when we refuse to challenge evil."[52] Hospitality is leavened, therefore, with expectations that guests will provide adequate self-disclosure and even penance where required.

Beyond protecting the welcome space by testing the guest, the host also protects the safety and voice of the guest. Welcoming the guest requires careful attention to issues of power, inequality, and negative "othering."[53] Letty Russell points out that a "just hospitality" insures that those without power (technology, economic/social/class/racial/gender/sexual orientation, status, age,

ability) are included in the conversation.[54] The host has a prophetic responsibility, therefore, to help the community remain
constantly aware of the potentially dominating and excluding
aspects of testing the stranger, and to find ways to overcome forms
of exclusivity that marginalize forms of difference.

Within the vast sea of mediated social networks and the communities of taste or fandoms they house and foster, the local fan
culture of congregation, seminary, group, or gathering, which represents traditional religious resources, plays a potentially important role. On the one hand, bearers of religious traditions can
and should become guests in places hosted by others, placing
their invented theological artifacts as small nodes of complexity
directly into the social networks in which fandoms are being nego-
tiated as intentional nodes of complexity. For instance, theological
responses to the work of popular musicians might be uploaded
to YouTube and linked on the Facebook sites of fans. Theologians
could also blog on the key websites of those involved in various
fandoms, or blog on their own websites in ways that deepen and
add complexity to the work of various artists. Theologians can also
take the time to attend or speak at concerts, festivals, and other
pilgrimage sites associated with various popular musicians.

At the same time, however, ministers and educators can host
a local fan culture in their congregations, communities, or online
forums, welcoming the basic mattering maps and potential theological resources (breaks and beats) represented by the other fan cultures of those they welcome, and inviting conversations about the
ideas associated with these various fandoms. As they do this, they
can invent theological ideas that respond to the ideas represented
within these various fandoms, adding depth, complexity, and steerage. This means inventing theological ideas in such a way as to signal that their religious institution, congregation, or community is a
safe place (home) for affirmative, yet critical conversation about the
worldviews mediated by fandoms.

Participating in the Symbolic Production of Theology's Value

As we have already noted, we are talking at this stage of song-
making about the symbolic production of the song, not its material

production. Bourdieu suggests that those who are most involved in the reception of a work of art, "art critics, dealers, patrons," along with those whom we've been referring to in relation to popular art as fans (including executive fans), are the ones who ultimately define the "value of the work."[55] This is highly suggestive for theological invention. Sociologically, in a media-saturated context, theological compositions, like works of art, require some real-time "crowd-sourced" *production of value* within a community of listeners, in order to be *listened to* and appropriated as religious truth.

Some theologians, especially road-show (itinerant) communicators, spend most of their lives cultivating this kind of fan-value, which works to create their name recognition and fame as a great preacher, powerful revivalist, or famous speaker. As Bourdieu points out, this kind of symbolic value is based on two things: (1) success or "book sales, number of . . . performances, etc., or honours, appointments, etc.," and (2) legitimation or the "degree of specific consecration (literary or artistic prestige)."[56] The production of value for such communicators is largely a matter of self-promotion—being published in periodicals with the largest subscription base, increasing book sales, capturing Internet downloads, garnering recognition among recognized critics (executive fans), and speaking in ways that attract the broad interest of relatively uncritical masses.

These few communicators, I would argue, are operating within an entirely different field of cultural production than most theologians, who operate within more localized or specialized communities of discourse, whether geographic or online. The production of belief in the religious value of theological ideas in the local church, synagogue, or mosque, for instance, scales the process of legitimization down considerably. Book sales, public performances, honors, appointments, prestige, and a national or international fan base, while helpful, are less important than whether the religious leader and community invents messages that function well in relation to local fandoms for local religious leaders, local authors and artists, local products, locally produced music, and so on.

In local congregations or theological institutions, therefore, it is important to seek out the unique theological value of one's theological invention within the actual, local, and regional mattering maps of one's audience, without, of course, forgetting elements of those mattering maps that function at a national and global level. A local ethnography will help the theologian operating on a smaller scale discover how *they* (your particular audience) are consecrating your words, actions, and intonations, knowing and recognizing the symbolic value of those things in *this* place.

The Theologian as Ethnomusicologist

Perhaps the most important thing to realize about the religious reception of popular music is that it cannot be understood by simply analyzing the authors or performers (celebrities) or the texts (lyrics, sounds, or visual images) produced by the musicians. In order to understand the religious influence of fandoms, theologians must spend time doing basic fan ethnography, studying the ways music and other cultural artifacts are received and used by the fans in their midst, listening for the religious or quasi-religious desires expressed by commitments to these artifacts. Theologians can try to understand how their audiences are functioning as bricoleurs, constructing religious narratives and worldviews. They can ask why their theological inventions should be added to the mattering maps of these people, and how it should best be accomplished.

It is a good idea, therefore, for theologians to learn methods for discovering and analyzing the fan cultures represented within their classrooms, audiences, or congregations, with an eye to determining more clearly the roles their remixes or mashups of religious traditions are already playing and might potentially play in relation to the fandoms within the audience and beyond. Theologians do not have to be trained sociologists or ethnographers to do basic research into the ordinary theologies around them. Here are two examples of ways fan culture analysis can be done with individuals, small groups, classes, or entire congregations.

Auto-Ethnography

In a course I teach on Popular Music and Religious Identity at Vanderbilt Divinity School, I ask students at the beginning of the course to perform an "auto-ethnography,"[57] in which they are required to look around their apartments, houses, yards, and driveways and identity all the consumer objects or artifacts that indicate their fandoms. I encourage them to be selective. We are not fans of everything we consume. Fandom is not simply product loyalty; it involves active, ongoing participation in an entire community of fans, including regular attentiveness to the object of fandom, pilgrimages to key sites (either geographic, journalistic, or cyber sites), critical reflection on what it means to be a fan or insider, and real emotional and behavioral investment in remaining a fan. I encourage them to include any church, synagogue, mosque, religious movement, tradition, or religious personality or leader they would identify as the locus for fandom.

Once these fandoms are identified, I have students chart them in relation to a timeline of their personal development, as well as in terms of gender, class, race, and geographic upbringing. More importantly, we discuss ways in which each of these fandoms involves certain emotions, memories, regular pilgrimages to concerts or retreat centers, attendance at trade shows or product releases, subscriptions to fanzines, participation in blogs or online communities, and so on. I encourage them to reflect on what each fandom has meant to them and how it might relate to the other fandoms listed.

Finally, we begin to discuss what each of these fandoms, especially those associated with music, adds to the feeling tones, spiritual longings, yearnings, and hopes in each person's life. How do these fandoms contribute to an understanding of the human condition, sin, evil, the environment, and creation? What yearnings, longings, and visions are associated with these fandoms, including ideas of redemption, hope, salvation, and new or alternative kinds of community? And what forms of action, behavior, and social agency are being learned in pursuit of these visions? What do people do and not do who participate in these lifeworlds? What practices does this mosaic of fandoms encourage? What role does institutional religion play in their fandoms, if any? What theologians or explicitly spiritual voices are included in these fandoms? What do they think that I can add to the mix as a theologian? It is at this level that we begin to see some of the connections between these various fandoms and how they work together to represent particular religious desires and support something like a spiritual habitus, and even a theology. We can also begin to see some of the ways that theologians, or the ideas of theologians, are being incorporated into the remixes of religion that are occurring in our midst.

Musical Religious Autobiography

In the spring of 2007, colleague Allison Pingree and I tried an experiment in musical religious autobiography with an adult education class at Second Presbyterian Church in Nashville.[58] We entitled the course Popular Music and Religious Identity. There were thirty adult members of the class (a bit large for our initial plan, but we managed). They ranged in age from twenty to eighty-three. Sadly, the class was not racially mixed, bearing witness to the all-white racial composition of our Nashville congregation. We invited each member of the class to bring to us a musical artifact (on CD or cassette tape), e-mail us an mp3 file, or simply tell us the name of a song and artist so that we could purchase the track from an Internet service such as iTunes or Rhapsody. This song was to be chosen by virtue of its importance to each person spiritually, either at an earlier point in life or in the here and now. Each person was to write a brief one- or two-paragraph liner note saying something about why this song meant something important to him or her spiritually. We collected all of the songs and burned them onto two CDs so that each person had both CDs and the liner notes for all tracks. We then asked them to read the liner notes and listen to each other's songs in their cars or at home for two weeks, as often as they could.

As it turned out, the range of music chosen by the class was fairly broad. Coupled with the liner note–styled testimonies and the different musical feels, the result was astonishing. Included were Bob Marley, John Denver, the Dixie Chicks, Bill Gaither, a German ensemble singing a South African liberation song, a Russian Orthodox chant, George Harrison, Alison Krauss, White Stones, Dar Williams, Cat Stevens, Bonnie Raitt, Chris Tomlin, Mercy's Mark, Judy Collins, Kate Campbell, the Kingston Trio, Aaron Copland, and several public domain hymns. The interesting thing about the testimonies included in the liner notes is that most of them identified specific emotions, feelings, memories, or attitudes that accompanied hearing the song.

In the following weeks, we discussed something of the feeling and ideas that these songs generated, and the different spiritual worlds in which each of us lived. Class participants got to know each other in deeper and more profound ways. They also began to identify different, but often convergent, religious desires—things that were wrong or missing in their lives, forms of transcendence that they desired, ways that they desired to be different from the larger culture, and critiques of religious experience that were important to them. Most importantly, the class discovered very different, sometimes conflicting, but often complementary things that mattered spiritually to them and began to see why Second Presbyterian Church was a good, or at least partially adequate, home for these things.

Questions for Reflection

Once some basic ethnographic study has been accomplished, seven questions will be helpful for the theologian who proposes to invent theology for this audience.

First, what is the emotional and spiritual feel or affect of peoples' lives? When we look around us in our classrooms, churches, circles of friends, or congregations, we are looking at people whose lives have a lot of different soundtracks. When they turned off their car radios and walked into the classroom or sanctuary to hear us hold forth, turned on our music, or clicked their way to our blog, what was playing on the radio or mp3/CD player? Kenny Chesney? Tupac? Public Enemy? Bob Marley? Patty Griffin? Red Hot Chili Peppers? Aaron Copland? Kanye West? Eminem? Van Morrison? What do audience members identify as the emotions and affective states that are being expressed in these musics? Anger? Pain? Longing? Fear? Hope? Exclusion? Lust? All of these emotional and affective elements contain profound theological overtones. They speak to both the need for God and the understanding of who God is.

Second, if we look at the ten to twenty top fandoms in our audience, what *matters*? And how would we map what matters? For example, if the top fandoms cluster around Volvo automobiles, Macintosh computers, progressive bluegrass music, and introspective folk music, we are on our way to discovering what matters. Or if we discover that the top twenty fandoms include Harley-Davidson motorcycles, Dierks Bentley, Big and Rich, hunting and fishing, NASCAR racing, and Lynyrd Skynyrd, we will likely stumble onto a very different set of things that matter. What do we hear people saying regarding why they like these things? How would we summarize what we hear?

Third, what are people *leaving* in order to go on these fan pilgrimages? What are the things within our larger cultural home that people feel compelled to get away from in some form of alternative community? Is the Volvo/bluegrass fan leaving behind a life of rootless corporate power? Or is this fan striving to leave a world in which the environment is poisoned and polluted? Is the Dierks Bentley/ Harley fan leaving a world of hard labor in which someone else has complete control? Is this fan primarily leaving a life of perceived loss of white male power and privilege? In other words, what can we learn about the *human condition*, about the deepest desires people are experiencing and the shape that evil, suffering, pain assume in their lives?

Fourth, what are the forms of transcendence that people seek to experience in these fan cultures? Is it transcendence through beauty? Anger? Redemptive violence? Empowerment? Empathy? Humor? Sheer energy or power? Volume or amplification? Speed? Emotional catharsis? Resistance? Liberation? The body? Ecstasy? Reconnection with roots? Control? Justice? Or just the transcendence of community and connection itself? In other words, what are the promised lands all around us that people are seeking and experiencing in these fan cultures? How do these connect with our ideas? What challenges do they present for the invention of theological meaning?

Fifth, what do people seem to take home with them? What changes in a person's life as a response to these fandoms? What commitments do they form or are they a part of? What kinds of attitude, values, ideas, lifestyle, manner, approach, practice are confirmed or flirted with by virtue of participation in these fandoms? Ideas about God and country (John Cougar Mellencamp, Toby Keith, Bruce Springsteen); empathy for those in the world who are suffering (U2, Sinéad O'Connor, Buddy and Julie Miller), attempts to integrate body and spirit (Madonna, PJ Harvey, Marvin Gaye, Al Green),

eco-theology (Jack Johnson, Willie Nelson, Pearl Jam), apocalypti-
cism (Radiohead, Beck), religious and political antinomianism and
anarchism (Sex Pistols, Legendary Shack Shakers, the Clash, Patti
Smith, Green Day), liberation, humanization, and justice (Pete
Seeger, Joan Baez, P. Diddy, Public Enemy, Common), and so on. I
will come back to some of these in the next chapter.

Sixth, what are the critiques of the dominant culture and religion that are implicit in these fan cultures? Is the Volvo/bluegrass fan
performing a small critique of rootless, institutional, corporate life in
which the office might learn some of the more organic ways of thinking about community and lifestyle? Is the Dierks Bentley/Harley fan
performing a small critique of a world in which freedom has been
reduced, in the words of Kris Kristofferson, to "nothing left to lose?"
And what are the self-reflexive critiques of the fan culture itself that
exist within the fan culture? In other words, what are people learning
about themselves and the culture around them through participation
in these fandoms?

Even more important, what do fans consider crucial about a song,
genre, or other artifact that makes its art worthy of fandom? What
constitute the key elements involved in legitimating a song or form
of music as art? In other words, what are critics within the fan culture arguing or pontificating about that reveals the norms involved in
valuing an artifact as art? What can you learn for inventing theology
from these norms for valuing other artifacts? Are the debates about
what constitutes legitimate value within fan cultures relevant to the
way you might shape your theological ideas?

Seventh, and most important, why are these people actually or
potentially adding you or your institution as a fandom to their mattering maps? How does your theological leadership, or the spiritual
dimensions of your institution, blog, discography, or website, fit amid
the fan cultures represented? What roles do your ideas, or the ideas
of the institution, congregation, or community you represent, seem
to play among these people's fandoms? What do they add? What do
people expect to find when they come to you or your home community? What is missing; what do other fandoms add that people think
they need? What opportunities exist to provide more depth, complexity, and steerage in relation to these mattering maps? What forms

of hosting will make you and your work a safe and just space for these particular bricoleurs as they build meaningful religious lives?

The process of getting on the mattering maps of others in a meaningful way can, of course, involve the theologian in multiple venues—books, blogs, newspaper articles, social networks—any place where crowdsourcing occurs. In all of this, however, it is important to remember that, in most instances, people are looking to theologians to provide depth, complexity, and steerage. When value is imputed to your work, and it is crated and remixed, it is important to respond critically to a value imputed, rather than pandering to that value. Not all values are theologically helpful. Not all are safe. Not all are genuinely just and open to the marginalized. The rap fan may be valuing your antiracist ideas, building you into his mattering map as an appendage in support of racial justice. The same rap fan may need to hear and act upon other values you communicate concerning gender justice and equality that grow directly out of the core values undergirding antiracism. The Toby Keith fan might value your jeremiads or prophetic warnings that the nation is falling out of covenant with God, forgetting its moral responsibilities and duties. The same fan, however, may also need to hear that restoration to covenant relationship with God is not a matter of avenging wrongs done to a nation, but of doing justice to the marginalized in the nation's midst. In other words, response to the ways fans are valuing your theological inventions could mean critiquing the values imputed, or working for other values entirely. You will never arrive at this point, however, unless you know what values are, in fact, being imputed to your words—what connections are being made within the audience's set of mattering maps, and how the religious desires in the audience are, in fact, producing the value of your theological ideas. Only then can your theological invention be shaped to add depth, complexity, and steerage.

In the end, there are at least three things that can be learned from thinking this way about music fandoms. First, fandoms give us access to the feeling tones, key mattering maps, and pilgrimages that shape and express the key religious desires around us. Knowing what these desires are will help theologians invent messages that will find their way onto these mattering maps and contribute to the mashup of religion that is taking place in a particular place and time.

Second, we can learn that everyday listening for a divine word is a consistent spiritual practice that takes place not only in religious institutions such as churches, synagogues, mosques, and seminaries, but outside of the formal structures of religious gathering in general. Listening for God in religious institutions, and from trained theologians, is part of a larger practice of listening for God in one's life, including listening to music (and lots of it), television pundits, documentaries, Internet blogs, good friends and family, and so on. This ongoing practice of discernment provides a tremendous opening for theologians to explore the genuine spiritual lives of those around them within the larger culture, in order to become more effective communicators. These broader practices of listening also invite theologians to use available technologies such as blogs and social networking Internet sites to place their ideas directly into conversation with the ideas promulgated within these other networks of information.

Finally, we need to understand how and why the religious communities and traditions we belong to are, in many ways, often imperfect, but not unlikely, spiritual and theological homes for the feeling tones and mattering maps expressed within the various fandoms within our larger culture. It is important for theologians to get a sense of why people find their way into their classrooms, sanctuaries, websites, or lectures. Analyzing fandoms can help us understand why all of those diverse fandoms cross, intersect, and connect in *our* communities of belonging, and, in fact, *constitute* those communities as a constellation of very particular cultural leavings, transcendings, critiques, and transformations. Once this is determined, theologians can begin to decide how best to make their places of work and performance into safe places, homes that offer significant depth, complexity, and steerage within the great ocean of fandoms.

In the next chapter, I want to shift gears slightly but continue to build on this process of understanding the role of fandom in our lives. Instead of focusing on the ethnographic analysis of fandoms, how popular music fandoms (and other fandoms) are being used to express and shape spiritual identity, I want to focus on the analysis of popular music texts and the theologies I believe are being expressed in those texts. I will shift, therefore, from an emphasis on *ethnography* (the study of the people who consume music as fans) to *textual analysis*. By doing so, I hope to demonstrate what happens when we ask ourselves more broadly what are some of the key theological narratives, faith stories, or prototheologies that popular song-makers are telling folks these days, as found in their lyrics and performances. This requires that we look closely at the kinds of words that an artist produces, and how these cultural texts relate to larger religious narratives found today within popular culture. Then, if we consider ourselves as potential hosts in this context, adding depth, complexity, and steerage, we will consider several case studies that examine how, in fact, we might place theological invention in service to these tasks.

6

LYRICS
INVENTING THEOLOGY IN RESPONSE
TO POPULAR MUSIC

Myths are metaphors that stand for things other and greater than themselves.

—Peter R. Stillman, *Introduction to Myth*

In this final chapter, I want to shift focus from the analysis of musical fandoms (a form of theoethnographic study) to the analysis of musical texts (a form of theoliterary study). As a way of sharpening our understanding of the reception of the popular song, I want to focus on how to read and interpret the theology within lyrical content. I will begin by outlining a brief method of text analysis that will help us know what to look for in these texts. Then I will shift gears and demonstrate the method by unpacking several key forms of theology expressed in musical lyrics today.

This kind of analysis, of course, brings the lens of theology directly into play and invites a missiological and apologetic element into theological engagement with popular culture. The goal is to learn how to identify key clusters of theologically relevant ideas in the words of an artist in order to bring them into conversation with theological categories that belong to the Christian faith historically and confessionally. This, in turn, can help theologians invent theological messages that will connect to the religious desires expressed in popular music, while offering complexity, depth, and steerage that is resourced by a particular religious tradition.

In order to illustrate this method, I will use as case studies several quasi-theologies that are afoot in the popular music in and around my social location in Nashville. With the term "quasi-theology," I intend to designate a myth, root metaphor, or worldview having some resemblance to Christian theology and expressing what Bill Friskics-Warren calls an "urge for transcendence."[1] A quasi-theology potentially or actually connects with an aspect or model of Christian theology.

In each instance, I will use the music of one or two artists to tease out the contours of a quasi-theology. I will speak briefly about the general contours of these theologies, and then bring a Christian theological perspective to bear and indicate in broad terms what I think theologians (in my case Reformed theologians) might say in response. Remembering the goals of complexity, depth, and steerage identified in chapter 5, I will indicate how theologians can add more complexity and depth to these quasi-theologies, steering the religious impulses within them in a direction more conversant with Christian faith. This, I think, will provide some sense of how a theologian can both learn from and engage cultural theologies that are all around us today. My primary goal is to teach a simple method of theological text analysis. My responses to these artists' lyrics are simply one example of the kind of theological reflection and conversation that might ensue in relation to the lyrics of popular music.

Theological Analysis of Lyrics

With very few exceptions, most songs or catalogues of songs (discographies) can be best analyzed by making use of a narrative form of analysis. Before beginning such an analysis, however, it is helpful to assess two basic aspects of lyrics, ultimate concern and the idea of the holy, using categories I have adapted from Kelton Cobb's very helpful book *The Blackwell Guide to Theology and Popular Culture.*[2]

Ultimate Concern

First, the theologian can work to identify the ultimate concern within the lyrics. According to Paul Tillich, an ultimate concern is that which makes an unconditional claim upon us and is at the center of all other values. For Tillich there is no such thing as an unbeliever. Everyone has some sort of ultimate concern, and faith is a state of being ultimately concerned.[3] As Cobb states it, "An ultimate concern is one's weightiest conviction, loyalty, or interest that assigns the relative gravity to all other convictions, loyalties, and interests that one holds."[4] It is important to keep working until one is certain that the idea or value identified as ultimate within an artist's lyrics is not, in fact, secondary—or pointing toward something still higher. For instance, the analyst may not want to settle for categories such as sex or lust (unless clearly ends in themselves), but ask if love (either erotic or selfless) is the ultimate concern. Likewise, a concern with fairness or retribution may indicate that a larger issue of justice is the ultimate concern. In other words, the theologian should keep asking whether the category chosen is, in fact, the artist's *ultimate* concern.

The Holy: Ontological or Moral Faith

Philosopher of religion Rudolf Otto observed that the holy (sacred) is both *mysterium tremendum* (a terrifying mystery) *and mysterium fascinosum* (a fascinating mystery).[5] These two aspects of the holy, according to Cobb, correspond to two types of faith identified by Paul Tillich: ontological faith and moral faith.[6] Ontological faith is "enchanted by the fascinating face of the holy,"[7] by beauty, the erotic, and the sacramental, ways in which the lower becomes a vehicle for the higher. In other words, ontological faith is focused on the beautiful and awe-inspiring *presence* of God. Moral faith, on the other hand, is "attuned to the terrifying side of the holy," to how the finite falls short of the infinite.[8] This kind of faith is focused on the *goodness* of God.

The theologian should ask whether the story told by the artist is ontological or moral. Is the artist primarily concerned with being or becoming, beauty or goodness, awareness of God or conversion to God, dwelling more deeply in the world or changing the world? Once the artist's ultimate concern and type of faith has been identified, the theologian is ready to assess narrative elements. Here are a few basic categories of analysis that will help you discover the quasi-theological or theological story the lyrics are telling.

Human Condition (Problem). What is wrong according to these lyrics? What are the key problems, enigmas, desires, needs, anxieties, issues, troubles, or difficulties experienced? Loneliness? Abuse? Violence? Desire? Hope? Pain? Youthful growing pains? Broken relationships? The goal here is to get at the way in which the lyrics establish a particular plot requiring a hero, protagonists, helpers, and an ultimate source or giver of an answer or solution.

Reason for Human Condition (Villain). What is causing this problem? Who or what is at fault? Are the villains parents or the older generation? Perhaps the reason things have gone wrong is the inertia of age and tradition. Are the villains institutions that are stifling human freedom? Are they politicians? Perhaps they are those who abuse power.

Thing Most Desired (Desired Endpoint or Goal of the Story). Where is the story headed? What is the desired object in the narrative, the sought for (or assumed) end? Enlightenment? Peace? Love? Belonging? Hope? Escape? Wholeness?

Belief (Protagonist). This is usually the image of heroism or faithful action in the story: the image of who we are, should be, or can be within this narrative, in order to belong and sustain the story's action. How are we imagined as active—believing in a way forward or through? Are we being asked to convert to a new position? Are we being called to do something or become something different? Are we being asked to receive or accept something? Are we being invited to experience something new or helpful? Are we being invited on a particular journey? Are we being involved in something in a particular way? Are we being implicated in a way of life that requires us to reflect on our values and commitments?

Help (Helpers, Heroes). This is the image of powers or helpers without which the protagonist could not make progress. In Christian theology, for instance, helpers include Christ, Spirit, Scripture, sacraments, ministers, and church. In a cluster of song texts or within a fandom, the artist/performer often plays this role, and the artist will associate with a set of other helpers, for better or worse (drugs, family, political parties, movements, political figures, other artists, religious views, etc.).

God (Arbiter and Rewarder/Giver). God is the image of the one who, in the last analysis, sees to it that the goal of the story is met. God is the power that will give redemption to those who have been longing for it as they have struggled within the human condition. To some extent, God can be read backwards from the human condition and image of redemption, as that which is the only power capable of redeeming this situation (Lover, Judge, Creator, Peacemaker, Avenger, Healer, etc.).

As noted in chapter 5, it is important for theologians to ana-lyze the local and regional fandoms around them. In the second half of this chapter, therefore, I will make use of these categories and engage five quasi-theologies within the lyrics of popular music cur-rently prominent around me in Nashville. In order to save space (and avoid copyright issues), I will present mostly my narrative theologi-cal analysis, forgoing lengthy quotations of song lyrics. The reader is encouraged to go to the websites representing these artists in order to engage their lyrics more fully.

Patriotic Theology (John Cougar Mellencamp, Toby Keith)

Although moral faith will not be of primary importance for all theo-logical worldviews, it is certainly a driving force within the music of our first two theologians, John Cougar Mellencamp and Toby Keith. Both artists urge us in different ways to transcend ourselves through a God-infused, righteous patriotism. Mellencamp is a proud Mid-western Democrat who asked John McCain to quit playing his songs "Our Country" and "Small Town" at his political rallies during the 2008 election season.[9] His staunch patriotism is well documented in his lyrics. "Our Country" calls on the government to do more to provide assistance to low-income and poor people.[10] Mellencamp's post-9/11 protest song "To Washington"[11] pushed back at the sins of politicians in Washington and struck a chord with listeners on the

Left and Right alike. Those on the Right felt that he had gone too far in his indictment of the White House. Those on the Left felt that someone had finally represented their voice. For Mellencamp there was no paradox between hardcore blue-collar patriotism and being angrily against the Iraq war, George W. Bush's economic and foreign policies, and systemic racism. In more recent lyrics, Mellencamp is particularly interested in challenging and healing the racism that divides the country. In a song called "Jena,"[12] Mellencamp addresses the travesty of justice involving six African American teenagers in a small Louisiana town, calling for the town to take down their nooses.

Nashville's Toby Keith, on the other hand, is another kind of patriot. Keith's performance of "Beer for My Horses"[13] has raised eyebrows for its prolynching refrain encouraging the listener to gather up all the "bad boys" and execute them at a public hanging. In the face of his detractors, Keith has fought back, saying that the lynching refrain was "about the old west and horses and sheriffs and posses and going and getting the bad guys. It's not a racist thing or about lynching."[14] Keith has also made proud statements that he is "white trash with money,"[15] and his comments in an interview with Glenn Beck raised the racist suspicion again when he remarked, "I think the black people would say he [Obama] don't talk, act or carry himself as a black person. . . . I think that that's what they would say. Even though the black society would pull for him I still think that they think in the back of their mind that the only reason he is in [the general election] is because he talks, acts and carries himself as a Caucasian."[16]

In 2002 Keith recorded "Courtesy of the Red, White and Blue (The Angry American),"[17] a response to September 11. The song became an overnight sensation among politically conservative listeners. In it, Keith encouraged immediate retaliation in order to serve up justice, providing an image of a fist-shaking Statue of Liberty and the American eagle swooping in for attack against America's enemies.

Both Mellencamp and Keith promote a deeply moral faith and play upon biblical ideas of covenant and jeremiad. These are ideas well developed within Christian theology, especially by Reformation theologian John Calvin, and have become deeply embedded within the American psyche. According to Kelton Cobb, for Calvin the idea of covenant explained how God had made a pledge to "deal with creation according to certain constant purposes—purposes, it is important to note, that are primarily concerned with justice."[18] Perry Miller shows how the Puritans, theological heirs of Calvin, further developed the covenant idea to indicate that "God pledged Himself not to run tyrannically athwart human conceptions of justice. The creator was represented as agreeing to abide by ideas comprehensible to [humanity]."[19] Jeremiads, in this context, hearken back to the prophet Jeremiah, who encouraged a covenant people who know the ways of God's righteousness and justice to repent and change their ways in order to remain the covenant people. James Morone argues that "the jeremiad became a kind of American anthem."[20] According to Cobb, it became "the idiom into which we habitually slip when reality falls short of our utopian aspirations."[21] Cobb concludes that "the fear of being forsaken by some kind of guiding purpose if we forsake the principles enshrined in our founding documents haunts conservatives and progressives alike."[22]

In different ways, both Mellencamp and Keith represent this fear of abandoning and losing our covenant identity and status. Both seek to represent the nation's divine calling and status as a beacon of covenant light to the nations. Mellencamp and Keith disagree on the nature of faith or the ways in which we are to be a light to the nations, but they take this role seriously—Mellencamp through embracing otherness and diversity and advocating negotiation and cooperation, and Keith through putting our lives on the line for democracy around the world.

Using our narrative categories of analysis, for both Mellencamp and Keith the human condition is one of straying from the covenant granted to our nation. The reason for this condition looks different, however, to each artist. For Mellencamp, this condition is caused by injustice to the poor and disenfranchised in our midst. For Keith, this condition is caused by cowardliness in the face of our enemies, outer and inner. For both artists, the desired goal or redemptive vision is the restoration of our divine covenant as a nation. For Mellencamp, restoration is found in a vision of justice and human equality bequeathed to us by the Constitution and Bill of Rights. For Keith, restoration is found in a vision of national strength and the power to protect democracy worldwide. Belief is also quite different for each artist. For Mellencamp, belief is expressed in acts of speaking out against injustice and working to bring justice to all. For Keith, belief is expressed in acts of strong, assertive defense of the nation and democracy. In expressing this belief, these artists appeal to very different helpers or redeemers. Mellencamp finds help in regional, Midwestern values of frontier solidarity: working alongside one another to forge a way in the wilderness. Keith looks to the military and other images of physical and emotional power in facing down enemies. There is also a vigilante-helper in Keith's lyrics—a hero who works to avenge wrongs done, in spite of the laws of the land. For both artists, God is a God of justice, yet a different form of justice informs each. For Mellencamp, it is redistributive justice, working, in Walter Brueggemann's words, to "sort out what belongs to whom and to return it to them."[23] For Keith, it is retributive justice, a scorekeeping God who works to avenge and even up the score.

Idolatry is a pervasive issue in relation to most popular music quasi-theologies, since, from a Christian confessional standpoint, the very nature of idolatry is, in Tillich's words, "the elevation of a preliminary concern to ultimacy."[24] In this regard, Christian theologians will worry that both Mellencamp and Keith miss the potentially idolatrous role the nation (including its Constitution and key documents) plays in their lyrics. They permit perilously close associations to persist between God and nation, making it possible for listeners to lose sight of a nation in covenant relationship to God and to instead place God and nation on equal par. Most Christian theologians will prefer Mellencamp's take on the nature of the covenant and jeremiad, if only because Mellencamp remembers more immediately and forcefully that at the heart of the covenant for Jeremiah was justice; not retributive justice grounded in anger, but redistributive justice grounded in love. In the words of Jeremiah, the covenant obliged the people of Israel not to oppress the alien, the orphan, and the widow, not to shed innocent blood, and not to go after other gods (Jer 7.6). Perhaps the reason Toby Keith misses this is because he is, as he himself admits, telling an "old west . . . sheriff and posse" story, using what theologian Walter Wink calls "the myth of redemptive violence,"[25] the idea that killing the gunslinger is the key to redemption. The power of this myth, which controls the imagination of many Americans, often short-circuits the deeper justice requirements within America's covenant with God. It is, however, a dominant mythology within American popular culture and needs to be addressed and reshaped by theologians.

Although it is easy to be critical of this form of nationalistic moral theology, it has a long history, especially within the Protestant tradition, and its popularity speaks to the need for theologians to add more depth and complexity to the ways popular music audiences frame a healthy patriotism in an increasingly xenophobic and politically polarized culture. Moral forms of faith attach easily to social, political, and national agendas, and are easily co-opted by patently anti-Christian myths of redemptive violence. These two artists remind theologians that many people live into powerful forms of *moral faith* and a sense of moral consequences on a social scale. Christian theologians should not shy away from inventing messages that engage this form of faith, addressing its tendencies toward idolatry, and steering it in the direction of a covenant grounded in God's redistributive justice.

Prophetic Theology (Johnny Cash)

While we might focus on a number of artists here, including, but not limited to, Pete Seeger, Bob Marley, P. Diddy, Public Enemy, or U2, I have chosen to focus on Johnny Cash, given my Nashville context. Bill Friskics-Warren compares Cash to Curtis Mayfield as someone who "was in it for the long haul."[26] According to Friskics-Warren, "Until his death in 2003, he stood resolutely with people on society's margins, giving voice to their often silent cries and struggles and witnessing to the need for justice, tolerance, and decency on their behalf."[27] When he became the "Man in Black," Cash began a process of identifying himself with the marginalized. In the song "Homeless,"[28] he identified with those experiencing abject poverty. The song reminds the listener that we are all not far from the life of the homeless person. In "Folsom Prison Blues,"[29] he reached across polite social boundaries and placed himself in the shoes of the incarcerated. Choosing to perform Peter La Farge's "The Ballad of Ira Hayes,"[30] Cash connected with the lonely and alcoholic, especially among Native Americans

and war veterans. Cash may also have seen himself in a modestly sal-
vific, Christ-like role. As he explains in "Man in Black,"[31] his goal was
to become a scapegoat, someone who placed some of the darkness
and difficulty in the world on his own back in order to carry it away.

Friskics-Warren notes that the gothic and punk scenes picked up
on Cash's slightly anarchic "bad to the bone" way of identifying with
the outcast and the underside of life and made it into a mode of
expressing irony. He correctly points out that for Cash, this outcast
identification was not a way to ironically reflect society back to itself
as something grotesque. It was as if, by connecting himself to these
people, he could keep society somehow connected as well—keep the
outcast from being forgotten as real human beings in need of recognition and healing. It was, therefore, a very unusual way of offering prophetic resistance, resisting our tendency to forget and discard
others and offering hope to the countless people who live in poverty,
incarceration, loneliness, addiction, and despair. Cash wanted to level
hierarchies, to help us to see our common humanity and embrace a
social "priesthood of all believers." He became the Robin Hood or
Zorro of country music,[32] robbing the rich to give to the poor by
creating a powerful and empowering music of the people. When one
listens to Cash's lyrics, Acts 10:34 comes immediately to mind: "God
is no respecter of persons."

Similar to most theologians of Christendom, Cash believed in the
social order. He was no apocalypticist, even though some of his later
songs, such as his cover of Trent Reznor's "Hurt" and Nick Lowe's
"The Beast Within" or his own "The Man Comes Around," seem to
push in that direction. Instead of heaping apocalyptic despair upon
listeners, these songs should be seen more as glimpses into Cash's
own inner spiritual struggles and his own willingness to identify with
the darkest elements within the human condition—again, a move of
solidarity with others in a common humanity, not a statement of the
hopelessness of all humanity. Cash seemed to agree with Calvin's
view that our sin sits upon us as a deformity of the divine image. This
sin is common to us all, not just those who are incarcerated or who
have fallen under the power of addiction and despair. When wedded
to a prophetic vision, awareness of shared sin is transformed into a
sense of connection with those who are most marginalized and who

can fall from sight, as well as an awareness of our complicity in creating the conditions in which persons become lost and hopeless.

Using our narrative tool for analyzing lyrics shows us that the human condition in the music of Johnny Cash is invisibility, not belonging. This condition is caused by forgetfulness, willfully neglecting the poor and outcast of society. Religious desire is directed toward reconnection within one human family, a world in which people of all walks of life recognize and remember one another. Belief takes the shape of solidarity with the poor and estranged, putting oneself in the shoes of those who are lost and alone. Helpers take the form of conscience and memory, anything (a song, image, or encounter) that calls to mind the fact that we belong to one another as human beings. God is a God of inclusion, who welcomes all to the table of fellowship and belonging.

Cash's vision matches, in some ways, the process-relational theologian's theological worldview.[33] For the process-relational theologian, isolation, loneliness, and broken relationality define a sinful human condition, and restored connection with the world, others, and God is crucial to experiencing redemption. Within this theological framework, however, solidarity with the oppressed or remembering their plight is only one piece of the life of faith. It is also important, in process-relational Christian theologian Marjorie Suchocki's words, to offer "resurrection alternatives" and "structures that promote inclusive well-being" to those who experience suffering.[34] The album *At Folsom Prison* reminds us of the plight of prisoners, but does little to point to the resurrection opportunities and alternatives that exist within that context. The same can be said about songs such as "Homeless" and "The Ballad of Ira Hayes."

At the same time, forgetting the outcast is only half the problem, a symptom of a deeper malady. Suchocki speaks of a tragic and demonic element within society creating structures and modes of being that work to deny our interdependence, teaching us from birth to live "against the grain of relational existence."[35] For Christian theologians it will be crucial to identify this larger evil and the narcissistic, solipsistic modes of being that lead us to imprison one another (not just the outcast) within high walls of isolation and loneliness.

It is likely that Cash's vision grew not only out of his own experiences of isolation and distance, but out of his Christian commitments, though he chose mostly to separate his sacred and secular music from one another. Cash, and those who promote fan cultures similar to his, do a tremendous service to society in keeping the outcast in the public eye, sharpening our memories of one another as human beings. Theologians can learn from Cash not just to mention the marginalized, but to *engage* them emotionally and physically (on location) and *represent* them in theological invention. At the same time, Christian theologians can present a more complex vision of the ways in which the fabric of mutual belonging is broken, and steer this quasi-theology in the direction of clearer resurrection alternatives.

Theologies of Love: Erotic (Madonna), Empathic (Sinéad O'Connor, Julie Miller)

Kelton Cobb points out that when St. Augustine observed the symbols of pagan mystery religions in his day, many of which were images of sexuality and fertility and attempts to redirect erotic impulses toward the divine, he saw expressions of the God-shaped hole in each of us, the heart that is always restless until it finds peace in God.[36] For Augustine *all* human desire was in some sense a reflection of our endless desire for God, and Augustine wrestled in his own life with how to direct that desire. This same quandary finds expression in the works of many popular musicians today.

Bill Friskics-Warren asserts that for the post–rock-'n'-roll generation, we find this expression of restless human desire (*eros*) most powerfully in the commingling of sex and spirituality in the music of artists such as Marvin Gaye, who gave us the song "Sexual Healing," the Reverend Al Green, who gave us "Love and Happiness," and Madonna, who gave us "Like a Prayer." According to Friskics-Warren, "Madonna's music frequently exhibits a yearning for spiritual renewal rooted in sensuality. . . . Madonna conveys a hunger for personal wholeness that hinges on but often transcends sex."[37] One way love is given quasi-theological voice in popular music today is through the merging of sexual and spiritual categories of desire.

In this music, the human condition is defined by a deep desire for touch. In "Like a Prayer,"[38] Madonna sings that she is so desperately in need of human connection that she is literally dying for a lover's kiss. The belief that is being solicited is belief that sensuality is a good thing, not a bad thing. Getting in touch with one's body and personal longing for touch can lead to experiences of nearly mystical, ecstatic joy through immersion in another person and through opening oneself up to another. This process involves the pain of opening oneself up (physically and emotionally), but the promised results are transcendent in nature: perfect union with a lover. In the song "Erotica,"[39] Madonna tells lovers to put their hands into the flames of love. If they do, their lives will be forever changed. We can hear in Madonna's lyrics her own (priestly) sense that she is a redeemer or helper in the narrative told her listeners. She will show the way. The primary helper, however, is "the heart." In "Deeper and Deeper,"[40] Madonna encourages fans to get their minds out of the way and allow their hearts to take control of their lives. For Madonna, God is the womb of love, and the goal of her faith-story is to encounter the very source of love itself. In "Where Life Begins,"[41] she encourages lovers to go in search of this source of life and love, the place where her own love can be found.

This longing for connection with a love beyond yet within us does not have to be focused on the sexual. Bill Friskics-Warren points out that in the songs of artists such as Sinéad O'Connor, Moby, and Nashville's Julie Miller, the focus of erotic spirituality shifts from sensual/spiritual *connection with* the other to deep *compassion for* others in their suffering. For these artists, the quasi-theology of love shifts its locus from sexuality to sympathy, from physical desire to emotional self-giving. The human condition is defined by the need for healing compassion among those whose lives are filled with violence and other forms of suffering. The human condition is caused by any person or system that victimizes others. Sinéad O'Connor, for instance, in her song "Three Babies,"[42] sings entirely from the point of view of a homeless woman whose children are being taken from her. She enters completely into the consciousness of this mother: her pain, her helplessness in her addictions, her awareness of the smell and the feeling of her babies. In this song, and in many of her songs,

O'Connor seems to be trying to give herself entirely to another, in a form of substitution or what the great post-Holocaust philosopher Emmanuel Levinas calls being "torn up" for another.[43]

In a similar way, Nashville's Julie Miller, in her song "Rachel,"[44] mourns for Rachel Scott, the murdered Columbine High School student whose journal revealed a young woman of uncompromising character and goodness. In "All the Pieces of Mary,"[45] Miller pours out her heart to a homeless woman who is mentally ill. In this song, as in others, we hear the shape that belief takes—being someone who shoulders the pain of another, a person of compassionate solidarity in suffering. In "Maggie,"[46] Miller laments the situation of a friend's mother who was orphaned as a child and again sees hope only in finding a sympathetic or empathic helper who at least will listen to/ for Maggie's silent pain.

Theologian Wendy Farley writes compellingly about this kind of empathic religious desire. When one is abused or subjected to radical suffering (violence, neglect, shunning, disconnection), it is as if one's very being has been de-created. What God has made in love and desire for relationship is undone, as relationality is violated and broken asunder. Only through encounters with compassion and trustworthy love can what evil has de-created be re-created.[47]

Within this worldview, God is perfect Empathy. Brandon Heath, whose song "Give Me Your Eyes"[48] was very popular on the Billboard Contemporary Christian charts, has a similar theology. Heath prays that God will grant him the gift of God's eyes, love, arms, and heart. He desires a more perfect empathy so that he can more adequately pour out his life for the wounded.

Madonna and Julie Miller represent two very different theologies of love: one erotic, one empathic. To use our narrative categories, the human condition is defined for both musicians as a need for love. For Madonna, what is needed is intimate physical connection with the human other. For Miller, what is needed is the compassion that will heal the human other. The reason for this human condition wears different faces for Madonna and Miller. For Madonna, the reason is repression, the denial of the natural desires of the body. For Miller, the reason is violence or abuse that destroys the body, which is created for relationships of love. For Madonna, belief is a matter of getting in touch with one's erotic desires and giving oneself to another in love. For Miller, belief is demonstrated through empathic self-giving. For Madonna, the primary helper is the desiring heart, inasmuch as it helps one overcome the strictures of the repressive conscience. Miller finds help in a community of empathy, those who join her in seeking healing and wholeness for others. For both, redemption is found in a life of intimacy and wholeness. Madonna seeks personal wholeness through mystical-sensual connection with a barely attainable other. Miller seeks wholeness and restored intimacy for the suffering, inconsolable other. Both partake of a deep desire to fill the God-shaped yearning (*eros*) for the divine that controlled so much of Augustine's early life and writing.

What would Christian theologians have to say to these popular theologies of love? At the outset it is clear that most would not, on the surface of things, be avid Madonna fans. In *The Institutes of the Christian Religion*,[49] Calvin says, "Let neither your heart burn with wicked lust within, nor your eyes wantonly run into corrupt desires, nor your body be decked with bawdy ornaments, nor your tongue seduce your mind to like thoughts with filthy words, nor your appetite inflame it with intemperance" (II.8.45). If we dig a little deeper within the Christian tradition, however, we see that mystical visionaries such as Julian of Norwich often mixed together a bodily, sensuous desire for God with a sense that life is nurtured through compassion that moves us toward (or into) God.[50] In this sense, the intense desire to connect with God, while easily displaced and focused solely on the human body, is, nonetheless, expressed in human-to-human love, and often finds itself in this exchange.

When theologians speak of love for neighbor, they sound a lot like Julie Miller. "We ought to embrace the whole human race without exception in a single feeling of love; here there is no distinction between barbarian and Greek, worthy and unworthy, friend and enemy, since all should be contemplated in God, not in themselves" (Calvin, *Institutes*, II.8.55) At the same time, theologians, citing the apostle Paul (Phil 2:1-5), might encourage Miller to remember that her deep outpouring of love is a part of the *kenosis* or self-giving of Christ. This would save her and her fans from what in her lyrics sometimes feels like depletion and exhaustion in self-giving. In other words, through connection with *divine empathy* it is possible to find resources of compassion that cannot be depleted.

In the end, the pervasive quasi-theologies of love within the popular music soundscape encourage Christian theologians to remember that desire for the other, and the Holy Other, are, as the great commandment suggests, coextensive. Popular music of this type can teach us to take the body, both the erotic and the suffering body, seriously as theologians, and not to shy away from speaking about both in the context of God's unconditional love. Christian theologians can promote a deeper awareness of the ultimate source of this *eros* in our longing for unconditional love, and they can steer this *eros* toward the resources of unconditional love found in the divine empathy expressed through the life, death, and resurrection of Jesus Christ.

Theologies of Negation (the Legendary Shack Shakers, Eminem)

One of the good things about covenant theology, and moral forms of faith that are formed in response to prophetic jeremiads, is the overall sense that we live within a God-ordained and God-ordered universe. We may be disappointed with the way things are going, but at least we believe that God is involved, and patiently waiting for us to get it right. Kelton Cobb, however, argues that gothic faith is a form of negative moral faith lived out within a more nihilistic context in which we are "buffeted by powers whose intentions are unknown, and judging from the body-count of innocents, probably capricious."[51] He goes on to say, "Evil no longer occurs in a providential order that we can trust will ultimately contain it and even bring good out of it. More and more it occurs in a nihilistic universe where anything can happen."[52]

Musically, gothic ideas can be found in groups like Echo & the Bunnymen, Joy Division, the Cure, Nick Cave, and the Psychedelic Furs. In Nashville, the inheritors of this worldview can be found in a band called the Legendary Shack Shakers. Religion and culture scholar David Perkins has researched this band's work, along with a range of other similar groups. The Legendary Shack Shakers are part of a larger national music scene Perkins calls "Southern gothic," a style that, like the novels of Flannery O'Connor, captures what Tennessee Williams once called "an intuition of an underlying dreadfulness in modern experience."[53] Other bands making similar music include Cicada Omega, 16 Horsepower, Slim Cessna's Auto Club, Creech Holler, Munly and the Lee Lewis Harlots, Drunken Prayer, and Palodine. The music of all these bands brings together elements of revivalism and darker gothic moods and themes.

In a MySpace video, the Legendary Shack Shakers say that they are "southern by the grace of Goth."[54] The band's lead singer and principal songwriter, Colonel J. D. Wilkes, in another video interview, observes in an offhanded manner that if he were not playing this music he would "probably be a serial killer."[55] According to Perkins, nearly all of these southern gothic bands trade in southern stereotypes and make use of the performance dynamics of southern revivalism.[56]

> Anyone who has heard a live performance of Ralph Stanley's "Oh Death," from the movie O *Brother Where Art Thou*, has experienced something of this strange blend of gothic, country, and punk. These bands' lyrics take fans into the bizarre world of Pentecostal healings, being "slain in the Spirit," serpent handlers, and arsenic drinking—anything that will help to exorcise the demons of America. Instead of snakes and arsenic, this exorcism comes through frenzied LOUD music, frantic dancing, the smashing of musical instruments and other props, and other performance rituals. A member of the band Cicada Omega says, "When we're in these bars, I feel like we're not so much working for the Lord, but, sometimes we're working for the devil instead. We represent both sides in the same show. As a human being, I feel both angels and devils in me. And, that's what gospel music is about, shouting it [all] out."[57]

Perkins argues that this music and its growing fan base indicate an urge for "freedom from forces that come part and parcel with contemporary cultural citizenship. And ironically, religion is one of those forces."[58] These bands preach the "church without Christ—no salvation—and no redemption from the hard facts of human experience."[59]

Southern gothic music is very much within both the punk and gothic traditions of popular music. In terms of our narrative categories of analysis, the human condition is one of meaninglessness, death, and despair—a funeral or graveside service for a world rotting in its own juices. In the song "Ichabod,"[60] Wilkes, recalling the famous sermon by Jonathan Edwards, asserts that he is "a sinner in the hands of an angry God." When he dies, he should rot in the barren ground. This human condition is caused by betrayal. Those trusted with our welfare have betrayed us all and led us into a wasteland of toxic dumps, phony religion, and economic instability. Perhaps the best expression of this is the song "Somethin' in the Water,"[61] written after public exposure of the environmental crimes at the Martin Marietta/ Union Carbide plant in Paducah, Kentucky. The song encourages the listener to be wary because there is "somethin' weird" in the ground water, a powerful metaphor for life victimized by evils beyond our control.

According to Cobb, Gothic music expresses faith in an end-story, an apocalyptic tale in which fans tell themselves that they "live in the worst and most barbaric of times, that all is broken never to be mended, that things are bad and fated to be, that significant hope is a sorry joke, the prerogative of suckers."[62] We live in poet John Milton's "paradise lost" with no way out.

Redemptive help is found in the form of priests of exorcism who will help believers shake the devil out in a variety of ways. The best that can be done is, as J. D. Wilkes says in an interview, to "push it out,"[63] with little or no hope of actual redemption beyond exorcism itself. In the song "Angel Lust,"[64] Wilkes wants us to force the devil to "eat his hat." In the end, however, the song expresses resignation. No matter what one does, things always turn out the same. Ultimately, both God and the redemptive goal of one's faith reside beyond any story that can be told—mysteries shrouded in darkness.

If gothic music is an attempt to transcend ordinary experience through negation or negative faith, anarchic bands such as the Stooges, the Sex Pistols, and Eminem's early work seem to represent another form of negative transcendence. Instead of submitting to the human condition as the ultimate victim, these bands push back against the forces of nothingness. Faith takes the form of aggressive, if not violent, negative resistance. As Bill Friskics-Warren points out, these artists use their music as a way of "confronting the degradation that surrounds [them] in hopes of divesting it of its power."[65] For these artists, expressions of negative resistance seem to contain a deep longing for something more, something better. At times the negative voice can push into realms of violence that border on sickness. In his music, for instance, Eminem threatens to destroy every person or thing that has ever humiliated him, including his mother and his wife. He devises an alter ego, Slim Shady, who "becomes the repository of the sickness and non-sense that has plagued him."[66] He tries to use Slim Shady and his invective to impel him somehow through and beyond the deep pit of negation at the center of his life. Although this is, in and of itself, theologically problematic, Friskics-Warren argues that, at least in the Slim Shady guise, Eminem "does not want to kill anyone. More than anything else he wants to get inside people's heads and, from misogyny to self-loathing, to eradicate the dis-ease that has taken root there, or at least to alert people to the dangers of it."[67] In some ways, this mirrors the exorcisms attempted by the Legendary Shack Shakers, but Eminem's use of Slim Shady in this way seems to indicate that exorcism need not be an end in itself, but a possible gateway to something better, something more.

It is clear that transcendence through forms of negation is an important aspect of popular music and the fandoms that are around us in our culture. In his exposition of "gothic faith," Cobb points to the work of Tom Beaudoin, who claims that the gothic imagination is a fundamental worldview for many Gen Xers who have been handed a failing economy, lingering nuclear threats, AIDS, overwhelming tuition debt, uncontrollable and even addictive consumerism, and a ruined environment.[68] This is a worldview that theologians need to take seriously. At the heart of the human condition is a deep-seated existential mistrust and despair at all reigning metanarratives, including the grand narratives provided by the Enlightenment, Christendom, evangelical Christianity, and the soft religions of New Ageism. This worldview has some affinities with the death-of-God theologies of Dietrich Bonhoeffer, Thomas J. J. Altizer, William Hamilton, Charles Winquist, and more recently the secularist theology of Gianni Vattimo.[69] It also reflects the early deconstructive philosophy of Jacques Derrida and the sociological nihilism of Jean Baudrillard.[70] This is not the soft take on deconstruction that we find in post-evangelical or emerging church theologies,[71] but a darker, more radical form of deconstructive thinking.

In order to find a Christian theology that corresponds to the Legendary Shack Shakers' theological worldview, we might appeal to Karl Barth, since Barth, like the southern gothic believer, is quick to assert the absence of final revelation in nature and the complete bankruptcy of human reason to deliver any real knowledge of God. Barth's theology permits atheism and nihilism, therefore, and would allow for the gothic as a genuine form of atheism, a complete and absolute separation from God. Here the Legendary Shack Shakers find a kindred spirit—better to exorcise "the world" and seek (divine) revelation than to rely on any form of human reason or "religion."

Tillich, like Augustine and Calvin, denies the ultimate possibility of such atheism, arguing that God is hidden behind all distortions of sin and evil in the world, and behind even the asserted atheism of the nihilist. Tillich might show more interest in the music of Eminem. Even if negation is misplaced, it is at least negation as an attempt to *drive out* the lesser gods while retaining some remnant of hope that the true God will appear from beneath the rubble. Within this theological context, any celebration of the absence of God leads in the end to a celebration of the radical otherness of and eventual sovereignty of the one true God, or the God beyond the gods.

What appears to be missing within these gothic forms of faith, from a larger Christian perspective, is not so much a lack of knowledge about the false gods that have made victims of us all as a lack of *self-knowledge* regarding the limitations of our own thinking and resources. There is something smacking of hubris in assuming that victimization and negativity in life *necessarily* leads to nihilism, or in assuming that we could push through to either the *nihil* or the one true God through rituals or methodologies of negation alone. In the end, the gothic musician is what scholar of mythology Erich Neumann calls a "permanent revolutionary," who, like the "dragon-slaying" hero in mythology, refuses "to become a father (or mother) and assume power," which would mean accepting limitations.[72] The

Christian tradition knows that ultimately knowledge of God and ourselves requires accepting the limitations of human knowledge and pursuing a fuller and more complete openness to revelation testified to in Incarnation, Resurrection, and the community of witnesses. True self-knowledge acknowledges the limits of self-knowledge, as well as our own ultimate dependence on the witness of others and the God who finds us through that witness.

In the case of Eminem, another element is troubling from a Christian perspective. The pathological push to get through to what Jim Morrison once called "the other side" should not require forms of violence against others that support abuse or misogyny. It is not at all clear for most listeners whether Eminem and other artists in this mold are working out their own salvation or trafficking in the dominant culture's patriarchal misogyny, homophobia, and bullying bravado in order to sell records. A more recent recording by Eminem, *Love the Way You Lie*, seems to indicate that little progress is being made in the direction of healing, and that in fact Eminem is simply wallowing in his own disease. In the Christian vision, confronting one's demons does not mean externalizing those demons and perpetuating attacks on others who are innocent victims or bystanders. Confronting the rage within one's own psyche does not mean promoting rage as a way of life or as a core element in human relationships.

There is much to learn as theologians from these theologies of negation. Theologians invent theological messages in a culture in which experiences of victimization, meaninglessness, and cynical suspicion of persons and structures are increasingly dominant. The popularity of these quasi-theologies invites theologians to consider what forms of priestly exorcism and prophetic pushing through are available within the Christian tradition if these fans are to begin to find Christian faith at all helpful or transformative in their lives. In this context, Christian theologians need to find ways to demonstrate that nihilism is an assumption that is not altogether necessary, even within a worldview in which one believes oneself to be victimized by forces beyond one's control. The Cross and Resurrection of Jesus Christ present another way to think about living through and beyond victimization.

Therapeutic Theologies of Recovery (Praise and Worship Music)

It is clear from the proliferation of self-help and recovery groups in congregations, and especially in the small group movement within evangelical megachurches, that there is much interest today in theologies that place personal wholeness, rather than self-denial or self-giving, at the center of what it means to be a religious person. This is not an improper motivation for theology, especially for those whose selves have been ripped from them by having grown up in, or married into, addictive, abusive, or shame-based situations. Although this worldview shows up in a variety of different forms of music today, we will focus on its expression in praise and worship music. Most praise and worship (popularly known as P&W or PW) music is produced and recorded in Nashville. As a genre, P&W should be distinguished from the broader spectrum of contemporary Christian music (CCM) because it is focused exclusively on either individual or corporate devotion, praise, and worship.

The human condition within this worldview is one of lost wholeness of self. This condition is caused by any activity (shame, abuse, fear, addiction) that strips the self of its powers and sends the self into hiding. The goal of this theology is wholeness or recovery of lost selfhood. Since the self is lost through self-perpetuating cycles of violence, codependency (mutually destructive relationships), or addiction, help must come from beyond the situation. Although the compassion of others such as the Julie Millers or Brandon Heaths of the world is essential to the healing, restoration, and recovery of the self, 12-step programs have made it clear that, in the last analysis, breaking out of a cycle of addiction or violence is likely to require a higher, personal power who will accept the shame-based self, embrace it, and provide it with the spiritual and emotional power to begin to re-create itself.

Although theologies of self-fulfillment can be shallow in nature, focusing on no greater good than the fulfillment of oneself in and of oneself, scholars from evangelical (Richard Mouw) to feminist (Marie Fortune) argue that there is an appropriate use of the therapeutic within theology, in the "training of the self to come to value itself and all things . . . in light of their relation to God."[73] The ultimate goal of salvation, in this light, is not simply self-fulfillment, but includes reconnection with others in healthy relationships, nondestructive patterns of behavior, and communities of mutual support.

Seen in this perspective, praise and worship music, in its best sense, is about opening a wounded self to the healing power of God, who is often seen, within these songs, as a mighty creating power: majestic, awesome, indescribable, utterly holy, and worthy of commitment. This opening up to God is done in the context of the community at worship, where others are also reconnecting with a higher power and hopefully discovering new ways to be in relation to one another in worship and small groups. There is no need in this music to tell a story or speak to issues. The goal is not a moral form of faith, but an ontological faith, one which regrounds the self in the one power that can give it what theologian Paul Tillich calls the "courage to be."[74] This is at least one reason for the hyperverticality of this kind of music, and its repetitive, contemplative, mantra-like quality. The exclusive goal is divine connection and empowerment.

Chris Tomlin's popular rendering of Laura Mixon Story's "Indescribable"[75] calls for utterly vertical worship of God, without reference to any of God's works or to any human story. God is the object of praise through five hyperbolic adjectives: indescribable, uncontainable, amazing, all-powerful, and untamable. In Tim Hughes' "Here I Am to Worship"[76] we can hear strong overtones of intimate human relationship turned and fixed upon God. Hughes uses first-person language, addressing God directly and personally as "lovely," "worthy," and "altogether wonderful." God's incredible beauty evokes pure adoration. Matt Redman's "Blessed Be Your Name"[77] locates this God in the deserts and wilderness places of our lives. In "Lord, I Lift Your Name on High,"[78] Rick Founds asserts that since so many of us find ourselves in these difficult places he is glad God has come to save us.

Reformed theologians would find much to work with in this popular theological movement. The emphasis on the need to admit one's helplessness apart from God is at the heart of Calvin's theology and of Reformed liturgics. Calvin would find some resonance with the emphasis on a higher power. He felt strongly that it is the sovereignty of God in one's life that makes all good things possible and ultimately leads to salvation. Likewise, Calvin's emphasis on original sin and total depravity (or our utter inability *not* to sin) has many rough parallels with the family systems view that sin is a larger web of social and familial dysfunctionality in which we are already enmeshed when we are born and which completely controls us.

Christian theologians will worry, however, about several things. First, by focusing on *praise* and the need for a higher power, this music elides any attempt to *name* the evils that have taken over one's life. This naming, of course, may take place in small groups of various kinds, in which one's need for a higher power is confessed. One might also listen to forms of music (such as Julie Miller's or Johnny Cash's) that articulate something of the specific suffering endured by one who has been abused, shamed, or trapped in addiction. Where praise and worship music predominates, however, this naming of sin is often excluded from practices of worship. It could, of course, be included through corporate prayers of confession and thanksgiving. At the very least, praise (*doxa*) should be linked closely to thanksgiving (*eucharistia*), which references the specific nature of God's helping agency. In the real world, one is thankful for *something specific*, not just for God's "Being *qua* (understood as) Being." In the classical form of Christian prayer (the collect), unconditioned adoration is always linked immediately to conditioned thanks: "Almighty and everlasting God (invocation, praise), who brought us out of shame and abuse into wholeness . . ." (conditional clause, thanksgiving). The prayer then moves on to articulate petitions ("help us to take care of ourselves . . ."), anticipated results ("so that we might find wholeness in our lives and be witnesses to justice in the world . . ."), and a closing benediction ("in the name of the triune God . . ."). Even in the most praise-filled moment within the Christian gospel, when Thomas exclaims, "my Lord and my God," he is staring at the wounds (*stigmata*) on the resurrected body. According to theologian Marjorie Suchocki, this means that the victory for which we praise Christ is fitted to our wounds, not a generalized, otherworldly escape from our wounds.[79] Praise, therefore, is praise for this particular transformation and not just broadly referenced, free-floating devotion.

Christian theologians will also worry that any attempt to focus the Christian faith on forms of self-fulfillment (even in the recovery mode) could easily be co-opted by consumerism, prosperity gospel, and narrowly therapeutic understandings of salvation that circumvent the gospel's social and cosmic proportions. In these models, confession disappears and the higher power is reduced to the many idolatrous gifts of prosperity and health that God wants to give to you. How can this error be avoided? One key addition becomes important. Sanctification (the work of discovering God's re-creating and regenerating work in our lives) can be closely linked to our awareness of justification (God's prior, cosmic work of reconciliation and forgiveness in Christ, which extends to the whole creation). This will help recovery thinkers remember that it is not possible to pursue our self-fulfillment apart from the reconciliation and fulfilling of the entire creation. In the last analysis, our regeneration is not only about us, but about God's reconciling of all things in Christ.

In the end, praise and worship music reminds theologians of the importance for many today of an ontological faith, which grounds the believer in the very *Being* of God as a higher power. This is especially true for those who are seeking the power to re-create or recover selves torn from them by abuse, shame, or addiction. Theologians can think of ways to bring vertical connection with an awesome God into theological invention, perhaps even voicing portions of their work as praise. At the same time, they can connect praise to the specific ways in which selfhood has been de-created and hidden, identifying the complex and often systemic sins (abuse, addiction, shaming, etc.) that diminish selfhood, and articulating specific forms of thanksgiving for God's redeeming work. Theologians can also connect our recoveries of selfhood to the larger work of redeeming victims of abuse, shame, and addiction in the larger community, nation, and world.

In chapter 5, I argued that we are surrounded by a range of fan cultures—musical pilgrimages through which people seek to interpret and transcend their ordinary experience. I argued that it is possible for theologians to host these fans and consider how their places of life and work (whether geographic or online) can function as a home for many fan pilgrimages. At the same time, I invited theologians to consider how they can invent messages that add depth and complexity to the pilgrimages of these fans and provide steerage through the many fan cultures vying for their attention. With this in mind, in this final chapter I have provided a method for analyzing the lyrics listened to within musical fan cultures, and used the method to analyze lyrics I hear often in and around Nashville. I have engaged these lyrics missiologically through lenses provided by Christian theologians, highlighting a small set of select messages that theologians within my theological tradition might want to communicate to those who are living into these worldviews through music on a daily basis. In the end, I want to invite theologians to consider which quasi-theologies are most significant in the fan cultures active within their congregations. Then, from within their theological tradition, theologians can both honor and embrace aspects of these quasi-theological narratives and the ideas, urges, desires, and concerns they address. At the same time, the theologians can add depth, complexity, and steerage, bringing these religious desires into a mutual teaching-learning interaction with the traditions they represent. At the end of the day, although religion remains a mashup affair, it may be a mashup leavened by well-considered theological messages invented to be appropriate to the popular music that is mashed up.

Appendix 1

THE MULTITRACK SERMON

A HOMILETICAL CASE STUDY

In chapter 2, theological invention was broken into four layers of tracks: Scripture tracks, culture tracks, theology tracks, and message tracks. Although this model of tracking could relate to any theological composition, it is particularly applicable to the invention of sermons. In this appendix, I will demonstrate the usefulness of the multitrack analogy for sermon invention and composition. In this example, I will track two sequences of a sermon. For a video demonstration of this method and the tracking of an entire sermon, go online to the YouTube account for "Jonymac2" and search for my videos on "The Multi-track Sermon."

The Multitrack Sermon

Let's begin with a paraphrase of a biblical text, the story of the feeding of the five thousand in Matthew 14:13-21. Jesus, having heard that John the Baptist has been beheaded by Herod, withdraws in a boat to a lonely place. A large crowd of people discovers where he has gone, and they follow him. When he goes ashore, he sees the crowd and out of compassion heals many of the sick. Soon it is growing late in the day, and the disciples are concerned about food. They implore Jesus to send the crowd into the villages to purchase food.

Jesus responds by telling the disciples to feed everyone. They remind him that they have only five loaves and two fish. He asks that these meager provisions be brought to him, orders the crowd to be seated, takes the loaves and fish, looks up to heaven, blesses and breaks the loaves, and gives them to the disciples who feed the entire crowd. Not only is the crowd satisfied, but the disciples collect twelve baskets of leftover pieces of food. In the end, five thousand men, women, and children are fed.

Message Track (Artistic Style, Enigma)

Having studied the biblical text and done some sampling and remixing to consider the best way to say what needs to be said, I decide to edit into this week's sermon a short snippet of audio:

> Compassion attracts those who are in need.

These are simply idea words, or thematic words. They are *my explicit message to today's listeners*. These words are already moving toward other harmonic layers of congregational hearing, straining for Scripture tracks, theology tracks, and culture tracks. But it is important to track my message so my listeners will know what it is I am actually saying to them. The message track is like a melody or vocal track, if you will. It lets my listener know what I am talking about.

Now let's move on to add other tracks.

Scripture Track (Dynamic Equivalence Style)

As I already mentioned, I arrived at this idea that "compassion attracts those who are in need" through theological reflection on a biblical text, Matthew 14:13-21. I am aware that there are important aspects of the scriptural text that I can draw forth into the sermon. I decide to layer in beneath the melody/message track ("Compassion attracts those who are in need") a brief paraphrased sample from the biblical text:

> When Jesus stepped forth from his boat, going to a lonely place, a great crowd gathered. They seemed to know what Matthew tells us, that Jesus would have compassion on them and heal their sick.

These words are recorded as part of the sermon's Scripture tracks. They are words that help the listener remember the foundational events of faith that underpin all Christian truth.

Theology Track (Equilibrist Style, Theology of Love)

For this sermon, I invited several laypersons to remix this portion of the sermon. I sent an e-mail to ten church members and asked them to track their theological ideas about this text by sending me thoughts on Jesus' compassion in this story. One track in particular seemed to jump out in the mix, so I decided to edit it into the song as a theology track at this point:

> Compassion is a sign of God's love for all of us. It attracts people because it says, "God has not forgotten you. In spite of what happens to you, God is there for you with saving, healing power."

Culture Track (Dialectical Style, Ordinary Experience)

As I reflect further on what I am communicating and on the theology of God's attractive love and compassion, I am aware of cultural and experiential connections for this idea. These connections lead me to track what is sometimes called an illustration because it illumines or throws light on my idea. This illustration is a story from my past experience. It narrates an experience with a small church that I sometimes drove past on my way to work. This exceptional church had initiated an exemplary gospel ministry to the homeless several years earlier. I decide to use this church as an example of compassion that attracts those who are in need.

> There is a small urban church that I used to drive past on my way downtown called St. Anthony's. One year things began to change at St. Anthony's Church. The first thing they did was to paint the church sanctuary doors red, a bright red color, so that they would be noticed—and they made sure they were unlocked every day from eight in the morning until midnight. Within six months, I noticed that a wheelchair ramp had been added to the side entrance to the church. At about the same

time, I noticed a sign had gone up in the churchyard advertising a shelter for homeless women, a soup kitchen, and a regular Thursday evening celebration of worship and the Lord's Supper.

Within a year and a half, I heard that the shelter was filled every night with homeless women and children, and the soup kitchen was desperate for food and for volunteers. I also heard from several long-time members that the church's endowment was being seriously depleted.

I decided to attend one of their community Lord's Supper celebrations one Thursday evening. It was an overwhelming experience. The modest sanctuary was filled with people of all types. Wheelchairs blocked every aisle. The wealthy and the homeless sat side by side singing ancient hymns of the church. People of every race and nationality knelt at the communion rail.

The Sermon Sequence

I have now, in a simple way, tracked and edited one sermon sequence at all four levels. Although I could edit these tracks to occur in the sermon in any number of ways, if I simply read out in the order above what I have tracked, the first sequence of my sermon would sound like this:

Message track:
Compassion attracts those who are in need.

Scripture track:
When Jesus stepped forth from his boat, going to a lonely place, a great crowd gathered. They seemed to know what Matthew tells us, that Jesus would have compassion on them and heal their sick.

Theology track:
Compassionate action is a sign of God's love for all of us. It attracts people because it says, "God has not forgotten you." In spite of what happens, God is there for you with saving, healing power.

Culture track:

There is a small urban church that I used to drive past on my way downtown called St. Anthony's. One year things began to change at St. Anthony's Church. The first thing they did was to paint the church sanctuary doors red, a bright red color, so that they would be noticed—and they made sure they were unlocked every day from eight in the morning until midnight. Within six months, I noticed that a wheelchair ramp had been added to the side entrance to the church. At about the same time, I noticed a sign had gone up in the churchyard advertising a shelter for homeless women, a soup kitchen, and a regular Thursday evening celebration of worship and the Lord's Supper.

Within a year and a half, I heard that the shelter was filled every night with homeless women and children, and the soup kitchen was desperate for food and for volunteers. I also heard from several long-time members that the church's endowment was being seriously depleted.

I decided to attend one of their community Lord's Supper celebrations one Thursday evening. It was an overwhelming experience. The modest sanctuary was filled with people of all types. Wheelchairs blocked every aisle. The wealthy and the homeless sat side by side singing ancient hymns of the church. People of every race and nationality knelt at the communion rail.

Similar to the first sequence of a song, what we now have is the first movement of thought, or the first sequence of a sermon. These four tracks appear at this stage in a short, partially edited way. They will be further edited and then performed with improvisational spontaneity and energy. They can also be expanded (tracks added) and woven together in a creative way in order to give body or fullness to this sermon sequence.

Notice three things. First, the content between the tracks harmonizes. Each track exists as a different *layer* of audio, a way of nuancing the same thing. Second, now that I have all four tracks written down, notice that the linear order or plotting of these tracks could be changed. I do not have to edit them in the order in which I wrote them down. If I wanted to emphasize the authority of Scripture and appear to be a more expository or text-based preacher, I could start with the Scripture track. If I wanted to sound more like a good topical preacher, I might start with the culture track or message track. Or, if I wanted to appear as a doctrinal preacher, I might start with the theology track. Third, the example I have provided demonstrates primarily a staggering of layers of audio. In other words, each track is presented in a linear fashion, one after the other, instead of being woven together to occur simultaneously. They tracks could, of course, be presented in a more simultaneous fashion, with each track flickering in and out of our hearing. Here, for instance, is how a portion of the first sequence might sound with the tracks unstaggered and woven together in a more simultaneous fashion.

> I used to drive past a little church called St. Anthony's. (*culture track*) The members of St. Anthony's experienced the attractive power of their own compassion. (*message track*) They discovered what Jesus' disciples learned when they followed him to a lonely place that day. Because of Jesus' compassionate healing of others, there would be no rest that day. (*Scripture track*) The members at St. Anthony's discovered the same thing. One year, things began to change at St. Anthony's. The first thing they did was to paint the church sanctuary doors red, a bright red color, so that they would be noticed—and they made sure they were unlocked every day from eight in the morning until midnight. Within six months, I noticed that a wheelchair ramp had been added to the side entrance to the church. At about the same time, I noticed a sign had gone up in the churchyard advertising a shelter for homeless women, a soup kitchen, and a regular Thursday evening celebration of worship and the Lord's Supper. (*culture track*) I remember thinking to myself, these people are putting themselves on the line! If they keep doing this, they're going to find themselves overrun with some pretty needy people. (*message track*)
>
> Sure enough, within a year and a half, I heard that the shelter was filled every night with homeless women and children, and the soup kitchen was desperate for food and for volunteers.

I also heard from several long-time members that the church's endowment was being seriously depleted. (*culture track*) People were coming, all right, (*message track*) desperately seeking God's healing power—wanting to know that God had not forgotten them. (*theology track*)

I decided to attend one of their community Lord's Supper celebrations one Thursday evening. It was an overwhelming experience. The modest sanctuary was filled with people of all types. Wheelchairs blocked every aisle. The wealthy and the homeless sat side by side singing ancient hymns of the church. People of every race and nationality knelt at the communion rail. (*culture track*) The people at this tiny church had discovered what Jesus and his disciples knew only too well on that day long ago. (*Scripture track*) If you put out the compassion shingle, you'll never get a moment's rest. (*message track*)

This is only one way to engage in simultaneous layering of tracks. Essentially, I have allowed the culture track to be dominant, layering in short flickers of my message track, theology track, and Scripture track along the way. The same could be done with any of the tracks. Sometimes one track is given more space, texture, and volume in the mix. At other times another track can be made more prominent.

Now let's explore moving from one sequence to another in a sermon. Sermon sequences are created by introducing and sustaining new content in one or more of the four layers or submixes of tracks. I can move on by way of any of the four layers of tracks. Here are four examples.

Moving on with a Message Track (Artistic Style, Enigma Deepened)

The first thing that I may want to do in the next sequence is to advance my message. For instance, I can say,

And that creates problems, doesn't it, because the need for compassion is overwhelming and there can't possibly be enough to go around!

I have now introduced new content through a message track, a further development of the sermon's central message about life today.

Moving on with a Scripture Track (Dynamic Equivalence Style)

I might use a Scripture track to lead the way, saying,

> Jesus' compassion attracted five thousand people! *But* dinnertime was coming. The disciples knew that there would never be enough food to go around. They ran to Jesus and warned him, "We have just five loaves and two fish!"

I have now introduced new content with a Scripture track, a further development of the relationship between my idea and the biblical text. In other words, I have moved on to a new sermon sequence scripturally.

Moving on with a Theology Track (Equilibrist, Theology of Love)

I could use a theology track to turn this corner.

> But is God's love too attractive? If we really become vessels for God's compassionate love, aren't we going to be empty vessels pretty soon? After all, we're not God!

I have now introduced new content in a theology track, a further development of the relationship between my idea and the theological worldview of my congregation. In other words, I have moved on to a new sermon sequence theologically.

Moving on with an Culture Track (Dialectical Style, Ordinary Experience)

I may, of course, choose to move on by way of experience. Here are three brief culture tracks that could be layered in to move the sermon forward at this level.

> How can I take a homeless person into my home when I've barely got enough emotional and financial resources to take care of my own family?

And if I donate that much money to our church's poverty fund, I may not be able to send my own child to the best school.

And if I give half my time to my family and my church, my career will suffer and so will our standard of living.

I have now introduced new content with culture tracks, a further development of the relationship between my message and human experience. In other words, I have moved on to a new sermon sequence experientially.

No matter which track leads the way, the key to establishing a new sequence is to introduce and sustain new content in one or more tracks. Each sequence contains shifts between and among parallel tracks. Brief indications of the presence of several tracks will occur in each sermon sequence. In most cases, it is the message track (melody) or the particular meaning that is being developed in a sequence that provides a rhetorical boundary for a particular sequence. This is true despite the fact that the message track may not appear at the beginning and end of the sequence but somewhere in the middle of the sequence itself, depending upon your style.

The Sermon Track Sheet

Before you prepare a sermon outline or manuscript or begin to practice your oral presentation, prepare a sermon track sheet to use as a guide. This track sheet directly parallels the edit window on a DAW and provides a visual picture of all of the audio tracks for your sermon. Take a piece of paper and turn it sideways. Along the left-hand side list the four submixes of tracks. You may want to draw straight lines from the top to the bottom and from the left to the right of the page, leaving several blocks into which you can jot your ideas, illustrations, scriptural information, and theological references. Figure A.1 shows what the first two sequences of our sermon on Matthew 14:13-21 would look like on a track sheet.

Some will want to turn this track sheet into a full-blown manuscript. Others will want to rearrange it in outline form. I would encourage you, if possible, *not* to use either a manuscript or outline but simply to preach across the track sheet, weaving the tracks together in ways that meet the immediate needs of the preaching

Layer or submixes of tracks	*Sequence 1*	*Sequence 2*	*Sequence 3*	*Sequence 4*
Theology tracks	Acts of compassion are signs of God's attractive love.	But is God's love too attractive?		
Message tracks	Compassion attracts those who are in need.	But the need for compassion is over-whelming!		
Experience tracks	St. Anthony's church	• Taking in a home-less person uses up resources. • Giving money and time to church, family suffers • Giving time to the church, career suffers		
Scripture tracks	A great crowd gathers and Jesus had compassion and heals many who are sick.	Only five loaves and two fish.		

Figure A.1. Sermon track sheet in process.

event in your church. All you need to take with you into the pulpit is the track sheet. I call this editing on the fly. It takes practice, but once learned, it provides a good method for preaching extemporaneously from notes.

This, then, is how sermon multitracking works. Each sequence is made up of an interweaving of four submixes of tracks, message tracks, Scripture tracks, theology tracks, and culture tracks. Most sermons will include from three to five sequences. As more layers of tracks are added to each submix or code, the sermon is filled out.

Permutations

Although we have been discussing this method of editing and organization in written form, with the advent of low-cost, simple-to-use digital audio workstations (DAWs: GarageBand, Acid Pro, Tracktion, etc.) and podcasting gear, this entire process might easily move into the audio recording domain. Preachers, making use of low-cost USB microphones, can now record audio directly into digital audio work-stations, tracking regions of audio that can be turned into sequences of sermon material. These regions of sound can be moved around within the mix window and placed in whatever order is preferred. The preacher can also audition samples of other sounds (audio from other sermons, music, news clips, interviews, etc.) that might be included in the presentation as well. Once the process is completed, the preacher has a rough audio mix of a presentation organized and ready to perform. Since the presentation will be performed live, the rough mix amounts to a complete audition of the presentation's audio content.

Any of the boxes on the track sheet could be given over to a different media of presentation: popular songs, audio or video clips from television, films, YouTube, or self-conducted interviews, drama, and so on. For instance, in sequence one of the sermon example above, the message track, "compassion attracts those in need," could be expanded slightly and performed as a rap or spoken word poetic monologue. The Scripture track could be performed as a short drama or dramatic reading. The culture track could be presented by show-ing a brief video of St. Anthony's Church and its Thursday evening service. The theology track could be performed as a song written for the sermon, or by covering a popular song that expresses the heart of God's compassion for us all. The preacher will not mix media too often, perhaps once per sermon, or per sequence at most, due to time constraints and sermon continuity, but varying the media used for each track has great potential to enliven sermon production. The sermon track sheet and the remixing concept of using others to track in the sermon studio help the preacher see many new ways in which the parts of the sermon can be edited in order to make a creative whole.

Digital technologies have greatly simplified the process of orga-nizing and editing audio and video. It is likely that in years to come the manipulation of audio and video will become even easier than it is today. Tracking presentations such as sermons entirely in the digital audio domain, and then organizing and reorganizing tracks of audio into multiaudio and multimedia presentations, has become a distinct possibility and is likely to be of significant interest to the next generation of preachers.

Appendix 2

MASHUP AND THEOLOGICAL INVENTION

AN ACADEMIC CASE STUDY

This appendix provides an example of an academic theological mashup in the form of a blog. In the blog referred to below is a mashup of a set of readings that were on my bookshelf and desk at home. I had been reading several journal articles and books on a variety of only partially related subjects: desire, love, modernity and postmodernity, mass communication, consumerism and religion, preaching, practical theology, the psychology of religious experiences, dialogue, ethics, public theology, deconstruction, ethics, the environment, the emerging church, cultural criticism, and theologies of the human condition. These readings were widely interdisciplinary in nature. Two of the primary theological books I chose to mash up were by Wendy Farley: *Eros for the Other* and *The Wounding and Healing of Desire*, along with Edward Farley's *Good and Evil*. In these books, Wendy Farley and Edward Farley argue that the basic rhythm of theology is the wounding and healing of desire for the human other and for God.

I was aware, as I read these materials, that there were some significant ways in which, using something similar to the audile technique possessed by many mashup artists, I might potentially make these readings work together in a mashup of Farley's work. Like a

DJ confronted with several crates of vinyl records, I saw my goal as finding the important "breaks" and "beats" in each work and beginning to integrate them into a unified composition, deconstructing, embellishing, and re-creating the Farleys' work. The mashup could have become an essay or lecture, but, given the range of materials, I decided to introduce the material on my blog, *Mashup Religion*, for comments, input, and further mashing up. As with any form of theological production, I endeavor to include all four tracks (see chapter 2): Scripture, theology, culture, message. The blog format permits me to track culture by including videos and links to other websites.

The reader can go to the blog to see items of interest. As with most blogs, the first post is the most recent, so if the reader desires to view this in a serial form, it will be necessary to begin with the final post and work backwards. It may be easier to accomplish this online.

NOTES

Preface

1 This CD is available through cdbaby.com and is entitled *God in Music City*.

2 The results of this are posted online at http://www.godinmusiccity.com.

3 For some of the published results of this project, see Ronald J. Allen, *Hearing the Sermon: Relationship, Content, Feeling* (St. Louis: Chalice Press, 2004); *Interpreting the Gospel: An Introduction to Preaching* (St. Louis: Chalice Press, 1998); "The Turn Toward the Listener: A Selective Review of a Recent Trend in Preaching," *Encounter* 64 (2003): 165–94; John S. McClure, Ronald J. Allen, L. Susan Bond, Dan P. Moseley, and Lee G. Ramsey Jr., *Listening to Listeners: Homiletical Case Studies* (St. Louis: Chalice Press, 2004); Mary Alice Mulligan and Ronald J. Allen, *Make the Word Come Alive* (St. Louis: Chalice Press, 2005); Mary Alice Mulligan, Diane Turner-Sharazz, Dawn Ottoni Wilhelm, and Ronald J. Allen, *Believing in Preaching: What Listeners Hear in Sermons* (St. Louis: Chalice Press, 2005).

Introduction

1 See Nicola Vicentino, *Ancient Music Adapted to Modern Practice*, ed. Claude V. Palisca, trans. Maria Rika Maniates (New Haven: Yale University Press, 1996); Matthew Gelbart, *The Invention of "Folk Music" and "Art Music": Emerging Categories from Ossian to Wagner*, New Perspectives

in Music History and Criticism 16 (Cambridge: Cambridge University Press, 2007).

2   See Jeff Howe, "The Rise of Crowdsourcing," *Wired*, June 2006.

3   Leigh Eric Schmidt, *Hearing Things: Religion, Illusion, and the American Enlightenment* (Cambridge, Mass.: Harvard University Press, 2000).

4   Walter Ong, *Orality and Literacy: The Technologizing of the Word* (New York: Routledge, 1982); idem, *The Presence of the Word: Some Prolegomena for Cultural and Religious History* (New Haven: Yale University Press, 1967); Marshall McLuhan, *The Gutenberg Galaxy: The Making of Typographic Man* (Toronto: University of Toronto Press, 1967); Michel de Certeau, *The Practice of Everyday Life* (Berkeley: University of California Press, 1984); Alain Corbin, *Village Bells: Sound and Meaning in the Nineteenth-Century French Countryside*, trans. Martin Thom (New York: Columbia University Press, 1998); Julian Jaynes, *The Origin of Consciousness in the Breakdown of the Bicameral Mind* (Boston: Houghton Mifflin, 1976).

5   Schmidt, *Hearing Things*, 30. Schmidt identifies in the eighteenth and nineteenth centuries a shift in the way God speaks, away from the more orderly "communal call" to an "immediate call" in Evangelical and especially Wesleyan piety.

6   Schmidt, *Hearing Things*, 54.

7   Schmidt, *Hearing Things*, 11.

8   James W. Carey, "A Cultural Approach to Communication," *Communication* 2, no. 2 (1975): 1–25; idem, *Communication as Culture: Essays on Media and Society* (Boston: Unwin Hyman, 1989).

9   Carey, *Communication as Culture*, 18–19.

10 Birgit Meyer and Jojada Verrips, "Aesthetics," in *Key Words in Religion, Media, and Culture*, ed. David Morgan (New York: Routledge, 2008), 27.

11 Meyer and Verrips, "Aesthetics," 27–28.

12 Jeremy Stolow, "Technology," in Morgan, *Key Words in Religion, Media, and Culture*, 189.

13 Dorothea E. Schulz, "Soundscape," in Morgan, *Key Words in Religion, Media, and Culture*, 178.

14 Pierre Bourdieu, *The Field of Cultural Production: Essays on Art and Literature* (New York: Columbia University Press, 1993), 76–77.

15 Walter Benjamin, "The Work of Art in the Age of Mechanical Reproduction," in *Illuminations*, ed. Hannah Arendt, trans. Harry Zohn (New York: Schocken, 1969).

16 Theodor W. Adorno, *The Culture Industry: Selected Essays on Mass Culture*, ed. J. M. Bernstein (New York: Routledge, 2001).

17 Kelton Cobb, *The Blackwell Guide to Theology and Popular Culture* (Malden, Mass.: Blackwell, 2005); Keith Negus, *Popular Music in Theory: An Introduction* (Middletown: Wesleyan University Press, 1996); Gordon

Lynch, *Understanding Theology and Popular Culture* (New York: Black-well, 2005); Stuart Borthwick and Ron Moy, *Popular Music Genres* (New York: Routledge, 2004); Simon Frith and Andrew Goodwin, eds., *On Record: Rock, Pop, and the Written Word* (New York: Routledge, 1990); Michael J. Gilmour, *Call Me Seeker: Listening to Religion in Popular Music* (New York: Continuum, 2005); Hanno Hardt, *Myths for the Masses* (London: Blackwell, 2004); Colin Larkin, ed., *The Encyclopedia of Popular Music*. 5th ed. (London: Muze UK, 2007); Diane Pecknold, *The Selling Sound: The Rise of the Country Music Industry* (Durham: Duke University Press, 2007); Thomas Turino, *Music as Social Self: The Politics of Participation* (Chicago: University of Chicago Press, 2008).

18 See R. Serge Denisoff and William L. Schurk, *Tarnished Gold: The Record Industry Revisited* (New Brunswick, N.J.: Transaction Publishers, 1997), 31.

19 Lynch, *Understanding Theology and Popular Culture*, 14.

20 Randal Johnson, introduction to Bourdieu, *Field of Cultural Production*, 5.

21 Pierre Bourdieu, *The Logic of Practice*, trans. Richard Nice (Stanford: Stanford University Press, 1990), 53.

22 John S. McClure, *The Four Codes of Preaching: Rhetorical Strategies* (Minneapolis: Fortress, 1991; repr., Louisville: Westminster John Knox, 2003).

23 Roland Barthes, "The Grain of the Voice," in *Image, Music, Text*, ed. Stephen Heath (New York: Hill & Wang, 1977), 179–89.

Chapter 1

1 For more on the bohemian tradition, see Hans Abbing, *Why Are Artists Poor? The Exceptional Economy of the Arts* (Amsterdam: Amsterdam University Press, 2002), 25–27. According to Frank Kermode, Victorian literary critic Walter Pater did much to promote this perspective. For Pater, the poet is marked by "sensibility," the "power of profoundly experiencing what is significant in life and art." According to Pater, the artist's "'whole nature' becomes one complex medium of reception; what he [*sic*] receives is the vision—the 'beatific vision,' if we care to make it such—of our actual experience in the world." This "demands an intense individuality, a cultivation of difference and indeed conflict with the world at large." Frank Kermode, *Romantic Image* (London: Routledge & Kegan Paul, 1957), 33.

2 Jeremy S. Begbie, *Resounding Truth: Christian Wisdom in the World of Music* (Grand Rapids, Mich.: Baker Academic, 2007), 245.

3 For more on Schleiermacher's musical aesthetic, see Abigail Chantler, *E. T. A. Hoffmann's Musical Aesthetics* (London: Ashgate, 2006), 1–32; for more on Schopenhauer's aesthetic, see Rüdiger Safranski and Ewald Osers, *Schopenhauer and the Wild Years of Philosophy* (Cambridge, Mass.: Harvard University Press, 1991); for Emerson's aesthetic see Sanja

Šoštarić, *Coleridge and Emerson: A Complex Affinity* (Boca Raton, Fla.: Universal, 2003).

4   Bourdieu, *The Field of Cultural Production*, 40.

5   Bill Friskics-Warren, *I'll Take You There: Pop Music and the Urge for Transcendence* (New York: Continuum, 2005).

6   See John S. McClure, "In Pursuit of Good Theological Judgment: Newman and the Preacher as Theologian," in *Loving God with Our Minds: The Pastor as Theologian*, ed. Michael Welker and Cynthia A. Jarvis (Grand Rapids, Mich.: Eerdmans, 2004), 202–19.

7   According to Gadamer, "The horizon is the range of vision that includes everything that can be seen from a particular vantage point." Hans-Georg Gadamer, *Truth and Method* (New York: Crossroads, 1975; 2nd rev. ed., New York: Continuum, 2004), xv.

8   Hans-Georg Gadamer, "Aesthetics and Hermeneutics," in *Philosophical Hermeneutics*, trans. and ed. David E. Linge (Berkeley: University of California Press, 1977), 96.

9   Ken Sharp, "Smokey Robinson: More Love," *Goldmine*, May 23, 2008, 43.

10 Sarah Chauncey, "Songwriters on Songwriting," *Canadian Musician* 20 (1998): 42.

11 Chris Smithers, "The King of California (Dave Alvin)," *Acoustic Guitar*, May 2007, 63.

12 Austin Scaggs, "Q & A: John Mellencamp," *Rolling Stone*, February 8, 2007, 28.

13 Richard Leiter, "Good News for Bad Lyric Writers: K. A. Parker Gives up the Secrets to Writing Great Lyrics," *Keyboard*, November 2001, 126.

14 Leiter, "Good News for Bad Lyric Writers," 126.

15 Paul Zollo, *Songwriters on Songwriting*, expanded 4th ed. (Cambridge, Mass.: Da Capo, 2003), 33.

16 Tom Russell and Sylvia Tyson, eds., *And Then I Wrote: The Songwriter Speaks* (Vancouver, Canada: Arsenal Pulp Press, 1995), 69.

17 Mark Simos, "The New Weird America: Songwriting In and Out of a Tradition," *Sing Out!* 46 (2002): 86.

18 Simos, "The New Weird America," 86.

19 Warren Hill, "Writing: Methods and Inspiration for Songwriting," *Canadian Musician* 22 (2000): 59.

20 Sharp, "Smokey Robinson," 44.

21 Russell and Tyson, *And Then I Wrote*, 164.

22 Sheff, David. "All We Are Saying: The Last Major Interview with John Lennon and Yoko Ono," *Playboy*, January 1981. http://www.john-lennon.com/playboyinterviewwithjohnlennononandyokoono.htm (accessed October 6, 2009).

23 Chauncey, "Songwriters on Songwriting," 47.

24 Tom Wilson, "We're Talking about Communication, We're Not Talking about Self-Indulgence, Part II," *Canadian Musician* 24 (2002): 58.

25 Russell and Tyson, *And Then I Wrote*, 161.

26 Zollo, *Songwriters on Songwriting*, 79.

27 Russell and Tyson, *And Then I Wrote*, 47.

28 Russell and Tyson, *And Then I Wrote*, 51.

29 Smithers, "The King of California," 61.

30 Smithers, "The King of California," 57.

31 Smithers, "The King of California," 77.

32 Russell and Tyson, *And Then I Wrote*, 56.

33 Zollo, *Songwriters on Songwriting*, 545–46; Russell and Tyson, *And Then I Wrote*, 45.

34 Russell and Tyson, *And Then I Wrote*, 133–34.

35 Russell and Tyson, *And Then I Wrote*, 48.

36 John Braheny, *The Craft and Business of Songwriting: A Practical Guide to Creating and Marketing Artistically and Commercially Successful Songs*, 3rd ed. (Cincinnati: Writer's Digest Books, 2006), 113.

37 In Vladimir Bogdanov, Chris Woodstra, and Stephen Thomas Erlewine, eds., *All Music Guide: The Definitive Guide to Popular Music* (Milwaukee: Hal Leonard, 2001), 818.

38 Steve Salzburg, "Carole King," in *Off the Record: Songwriters on Songwriting*, by Graham Nash (Kansas City, Mo.: Manuscript Originals, 2002), 137.

39 Russell and Tyson, *And Then I Wrote*, 59.

40 Russell and Tyson, *And Then I Wrote*, 59.

41 John H. Flavell and Patricia T. Botkin, *The Development of Role-Taking and Communication Skills in Children* (New York: John Wiley & Sons, 1968).

42 Kyle Swenson, "Sarah McLachlan: Tale of the Mastery Builder," *Keyboard* 23 (1997): 38.

43 Russell and Tyson, *And Then I Wrote*, 151.

44 Russell and Tyson, *And Then I Wrote*, 51.

45 Zollo, *Songwriters on Songwriting*, 118.

46 Russell and Tyson, *And Then I Wrote*, 59.

47 Kenneth Burke, *A Rhetoric of Motives* (Berkeley: University of California Press, 1969), 20–22.

48 Russell and Tyson, *And Then I Wrote*, 47.

49 Russell and Tyson, *And Then I Wrote*, 47.

50 Russell and Tyson, *And Then I Wrote*, 47.

51 Russell and Tyson, *And Then I Wrote*, 49.

52 Willie Nelson with Bud Shrake, *Willie: An Autobiography* (New York: Pocket Books, 1989), 175.

53 Leiter, "Good News for Bad Lyric Writers," 128.

54 Zollo, *Songwriters on Songwriting*, 273.

55 Russell and Tyson, *And Then I Wrote*, 50.

56 Russell and Tyson, *And Then I Wrote*, 176.

57 Russell Hall, "Mary Gauthier—the Philosophy of Songwriting and Starting Late," *Goldmine* 31, no. 16 (2005): 12.

58 Chauncey, "Songwriters on Songwriting," 43.

59 Zollo, *Songwriters on Songwriting*, 119.

60 Russell and Tyson, *And Then I Wrote*, 59.

61 Smithers, "The King of California," 59.

62 Jeffrey Pepper Rodgers, "Ring Some Changes," *Acoustic Guitar*, May 2006, 74.

63 In Chauncey, "Songwriters on Songwriting," 44–45.

64 Zollo, *Songwriters on Songwriting*, 22.

65 Russell and Tyson, *And Then I Wrote*, 137.

66 Russell and Tyson, *And Then I Wrote*, 54.

67 Russell and Tyson, *And Then I Wrote*, 137.

68 Russell and Tyson, *And Then I Wrote*, 138.

69 Daniel Johns, "Writing, Inspired by Disasters," *Canadian Musician* 25 (2003): 58.

70 Derek Richardson, "The Soul of the Song," *Acoustic Guitar*, December 2006, 55.

71 Adrianne Serna, "Letting It Rip: Patty Griffin," *Acoustic Guitar*, September 2007, 63.

72 Russell and Tyson, *And Then I Wrote*, 132.

73 Darrin Fox, "Paul Westerberg's Schizoid Craftiness," *Guitar Player*, March 2004, 20.

74 Zollo, *Songwriters on Songwriting*, 275.

75 Russell and Tyson, *And Then I Wrote*,108.

76 Tom Wilson, "We're Talking about Communication," 58.

77 Keith D. Miller and Elizabeth A. Vander Lei, "Collaboration, Collaborative Communities, and Black Folk Culture," in *The Right to Literacy*, eds. Andrea A. Lunsford, Helene Moglen, and James Slevin (New York: Modern Language Association of America, 1990), 55.

78 Gadamer argued that the crucial problem with Schleiermacher's, and later Hirsch's, view of "understanding" was that they accented the author's intentions to the exclusion of the historically situated nature of all understanding. See Gadamer, *Truth and Method* (New York: Continuum, 2004), 185–305.

Chapter 2

1 Current DAWs with sequencing features include Acid Pro, Cubase, Nuendo, Digital Performer, Ableton Live, Logic Pro, Logic Express, GarageBand, Pro Tools, Reason, Samplitude, Sonar, Tracktion, Storm, and Symphonia. Free open-source sequencers include Ardour, Frinika,

LMNS, MusE, Musescore, Musette, Qtractor, Rosegarden, SEQ24, and Hydrogen. Popular hardware sequencers include Akai MPC series, Alesis MNT-8, Roland MC-8 microcomposer, Roland MC-909, Yamaha PSR-3000, Roland Phantom X, and Yamaha QY-10.

2   From the *Pro Tools Reference Guide: Version 5.1 for Macintosh and Windows* (Palo Alto, Calif.: Digidesign, 2001), http://akarchive.digidesign.com/support/docs/PT_51_Reference_Guide.pdf (accessed September 8, 2009).

3   Benjamin, "The Work of Art," 228.

4   Lindsay Waters, "The Cameraman and Machine Are Now One: Walter Benjamin's Frankenstein," in *Mapping Benjamin: The Work of Art in the Digital Age*, eds. Hans Ulrich Gumbrecht and Michael Merrinan (Stanford: Stanford University Press, 2003), 134.

5   What follows is, in large part, a practical summary, revision, expansion, and application to the broader work of theological production of the ideas in my previous book *The Four Codes of Preaching*.

6   For more on this, see my book *The Four Codes of Preaching*.

7   Alfred North Whitehead, *The Aims of Education* (New York: Free Press, 1967), 12.

8   Craig Dykstra, "D. Min. Seminars and the Analysis of 'Style,'" ms., D. Min. Office, Louisville Presbyterian Theological Seminary.

9   See my essay "The Other Side of Sermon Illustration," *Journal for Preachers* 12 (Lent 1989): 2–4.

10 In spite of its age, and critiques suggesting epistemological biases, I will make use of H. Richard Niebuhr's categories for the relationship between Christ (in our case, religion) and culture to suggest styles of cultural tracking. I believe that these categories can be generalized to approximate the relationship between religion and culture within most theological composition. It should be remembered that I am treating religion as it is given over to rhetoric. I am fully cognizant of critiques of Niebuhr's categories by John Howard Yoder, Stanley Hauerwas, William Willimon, and others. While these are of some bearing in nuancing the "Christ/religion against culture" category below (separatist style) and avoiding the epistemic priority of the Christ transforming model, it is my belief that, in *practice*, separatist rhetoric, no matter how nuanced, continues to support a broadly countercultural model of religious experience. See H. Richard Niebuhr, *Christ and Culture* (San Francisco: HarperSanFrancisco, 1956); John Howard Yoder, "How H. Richard Niebuhr Reasoned: A Critique of *Christ and Culture*," in *Authentic Transformation: A New Vision of Christ and Culture*, ed. Glenn H. Stassen, D. M. Yeager, and John Howard Yoder (Nashville: Abingdon, 1996), 69ff.; Stanley Hauerwas, "The Democratic Policing of Christianity," *Pro Ecclesia* 3 (1994): 227–29; and idem, "Reinhold Niebuhr's Natural Theology," in *With the*

Grain of the Universe (Grand Rapids, Mich.: Brazos Press, 2001), 135–40. For a view more commensurate with my own on this issue, see John Gordon Stackhouse, *Making the Best of It: Following Christ in the Real World* (Oxford: Oxford University Press, 2008), 310ff.

11 W. Paul Jones, *Theological Worlds: Understanding the Alternative Rhythms of Christian Belief* (Nashville: Abingdon, 1989).

12 Lila J. Kalinich, "The Logos in Lacan," *St. Vladimir's Theological Quarterly* 32 (1988): 373.

13 See, for instance, Eugene Lowry, *The Homiletical Plot: The Sermon as Narrative Art Form* (Atlanta: John Knox, 1980).

14 Lowry, *The Homiletical Plot*, 28.

15 David Buttrick, *Homiletic: Moves and Structures* (Philadelphia: Fortress, 1987), 47.

16 See Robert Knudsen, "The Transcendental Perspective of Westminster's Apologetic," *Westminster Theological Journal* 48 (1986): 227–28.

Chapter 3

1 Eliot Wilder, *DJ Shadow's Endtroducing* (New York: Continuum, 2008), 18–24. See also the movie *Scratch* (2001), directed by Doug Pray, which chronicles the art of DJing and provides an excellent overview of its history, key influences, and methods, distinguishing DJing (the production of remixes from "breaks" and "beats") from MCing, (the overlaying of rap lyrics onto the DJ's remix).

2 Mikhail Bakhtin, *Problems of Dostoevsky's Poetics*, trans. and ed. Caryl Emerson (Minneapolis: University of Minnesota Press, 1984), 89. The word "intertextuality" was first introduced by Julia Kristeva in order to describe Bakhtin's dialogism, most notably in her essay translated as "Word, Dialogue and Novel," reprinted in Toril Moi, ed., *The Kristeva Reader* (London: Blackwell, 1986), 34–61.

3 Mikhail Bakhtin, *The Dialogic Imagination: Four Essays*, ed. Michael Holquist, trans. Caryl Emerson and Michael Holquist (Austin: University of Texas Press, 1981), 347.

4 Mary Minock, "Toward a Postmodern Pedagogy of Imitation," *Journal of Composition Theory* 15 (1995): 494; Bakhtin, *Problems*, 190.

5 Minock, "Toward a Postmodern Pedagogy," 495.

6 See James A. Berlin, "Poststructuralism, Cultural Studies, and the Composition Classroom: Postmodern Theory in Practice," *Rhetoric Review* 11 (1992); Ann E. Berthoff, "Learning the Uses of Chaos," in *Reinventing the Rhetorical Tradition*, eds. Aviva Freedman and Ian Pringle (Ontario: Canadian Council of Teachers, 1980), 75–78; John Shiga, "Copy-and-Persist: The Logic of Mash-up Culture," *Critical Studies in Media Communication* 24 (2007): 93–114; Jonathan David Tankel, "The Practice of Recording Music: Remixing as Recoding," *Journal of Communication* 40

(1990): 34–46; Rebecca Moore Howard, "Collaborative Pedagogy," in *A Guide to Composition Pedagogies*, eds. Gary Tate, Amy Rupiper, and Kurt Schick (Oxford: Oxford University Press, 2000), 54–70; Chris Leary, "When We Remix . . . We Remake!!! Reflections on Collaborative Ethnography, the New Digital Ethic, and Test Prep," *Journal of Basic Writing* 26, no. 1 (2007): 88–104; James E. Porter, "Intertextuality and the Discourse Community," *Rhetoric Review* 5 (1986): 34–47; Jeff Rice, "The 1963 Hip-Hop Machine: Hip-Hop Pedagogy as Composition," *College Composition and Communication* 54 (2003): 453–71.

7   For more on the idea of *chora*, see especially Gregory Ulmer, *Heuretics: The Logic of Invention* (Baltimore: The Johns Hopkins University Press, 1994), 61–78. According to Ulmer, quoting E. V. Walter, writers in the classical period "were inclined to call a sacred place a *chora* instead of a *topos*" (70). It is "a figure of spacing," not unlike Derrida's "differance" (73), and is the "'home of all created things'" (63), quoting Frank N. Magill, ed., *Masterpieces of World Philosophy* (New York: Harper & Row, 1961), 129.

8   See James L. Kinneavy and Catherine R. Eskin, "*Kairos* in Aristotle's Rhetoric," *Written Communication* 11 (1994): 131–42; Michael Carter, "*Stasis* and *Kairos*: Principles of Social Construction in Classical Rhetoric," *Rhetoric Review* 7 (1988): 97–112; Carolyn R. Miller, "*Kairos* in the Rhetoric of Science," in *A Rhetoric of Doing: Essays on Written Discourse in Honor of James Kinneavy*, eds. Stephen Witte, Neil Nakadate, and Roger Cherry (Carbondale: Southern Illinois University Press, 1992), 310–27.

9   According to linguist Ferdinand de Saussure, "signs function, then, not through their intrinsic value but through their relative position" within language. Ferdinand de Saussure, *Course in General Linguistics*, eds. Charles Bally and Albert Sechehaye, trans. W. Baskin (London: Peter Owen, 1974), 118.

10 Kinneavy and Eskin, "*Kairos* in Aristotle's Rhetoric," 141.

11 Miller, "*Kairos* in the Rhetoric of Science," 313.

12 Miller, "*Kairos* in the Rhetoric of Science," 313.

13 Bitzer quoted by Miller, "*Kairos* in the Rhetoric of Science," 313. See also Lloyd Bitzer, "The Rhetorical Situation," *Philosophy and Rhetoric* 1 (1968): 6.

14 Miller, "*Kairos* in the Rhetoric of Science," 313.

15 According to hooks, "the black poet . . . had many voices—with no single voice being identified as more or less authentic. The insistence on finding one voice, one definitive style of writing and reading one's poetry, fits all too neatly with a static notion of self and identity that was pervasive in university settings. It seemed that many black students found our situations problematic precisely because our sense of self, and by definition our voice, was not unilateral, monologist, or static but rather

multi-dimensional." bell hooks, *Talking Back* (Boston: South End Press, 1989), 11–12. In many ways this mirrors Bakhtin's "dialogism," in which selves emerge only through complex interactions with others—as sites of struggle, requiring one to engage the heteroglossia within language— "between languages and dialects, between hybridizations, purifications, shifts, and renovations." Bakhtin, *The Dialogic Imagination*, 66. According to Bakhtin, "only polyglossia fully frees consciousness from the tyranny of its own language and its own myth of language" (61). Similar to philosopher of language Valentin Volosinov, hooks advocates a shift away from univocal language use (*langue*), to intertextual, interactive, plurivocal, and co-inventive speech (*parole*). See V. N. Volosinov, *Marxism and the Philosophy of Language*, trans. Ladislav Matejka and J. R. Titunik (Cambridge, Mass.: Harvard University Press, 1929). Volosinov argued, against Ferdinand de Saussure, that "signs are social phenomena living on the boundaries between individuals; and they are meaningful only in the context of social relations among people." David McNally, *Bodies of Meaning: Studies on Language, Labor, and Liberation* (Albany: State University of New York Press, 2001), 112.

16 Paget Henry, *Caliban's Reason: Introducing Afro-Caribbean Philosophy* (New York: Routledge, 2000), 88. For a fascinating study of Paul's idea of reconciliation as "Creole consciousness," see Gilbert L. Bond, *Paul and the Religious Experience of Reconciliation: Diasporic Community and Creole Consciousness* (Louisville: Westminster John Knox, 2005). See also Charles Stewart, ed., *Creolization: History, Ethnography, Theory* (Walnut Creek, Calif.: Left Coast Press, 2007).

17 Minock, "Toward a Postmodern Pedagogy of Imitation," 493.

18 Minock, "Toward a Postmodern Pedagogy of Imitation," 499.

19 Françoise Deconinck-Brossard, "The Art of Preaching," in *Preaching, Sermon and Cultural Change in the Long Eighteenth Century*, ed. Joris van Eijnatten (London: Brill, 2009), 101.

20 Joseph Glanvill, *Essay Concerning Preaching: Written for the Direction of a Young Divine; and Useful Also for the People, in order to Profitable Hearing* (London, 1678), 67. Quoted in Deconinck-Brossard, "The Art of Preaching," 101.

21 Aleida Assmann and Jan Assmann, "Air from Other Planets Blowing: The Logic of Authenticity and the Prophet of the Aura," in Gumbrecht and Marrinan, *Mapping Benjamin*, 149.

22 Assmann and Assmann, "Air from Other Planets Blowing," 149.

23 Assmann and Assmann, "Air from Other Planets Blowing," 149–50.

24 Assmann and Assmann, "Air from Other Planets Blowing," 152.

25 Assmann and Assmann, "Air from Other Planets Blowing," 154.

26 Robert Hullot-Kentor, "What Is Mechanical Reproduction," in Gumbrecht and Marrinan, *Mapping Benjamin*, 161.

27 Barry Sandywell and David Beer, "Stylistic Morphing: Notes on the Digitisation of Contemporary Music Culture," *Convergence* 11, no. 4 (2005): 106.

28 Sandywell and Beer, "Stylistic Morphing," 110.

29 Sandywell and Beer, "Stylistic Morphing," 111.

30 Sandywell and Beer, "Stylistic Morphing," 111.

31 I am indebted to Ben Anthony for calling my attention to this wonderful film. *Scratch*, directed by Doug Pray (Palm Pictures, 2001).

32 Houston A. Baker Jr. "Hybridity, the Rap Race, and Pedagogy for the 1990s," *Black Music Research Journal* 11 (1991): 218.

33 Baker, "Hybridity," 218.

34 Baker, "Hybridity," 219.

35 Baker, "Hybridity," 220.

36 Baker, "Hybridity," 220.

37 Baker, "Hybridity," 221.

38 Baker, "Hybridity," 222. As the music became commercial, hip-hop musicians began to encounter copyright infringement issues over the use of sampled materials. This coincided with lawsuits regarding digital file sharing (Napster, Kazaa). See Dànielle Nicole DeVoss and James E. Porter, "Why Napster Matters to Writing: File-Sharing as a New Ethic of Digital Delivery," *Computers and Composition* 23, no. 2 (2006): 178–210.

39 Baker, "Hybridity," 226.

40 See Shiga, "Copy-and-Persist," 95.

41 Shiga, "Copy-and-Persist," 95.

42 Shiga, "Copy-and-Persist," 101.

43 Quoted in Leary, "When We Remix . . . We Remake!!!" 97.

44 Shiga, "Copy-and-Persist," 106.

45 John S. McClure, "Collaborative Preaching from the Margins," *Journal for Preachers* 22 (Pentecost 1996): 37–42.

46 Charles L. Campbell and Stanley P. Saunders, *The Word on the Street: Performing the Scriptures in the Urban Context* (Grand Rapids, Mich.: Eerdmans., 2000).

47 See John S. McClure and Nancy J. Ramsay, eds., *Telling the Truth: Preaching about Sexual and Domestic Violence* (Cleveland: United Church Press, 1998).

48 Carter, "*Stasis* and *Kairos*," 97–112.

49 Victor J. Vitanza, "From Heuristic to Aleatory Procedures: or Toward "'Writing the Accident,'" in *Inventing a Discipline: Rhetoric Scholarship in Honor of Richard E. Young*, ed. Maureen Daly Goggin (Urbana, Ill.: National Council of Teachers of English, 2000), 188.

50 Vitanza, "From Heuristic to Aleatory Procedures," 188.

51 Vitanza, "From Heuristic to Aleatory Procedures," 188.

52 Quoted in Ulmer, *Heuretics*, 47–48.

53 Ulmer, *Heuretics*, 48.

54 Jürgen Habermas, *The Theory of Communicative Action*, trans. Thomas McCarthy, 2 vols. (Boston: Beacon Press, 1984–87).

55 See Terrence W. Tilley, "Toward a Theology of the Practice of Communicative Action," in *Postmodern Theologies: The Challenge of Religious Diversity*, ed. Terrence W. Tilley (Maryknoll, N.Y.: Orbis Books, 1995), 5–16.

56 See, for instance, François Cooren, "Toward Another Ideal Speech Situation: A Critique of Habermas' Interpretation of Speech Act Theory," *Quarterly Journal of Speech* 86, no. 3 (2000): 295–317.

57 Habermas has responded with guarded optimism to queries about social networking as a potential key to the restoration of the public sphere. See Stuart Jeffries, "A Rare Interview with Jürgen Habermas," *Financial Times*, April 30, 2010, http://www.ft.com/cms/s/0/eda3bcd8-5327-11df-813e-00144feab49a.html.

58 Clive Thompson, "Live in the Moment: As a New Generation of Search Engines Mine the Signals of the Here and Now, Google Remains Stuck in the Past," *Wired*, October 2009, 46.

59 Vitanza, "From Heuristic to Aleatory Procedures," 197.

60 Ulmer, *Heuretics*, 36.

61 See Richard Kearney, *The God Who May Be: A Hermeneutics of Religion* (Bloomington: Indiana University Press, 2001).

62 Kearney, *The God Who May Be*, 37.

63 Kearney, *The God Who May Be*, 2.

64 Kearney, *The God Who May Be*, 1.

65 I have here in mind the social Trinitarianism of Jürgen Moltmann, which, as Veli-Matti Kärkkäinen puts it, "begins with three persons and works from that toward unity rather than vice versa." Veli-Matti Kärkkäinen, *The Trinity: Global Perspectives* (Louisville: Westminster John Knox, 2007), 110. See Jürgen Moltmann, *The Trinity and the Kingdom* (San Francisco: Harper & Row, 1981).

66 James E. Loder, *The Transforming Moment: Understanding Convictional Experiences* (San Francisco: Harper & Row, 1981), 115–16.

67 Loder, *The Transforming Moment*, 92.

68 Loder, *The Transforming Moment*, 92–121.

69 Loder, *The Transforming Moment*, 101.

70 Loder, *The Transforming Moment*, 102. Most profoundly, perhaps, in the Emmaus story, this is the moment of guest-host reversal, when, in the breaking of bread, Christ moves from being "guest" to being "host."

71 Loder, *The Transforming Moment*, 163.

72 See Benjamin Lee Whorf, "A Linguistic Consideration of Thinking in Primitive Communities," in *Language, Thought, and Reality: Selected Writings of Benjamin Lee Whorf*, ed. John B. Carroll (Cambridge, Mass.: MIT Press, 1973), 65–86.

73 See Saussure, *Course in General Linguistics*; Clifford Geertz, *The Inter-pretation of Cultures* (New York: Basic Books, 1973); J. L. Austin, *How to Do Things with Words*, eds. J. O. Urmson and Marina Sbisa (Cambridge, Mass.: Harvard University Press, 1975); Ludwig Wittgenstein, *Philo-sophical Investigations*, trans. G. E. M. Anscombe (New York: Macmillan, 1973).

74 See McClure, *The Four Codes of Preaching*.

75 Stanley Fish, *Is There a Text in This Class?* (Cambridge, Mass.: Harvard University Press, 1980); Robin Sylvan, *Traces of the Spirit: The Religious Dimensions of Popular Music* (New York: New York University Press, 2002).

76 Charles L. Campbell, *The Word before the Powers: An Ethic of Preaching* (Louisville: Westminster John Knox, 2002); Brian K. Blount, *Can I Get a Witness? Reading Revelation through African-American Culture* (Louis-ville: Westminster John Knox, 2005).

77 See William H. Willimon, *The Intrusive Word: Preaching to the Unbap-tized* (Grand Rapids, Mich.: Eerdmans, 1994); Stanley Hauerwas and William H. Willimon, *Resident Aliens: Life in the Christian Colony* (Nash-ville: Abingdon, 1989); Walter Brueggemann, *Cadences of Home: Preach-ing among Exiles* (Louisville: Westminster John Knox, 1997).

78 Thanks to Ted Smith for this way of shaping this idea.

79 See, for instance, Marla F. Frederick, *Between Sundays: Black Women and Everyday Struggles of Faith* (Berkeley: University of California Press, 2003); Mary McClintock Fulkerson, *Places of Redemption: Theology for a Worldly Church* (New York: Oxford University Press, 2007); Young Lee Hertig, *Cultural Tug of War: The Korean Immigrant Family and Church in Transition* (Nashville: Abingdon, 2002).

80 In *Other-Wise Preaching*, I attempted to take homileticans with me and follow Levinas on a journey through the semiotic realm, or what he calls "the said," toward the proxemic, pragmatic, and dialogic realm he calls "the saying." As I did so, I suggested that the cultural and linguistic practice of preaching, in our generation, was "exiting" itself, *in order to recover its deeper meaning and practice*. In part, what I hope to do now is to encourage preachers to re-enter the house of preaching (a house for me that now has no walls), but to do so precisely without the *dominance* of either language or culture controlling their assumptions and practices. John S. McClure, *Other-Wise Preaching: A Postmodern Ethic for Homiletics* (St. Louis: Chalice Press, 2001).

81 Some, such as Cheryl Bridges-Johns, would point us in this direction. See "Epiphanies of Fire: Paramodernist Preaching in a Postmodern World," paper delivered at the annual meeting of the Academy of Homiletics, Santa Fe, NM, December 1996.

82 Brian McLaren, *A Generous Orthodoxy* (Grand Rapids, Mich.: Zondervan, 2004). See also Dave Tomlinson, *The Post Evangelical* (Grand Rapids, Mich.: Zondervan, 2003); Pete Ward, *Liquid Church* (Peabody, Mass.: Hendrickson, 2002).

83 Many thanks again to Ted Smith for helping me articulate this felt tension in the work of post-evangelical emergents. See Ted Smith, *The New Measures: A Theological History of Democratic Practice* (New York: Cambridge University Press, 2007).

84 For the idea of "vintage Christianity," see Dan Kimball, *The Emerging Church: Vintage Christianity for New Generations* (Grand Rapids, Mich.: Zondervan, 2003).

85 Peter Collins, *How Not to Speak of God* (Brewster, Mass.: Paraclete Press, 2006), 3.

86 This final section reflects the fact that, at this point in time, I find myself happier with one of two very different options for thinking about language within human communication. One option is the almost apophatic form of ethical linguistics pursued by Emmanuel Levinas, for whom any substitution of word for thing always already stands under ethical erasure as potentially, if not actually, part of a linguistic totality. Another option is a straight pragmatist view of language, in which words are things in the world like anything else, a view in which the world and theological words codetermine one another. I now wonder whether both options could not function as mutually informing limit-conditions under the aegis of ethical and theological *desire.*

87 See, for instance, Thomas J. J. Altizer, *The Self-Embodiment of God* (New York: Harper & Row, 1977); idem, *The Gospel of Christian Atheism* (Philadelphia: Westminster, 1966); idem, *The New Apocalypse: The Radical Christian Vision of William Blake* (Lansing: Michigan State University Press, 1967); idem, *The Descent into Hell: A Study of the Radical Reversal of the Christian Consciousness* (New York: Seabury, 1979).

88 Rachel Muers, *Keeping God's Silence: Towards a Theological Ethics of Communication* (London: Blackwell, 2004), 119.

89 Muers, *Keeping God's Silence,* 121.

90 See Charles Winquist, *Epiphanies of Darkness: Deconstruction in Theology* (Philadelphia: Fortress, 1986), 11–12. See also Bernard Lonergan, *Insight: A Study of Human Understanding,* edited by Frederick E. Crowe and Robert M. Doran (Toronto: University of Toronto Press, 1957), 372–83.

Chapter 4

1 From the *Pro Tools Reference Guide: Version 5.1 for Macintosh and Windows* (Palo Alto, Calif.: Digidesign, 2001), http://akarchive .digidesign.com/support/docs/PT_51_Reference_Guide.pdf (accessed September 8, 2009).

2   David Buxton, "Rock Music, the Star System, and the Rise of Consumerism," in *On Record: Rock, Pop, and the Written Word*, eds. Simon Frith and Andrew Goodwin (New York: Routledge, 1990), 430.

3   See Mladen Dolar, *A Voice and Nothing More* (Cambridge, Mass.: MIT Press, 2006), 39–40.

4   Andra McCartney, "Soundscape Works, Listening, and the Touch of Sound," in *Aural Cultures*, ed. Jim Drobnick (Toronto: YYZ Books, 2004), 179. See also Kate Callahan, "Some Thoughts on Voice and Modes of Listening," http://www.sysx.org/soundsite/texts/02/VOICE. html (accessed September 29, 2009). Callahan points out that the famous soundscape musician John Cage noted that (for those with hearing) "as long as there is a bodied subject, there cannot be silence. An anechoic chamber still resonates with two sounds: of the nervous system and of the blood in circulation." See also Don Ihde, "Auditory Imagination," in, *The Auditory Culture Reader*, eds. Michael Bull and Les Back (Oxford: Berg, 2003), 61–66. Ihde argues that "unlike blindness, there is never a case of total deafness. . . . one listens with one's whole body. The folk music fan 'hears' the bass in his belly and through his feet, and the deaf child learns to 'hear' music through his hands and fingers" (66).

5   McCartney, "Soundscape Works," 179.

6   McCartney, "Soundscape Works," 179.

7   Dolar, *A Voice and Nothing More*, 163.

8   This, of course, has also led to concerns about eavesdropping and issues of surveillance and privacy.

9   Benjamin, "The Work of Art," 223.

10 Hans Ulrich Gumbrecht and Michael Marrinan, "Aura," in Gumbrecht and Marrinan, *Mapping Benjamin*, 85.

11 Barthes, "The Grain of the Voice," 182.

12 Barthes, "The Grain of the Voice," 182.

13 Barthes, "The Grain of the Voice," 182.

14 Barthes, "The Grain of the Voice," 185.

15 Barthes, "The Grain of the Voice," 183.

16 Roland Barthes, "Rasch," in *The Responsibility of Forms*, trans. Richard Howard (Berkeley: University of California Press, 1991), 312. Quoted in David Székely, "Gesture, Pulsion, Grain: Barthes' Musical Semiology," *Contemporary Aesthetics*, December 18, 2006, http://www.contempaesthetics .org/newvolume/pages/article.php?articleID=409 (accessed September 29, 2009).

17 Székely, "Gesture, Pulsion, Grain," 2.

18 Peter Antelyes, "Red Hot Mamas: Bessie Smith, Sophie Tucker, and the Ethnic Maternal Voice in American Popular Song," in *Embodied Voices: Representing Female Vocality in Western Culture*, eds. Leslie Dunn and Nancy Jones (Cambridge: Cambridge University Press, 1994), 217

19 Dolar, *A Voice and Nothing More*, 71.

20 Dolar, *A Voice and Nothing More*, 14.

21 Dolar, *A Voice and Nothing More*, 16.

22 Barthes, "The Grain of the Voice," 182.

23 Dolar, *A Voice and Nothing More*, 50.

24 George Steiner, *In Bluebeard's Castle: Some Notes towards the Redefinition of Culture* (New Haven: Yale University Press, 1974), 117.

25 Gernot Böhme, "Acoustic Atmospheres: A Contribution to the Study of Ecological Aesthetics," trans. Norbert Ruebsaat, *Soundscape: The Journal of Acoustic Ecology* 1 (2000): 14.

26 Böhme, "Acoustic Atmospheres," 16.

27 Böhme, "Acoustic Atmospheres," 16.

28 Böhme, "Acoustic Atmospheres," 18. This, of course, is often exploited by market forces. Playlists are created for shopping environments, with the idea of creating an atmosphere conducive to the consumption of certain products and attitudes. See, for instance, Charles S. Areni and David Kim, "The Influence of Background Music on Shopping Behavior: Classical vs. Top-Forty Music in a Wine Shop," *Advances in Consumer Research* 20 (1993): 336–40.

29 Gabor Csepregi, "On Sound Atmospheres," in Drobnick, *Aural Cultures*, 173.

30 Csepregi, "On Sound Atmospheres," 173.

31 Csepregi, "On Sound Atmospheres," 174.

32 Charles Hirschkind, *The Ethical Soundscape: Cassette Sermons and Islamic Counter-Publics* (New York: Columbia University Press, 2006), 11.

33 For the way in which the voices around us in the soundscape "mediate everyday life" see Katharine Conley, "Radio and the Mediation of the Everyday," in *Robert Desnos, Surrealism, and the Marvelous in Everyday Life* (Lincoln: University of Nebraska Press, 2004), 87–120.

34 Burton Z. Cooper and John S. McClure, *Claiming Theology in the Pulpit* (Louisville: Westminster John Knox, 2003), 2.

35 See Rene Chun, "Fleeing Cold Perfection for Lovable Lo-Fi Sound," *The New York Times*, January 8, 1993, 33.

36 See David H. C. Reid, "Organizing Material," in *Best Advice for Preaching*, ed. John S. McClure (Minneapolis: Fortress, 1998), 65–84.

Chapter 5

1 Antoine Hennion, "The Production of Success: An Antimusicology of the Pop Song," in Frith and Goodwin, *On Record*, 204.

2 Bourdieu, *The Field of Cultural Production*, 37.

3 See Erik Erikson, *Childhood and Society*, 2nd ed. (New York: W. W. Norton, 1963); Rolf E. Muuss, *Theories of Adolescence*, 3rd ed. (New York: Random House, 1975).

4 See Matt Hills, *Fan Cultures* (London: Routledge, 2002).

5 Matt Hills, "Fandom between Cult and Culture," in *Fan Cultures*, 117–30.

6 Steve Buhrman, "Finding God in Momo's Music Scene: Theological Conversation and the Prospect of Authentic, Transformative Community in Post-Christian Society," a paper presented toward the completion of the Master of Theology (M.Th.) degree, University of Oxford, Hilary, 2008, 4.

7 Buhrman, "Finding God," 5.

8 David Lyon, *Jesus in Disneyland: Religion in Postmodern Times* (Cambridge: Polity Press, 2000).

9 Lyon, *Jesus in Disneyland*.

10 Stewart M. Hoover, "Audiences," in Morgan, *Key Words in Religion, Media, and Culture*, 31–32 (emphasis in the original).

11 Hoover, "Audiences," 34.

12 Sylvan, *Traces of the Spirit*, 4, 220.

13 Buhrman, "Finding God," 6.

14 Hoover, "Audiences," 34.

15 Vincent J. Miller, *Consuming Religion: Christian Faith and Practice in a Consumer Culture* (New York: Continuum, 2004), 159–62.

16 Miller, *Consuming Religion*, 162, 176.

17 Lawrence Grossberg, "Is There a Fan in the House? The Affective Sensibility of Fandom," in *The Adoring Audience: Fan Culture and Popular Media*, ed. Lisa A. Lewis (New York: Routledge, 1992), 50–68.

18 Grossberg, "Is There a Fan in the House?" 56.

19 The name of this band is the Soundtrack of Our Lives. See also Joke Hermes, "Media Figures in Identity Construction," in *Rethinking the Media Audience: The New Agenda*, ed. Pertti Alasuutari (London: Sage, 1999), 69–85.

20 Grossberg, "Is There a Fan in the House?" 57.

21 Paul Tillich, *The Dynamics of Faith* (New York: Harper & Row, 1956), 1–4.

22 Roger C. Aden, *Popular Stories and Promised Lands: Fan Cultures and Symbolic Pilgrimages* (Tuscaloosa: University of Alabama Press, 1999).

23 Aden, *Popular Stories*, 79.

24 Aden, *Popular Stories*, 80.

25 Noted in Aden, *Popular Stories*, 86. See Leah R. Vande Berg, "Living Room Pilgrimages: Television's Cyclical Commemoration of the Assassination Anniversary of John F. Kennedy," *Communication Monographs* 62 (1995): 47–64.

26 See Aden, *Popular Stories*, 88–110.

27 Friskics-Warren, *I'll Take You There*, 9–14.

28 Friskics-Warren, *I'll Take You There*, 12.

29 For more about symbolic capital within cultures of legitimation, see Bourdieu, *The Field of Cultural Production*, 29–73.

30 See Hills, *Fan Cultures*, 56–57.

31 John Tulloch and Henry Jenkins, *Science Fiction Audiences: Watching "Dr. Who" and "Star Trek"* (London: Routledge, 1995), 149. Quoted in Hills, *Fan Cultures*, 57.

32 Andrew Goodwin, "Sample and Hold: Pop Music in the Digital Age of Reproduction," in Frith and Goodwin, *On Record*, 271.

33 Nick Couldry, "The Hidden Injuries of Media Power," *Journal of Consumer Culture* 1 (2001): 161.

34 Couldry, "The Hidden Injuries," 162. See Richard Sennett and Jonathan Cobb, *The Hidden Injuries of Class* (Cambridge: Cambridge University Press, 1972).

35 Couldry, "The Hidden Injuries," 161.

36 Mark Deuze, "Toward an Ethics of the Sociable Web: A Conversation between Trebor Scholz and Mark Deuze," http://mailman.thing.net/pipermail/idc/2007-July/002652.html (accessed September 30, 2009).

37 Sean Redmond points out that this is a very complex process indeed, creating even more "desire" for the celebrity. At the same time, famous participants on these sites are able to use these forms of media to cross back over into the "profane" world and demonstrate that they are ordinary. See Sean Redmond, "Intimate Fame Everywhere," in *Framing Celebrity: New Directions in Celebrity Culture*, eds. Sean Su Holmes and Sean Redmond (London: Routledge, 2006), 27–43. See also Jo Littler, "Making Fame Ordinary: Intimacy, Reflexivity, and 'Keeping It Real,'" *Mediactive* 2 (2004): 8–25.

38 Nicole S. Cohen, "The Valorization of Surveillance: Towards a Political Economy of Facebook," *Democratic Communiqué* 22 (2008): 9.

39 Deuze, "Toward an Ethics of the Sociable Web." Quoted in Cohen, "The Valorization of Surveillance," 9.

40 For more on the "consecration" of an author or work of art, see Bourdieu, *The Field of Cultural Production*, 40–44.

41 Cohen, "The Valorization of Surveillance," 7–8.

42 Cohen, "The Valorization of Surveillance," 8.

43 Ward, *Liquid Church*; Tom Beaudoin, *Virtual Faith: The Irreverent Spiritual Quest of Generation X* (Chichester: Jossey-Bass, 1998).

44 Ward, *Liquid Church*, 25–26, 27.

45 My research is largely based on auto-ethnographies and autobiographies conducted in classes such as those mentioned later in this chapter. It is clear from these exercises that religious bricoleurs look to the church and other resources of institutional religious education for depth, complexity, and steerage amid the many options available within popular culture.

46 This thesis parallels Vincent J. Miller's concern that religious bricoleurs' ability to construct anything meaningful from the stuff of culture

"depends on the complexity of the building blocks." Miller, *Consuming Religion*, 162.

47 Roger Silverstone, *Media and Morality: On the Rise of the Mediapolis* (Cambridge: Polity Press, 2006), 139–44.

48 Silverstone, *Media and Morality*, 142.

49 Silverstone, *Media and Morality*, 142–43.

50 Amos Yong, *Hospitality and the Other: Pentecost, Christian Practices, and the Neighbor* (Maryknoll, N.Y.: Orbis Press, 2008), 123–26. This is a significant departure from Derrida's unconditional or pure hospitality, in which one must even welcome the devil. For an important outline of this view, based on the eschatology of Irenaeus, see Hans Boersma, "Irenaeus, Derrida and Hospitality: On the Eschatological Overcoming of Violence," *Modern Theology* 19 (2003): 163–80.

51 Christine Pohl, *Making Room: Recovering Hospitality as a Christian Tradition* (Grand Rapids, Mich.: Eerdmans, 1999), 140. Quoted in Yong, *Hospitality and the Other*, 123.

52 Hans Boersma, *Violence, Hospitality and the Cross: Re-appropriating the Atonement Tradition* (Grand Rapids, Mich.: Baker Academic 2004), 35. Quoted in Yong, *Hospitality and the Other*, 124.

53 See Rodney S. Sadler Jr., "Can the Cushite Change His Skin? Cushites, 'Radical Othering' and the Hebrew Bible," *Interpretation* 60 (2006): 386–403.

54 Letty M. Russell, *Just Hospitality: God's Welcome in a World of Difference*, eds. J. Shannon Clarkson and Kate M. Ott (Louisville: Westminster John Knox, 2009), 101–24.

55 Bourdieu, *The Field of Cultural Production*, 37.

56 Bourdieu, *The Field of Cultural Production*, 38.

57 For more on conducting auto- or "self-" ethnography, see Hills, *Fan Cultures*, 65–89.

58 Allison Pingree is Director of the Center for Teaching at Vanderbilt University and affiliated faculty at Vanderbilt in American Studies and Women's and Gender Studies as well as Assistant Professor of Medical Education and Administration. She also worked with me as co-director, along with Greg Barz, of the Music, Religion, and the South research project noted in the preface.

Chapter 6

1 Friskics-Warren, *I'll Take You There*. For more on myth, see Peter R. Stillman, *Introduction to Myth*, 2nd ed. (Upper Montclair, N.J.: Boynton/Cook, 1985). For more on worldview, see Geertz, *The Interpretation of Culture*. For more on root metaphors, see George Lakoff and Mark Johnson, *Metaphors We Live By* (Chicago: University of Chicago Press, 1980). See also John Dominic Crossan, *The Dark Interval: Towards a Theology of*

Story (Sonoma, Calif.: Eagle Books, 1988) and James F. Hopewell, *Congregation: Stories and Structures* (Philadelphia: Fortress, 1987).

2   See especially chap. 4, "Theological Tools," in Cobb, *The Blackwell Guide*, 101–32.

3   See Tillich, *The Dynamics of Faith*.

4   Cobb, *The Blackwell Guide*, 103.

5   Rudolf Otto, *The Idea of the Holy: An Inquiry into the Non-rational Factor in the Divine*, trans. John W. Harvey (Whitefish, Mont.: Kessinger, 2004), 8–40.

6   Tillich, *The Dynamics of Faith*, 55–73.

7   Cobb, *The Blackwell Guide*, 109.

8   Cobb, *The Blackwell Guide*, 214.

9   Belmont Mall Publishing, and EMI Full Keel Music, publishers, respectively.

10   Sony/ATV Tunes LLC OBO Belmont Mall Publishing, publishers.

11   Sony/ATV Tunes LLC OBO Belmont Mall Publishing, publishers.

12   Belmont Mall Publishing/EMI publishers.

13   Cowritten with Scotty Emerick, Sony/ATV Tree publishers.

14   "Toby Keith Hits Back at Accusation Song Is Pro-Lynching," August 8, 2009, http://www.foxnews.com/story/0,2933,400084,00.html (accessed August 31, 2009).

15   See Keith's CD by that title, released on Show Dog Nashville, April 2006.

16   See Max Blumenthal, "Lynching Advocate Toby Keith: Obama 'Talks, Acts, and Carries Himself as a Caucasian,'" *Huffington Post*, August 5, 2008, http://www.huffingtonpost.com/max-blumenthal/lynching-advocate -toby-ke_b_116995.html (accessed September 12, 2009); Evan Agostini, "Toby Keith in Middle of 'Lynching' Debate," August 7, 2008, http://blogs.usatoday.com/entertainment/office_gossip/ (accessed September 12, 2009).

17   Tokeco Tunes Publishing.

18   Cobb, *The Blackwell Guide*, 215.

19   Perry Miller, *The American Puritans: Their Prose and Poetry* (New York: Doubleday Anchor Books, 1956), 144. Quoted in Cobb, *The Blackwell Guide*, 215.

20   James A. Morone, *Hellfire Nation: The Politics of Sin in American History* (New Haven: Yale University Press, 2003), 45. Quoted in Cobb, *The Blackwell Guide*, 216.

21   Cobb, *The Blackwell Guide*, 216.

22   Cobb, *The Blackwell Guide*, 217.

23   Walter Brueggemann, "Voices of the Night—Against Injustice," in *To Act Justly, Love Tenderly, Walk Humbly: An Agenda for Ministers*, eds. Walter

Brueggeman, Sharon Parks, and Thomas Groome (New York: Paulist Press, 1986), 5.

24 Paul Tillich, *Systematic Theology*, vol. 1 (Chicago: University of Chicago Press, 1967), 13.

25 Walter Wink, "The Myth of Redemptive Violence: Exposing the Roots of 'Might Makes Right,'" *Sojourners* 21 (1992): 18–21, 35.

26 Friskics-Warren, *I'll Take You There*, 151.

27 Friskics-Warren, *I'll Take You There*, 151.

28 Written by Guy Clark and Ray Stephenson, EMI April Music Inc., publishers.

29 House of Cash, publishers.

30 Edward B. Marks Music Co., publishers.

31 Song of Cash Inc., publishers.

32 See Cobb, *The Blackwell Guide*, 183, for more on the significance of Robin Hood and Zorro in American popular culture.

33 See John Cobb, *Process Theology: An Introductory Exposition* (Philadelphia: Westminster John Knox, 1976); Marjorie Suchocki, *God, Christ, Church*, new rev. ed. (New York: Crossroads, 1989).

34 Suchocki, *God, Christ, Church*, 119.

35 Suchocki, *God, Christ, Church*, 27.

36 Cobb, *The Blackwell Guide*, 84.

37 Friskic-Warren, *I'll Take You There*, 63.

38 Written by Madonna Ciccione and Patrick R. Leonard, © Warner Bros. Music Corp.

39 Warner Bros. Music Corp., publishers.

40 Warner Bros. Music Corp., publishers.

41 Warner Bros. Music Corp., publishers.

42 Screen Gems/EMI Music Inc., publishers.

43 Emmanuel Levinas, *Otherwise than Being*, trans. Alphonso Lingis (The Hague: Martinus Nijhoff, 1981), 144.

44 Bughouse Music, Inc., publishers.

45 Bughouse Music, Inc., publishers.

46 Bughouse Music, Inc., publishers.

47 See Wendy Farley, *Tragic Vision and Divine Compassion: A Contemporary Theodicy* (Louisville: Westminster John Knox, 1990). See also idem, "Evil, Violence, and the Practice of Theodicy," in McClure and Ramsay, *Telling the Truth*, 11–20.

48 Written by Brandon Heath and David Jason Ingram, Sitka 6 Music, publishers.

49 John Calvin, *Institutes of the Christian Religion*, ed. John T. McNeill (Louisville: Westminster John Knox, 1960).

50 Julian of Norwich, *Showings*, trans. Edmund Colledge and James Walsh (New York: Paulist Press, 1978).

51 Cobb, *The Blackwell Guide*, 225.

52 Cobb, *The Blackwell Guide*, 226.

53 In David Perkins, "Hell Yeah! Pairing Southern Religion and Punk/Postmodern Aesthetics in the Construction of Southern Gothic Music," paper presented at the Forum on Music and Christian Scholarship, Yale University, March 9, 2007, 4.

54 The Legendary Shack Shakers, "Swampblood," http://vids.myspace.com/index.cfm?fuseaction=vids.individual&videoid=19101774&searchid=764cb745-1d2f-4bcf-9796-a05639b06365 (accessed October 5, 2009).

55 The Legendary Shack Shakers, dwarf footage, http://www.youtube.com/watch?v=mkv7CW6USNg&feature=youtube_gdata (accessed October 5, 2009).

56 Perkins, "Hell Yeah!" 4–11.

57 From a revision of Perkins' lecture, "Hell Yeah!" presented to the Popular Music and Religious Identity class at Vanderbilt Divinity School on September 16, 2008.

58 Perkins, "Hell Yeah!" Yale version, 10.

59 Perkins, "Hell Yeah!" Yale version, 11.

60 Bug Music, Inc., publishers.

61 Bug Music, Inc., publishers.

62 Cobb, *The Blackwell Guide*, 226.

63 The Legendary Shack Shakers, "Swampblood."

64 ICG Alliance Music, publishers.

65 Friskics-Warren, *I'll Take You There*, 119.

66 Friskics-Warren, *I'll Take You There*, 134.

67 Friskics-Warren, *I'll Take You There*, 136.

68 Cobb, *The Blackwell Guide*, 221.

69 See Dietrich Bonhoeffer, *Letters and Papers from Prison*, new greatly enlarged ed. (New York: Touchstone, 1997); Thomas J. J. Altizer and William Hamilton, *Radical Theology and the Death of God* (New York: Bobbs-Merrill, 1966); Winquist, *Epiphanies of Darkness*; Gianni Vattimo, *After Christianity*, trans. Luca D'Isanto (New York: Columbia University Press, 2002).

70 See Jacques Derrida, *Of Grammatology*, trans. Gayatri Chakravorty Spivak, (Baltimore: The Johns Hopkins University Press, 1974); Jean Baudrillard, *Simulacra and Simulation*, trans. Sheila Faria Glaser (Ann Arbor: University of Michigan Press, 1994).

71 See in particular James K. A. Smith, *Who's Afraid of Postmodernism? Taking Derrida, Lyotard, and Foucault to Church* (Grand Rapids, Mich.: Baker Academic, 2006).

72 Erich Neumann, *The Origins and History of Consciousness*, trans. R. F. C. Hull (Princeton: Princeton University Press, 1995), 190.

73 Cobb, *The Blackwell Guide*, 259. See Richard Mouw, *Consulting the Faithful: What Christian Intellectuals Can Learn from Popular Religion* (Grand Rapids, Mich.: Eerdmans, 1994); Farley, *Tragic Vision and Divine Compassion*; Marie Fortune, *Love Does No Harm: Sexual Ethics for the Rest of Us* (New York: Continuum, 2006).

74 Paul Tillich, *The Courage to Be* (New Haven: Yale University Press, 1952).

75 Gleaning Publishing/EMI, publishers.

76 Worshiptogether.com Songs/EMI, publishers.

77 Worshiptogether.com Songs/EMI, publishers.

78 Maranatha Praise, Inc., publishers.

79 Suchocki, *God, Christ, Church*, 114–17.

BIBLIOGRAPHY

Abbing, Hans. *Why Are Artists Poor? The Exceptional Economy of the Arts*. Amsterdam: Amsterdam University Press, 2002.

Aden, Roger C. *Popular Stories and Promised Lands: Fan Cultures and Symbolic Pilgrimages*. Tuscaloosa: University of Alabama Press, 1999.

Adorno, Theodor W. *The Culture Industry: Selected Essays on Mass Culture*. Edited by J. M. Bernstein. New York: Routledge, 2001.

Agostini, Evan. "Toby Keith in Middle of 'Lynching' Debate." August 7, 2008. http://blogs.usatoday.com/entertainment/office_gossip/. Accessed September 12, 2009.

Allen, Ronald J. *Hearing the Sermon: Relationship, Content, Feeling*. St. Louis: Chalice Press, 2004.

———. *Interpreting the Gospel: An Introduction to Preaching*. St. Louis: Chalic Press, 1998.

———. "The Turn Toward the Listener: A Selective Review of a Recent Trend in Preaching." *Encounter* 64 (2003): 165–94.

Allen, Ronald J., and Mary Alice Mulligan. *Make the Word Come Alive: Lessons from Laity*. St. Louis: Chalice Press, 2005.

———. "Listening to Listeners: Five Years Later." *Homiletic* 34 (2009).

Altizer, Thomis J. J. *The Descent into Hell: A Study of the Radical Reversal of the Christian Consciousness*. New York: Seabury, 1979.

———. *The Gospel of Christian Atheism*. Philadelphia: Westminster, 1966.

———. *The New Apocalypse: The Radical Christian Vision of William Blake.* Lansing: Michigan State University Press, 1967.

———. *The Self-Embodiment of God.* New York: Harper & Row, 1977.

Altizer, Thomas J. J., and William Hamilton. *Radical Theology and the Death of God.* New York: Bobbs-Merrill, 1966.

Antelyes, Peter. "Red Hot Mamas: Bessie Smith, Sophie Tucker, and the Ethnic Maternal Voice in American Popular Song." In *Embodied Voices: Representing Female Vocality in Western Culture*, edited by Leslie Dunn and Nancy Jones, 212–29. Cambridge: Cambridge University Press, 1994.

Areni, Charles S., and David Kim. "The Influence of Background Music on Shopping Behavior: Classical vs. Top-Forty Music in a Wine Shop." *Advances in Consumer Research* 20 (1993): 336–40.

Assmann, Aleida, and Jan Assmann. "Air from Other Planets Blowing: The Logic of Authenticity and the Prophet of the Aura." In *Mapping Benjamin: The Work of Art in the Digital Age*, edited by Hans Ulrich Gumbrecht and Michael Marrinan, 147–57. Stanford: Stanford University Press, 2003.

Austin, J. L. *How to Do Things with Words.* Edited by J. O. Urmson and Marina Sbisa. Cambridge, Mass.: Harvard University Press, 1975.

Baker, Houston A., Jr. "Hybridity, the Rap Race, and Pedagogy for the 1990s." *Black Music Research Journal* 11 (1991): 217–28.

Bakhtin, Mikhail. *The Dialogic Imagination: Four Essays.* Edited by Michael Holquist. Translated by Caryl Emerson and Michael Holquist. Austin: University of Texas Press, 1981.

———. *Problems of Dostoevsky's Poetics.* Translated and edited by Caryl Emerson. Minneapolis: University of Minnesota Press, 1984.

Barthes, Roland. "The Grain of the Voice." In *Image, Music, Text*, edited by Stephen Heath, 179–89. New York: Hill & Wang, 1977.

———. "Rasch." In *The Responsibility of Forms*, translated by Richard Howard, 299–312. Berkeley: University of California Press, 1991.

Baudrillard, Jean. *Simulacra and Simulation.* Translated by Sheila Faria Glaser. Ann Arbor: University of Michigan Press, 1994.

Bauman, Zygmunt. *Liquid Modernity.* Cambridge: Polity Press, 2005.

Bawarshi, Anis. *Genre and the Invention of the Writer: Reconsidering the Place of Invention in Composition.* Logan: Utah State University Press, 2003.

Beaudoin, Tom. *Virtual Faith: The Irreverent Spiritual Quest of Generation X.* Chichester: Jossey-Bass, 1998.

———. *Witness to Dispossession: The Vocation of a Post-modern Theologian.* Maryknoll, N.Y.: Orbis Press, 2008.

Begbie, Jeremy S. *Resounding Truth: Christian Wisdom in the World of Music*. Grand Rapids, Mich.: Baker Academic, 2007.

Benjamin, Walter. "The Work of Art in the Age of Mechanical Reproduction." In *Illuminations*, edited by Hannah Arendt, translated by Harry Zohn, 219–53. New York: Schocken, 1969.

Berlin, James A. "Poststructuralism, Cultural Studies, and the Composition Classroom: Postmodern Theory in Practice." *Rhetoric Review* 11 (1992): 16–33.

Berthoff, Ann E. "Learning the Uses of Chaos." In *Reinventing the Rhetorical Tradition*, edited by Aviva Freedman and Ian Pringle, 75–78. Ontario: Canadian Council of Teachers, 1980.

Birchall, Clare. *Knowledge Goes Pop: From Conspiracy Theory to Gossip*. Oxford: Berg, 2006.

Bitzer, Lloyd. "The Rhetorical Situation." *Philosophy and Rhetoric* 1 (1968): 1–14.

Blount, Brian K. *Can I Get a Witness? Reading Revelation through African-American Culture*. Louisville: Westminster John Knox, 2005.

Blumenthal, Max. "Lynching Advocate Toby Keith: Obama 'Talks, Acts, and Carries Himself as a Caucasian.'" *Huffington Post*, August 5, 2008. http://www.huffingtonpost.com/max-blumenthal/lynching-advocate-toby-ke_b_116995.html. Accessed September 12, 2009.

Boersma, Hans. "Irenaeus, Derrida, and Hospitality: On the Eschatological Overcoming of Violence." *Modern Theology* 19 (2003): 163–80.

———. *Violence, Hospitality, and the Cross: Re-appropriating the Atonement Tradition*. Grand Rapids, Mich.: Baker Academic 2004.

Bogdanov, Vladimir, Chris Woodstra, and Stephen Thomas Erlewine, eds. *All Music Guide: The Definitive Guide to Popular Music*. Milwaukee: Hal Leonard, 2001.

Bohlman, Philip V., Edith L. Blumhofer, and Maria M. Chow, eds. *Music in American Religious Experience*. New York: Oxford University Press, 2006.

Böhme, Gernot. "Acoustic Atmospheres: A Contribution to the Study of Ecological Aesthetics." Translated by Norbert Ruebsaat. *Soundscape: The Journal of Acoustic Ecology* 1 (2000): 14–18.

Bond, Gilbert L. *Paul and the Religious Experience of Reconciliation: Diasporic Community and Creole Consciousness*. Louisville: Westminster John Knox, 2005.

Bonhoeffer, Dietrich. *Letters and Papers from Prison*. New greatly enlarged ed. New York: Touchstone, 1997.

Borthwick, Stuart, and Ron Moy. *Popular Music Genres*. New York: Routledge, 2004.

Bourdieu, Pierre. *The Field of Cultural Production: Essays on Art and LIterature*. Edited by Randal Johnson. New York: Columbia University Press, 1993.

———. *The Logic of Practice*. Translated by Richard Nice. Stanford: Stanford University Press, 1990.

Boyle, David. *Authenticy: Brands, Fakes, Spin, and the Lust for Real Life*. New York: HarperCollins, 2004.

Bozarth-Campbell, Alla. *The Word's Body: An Incarnational Aesthetic of Interpretation*. Tuscaloosa: University of Alabama Press, 1979.

Braheny, John. *The Craft and Business of Songwriting: A Practical Guide to Creating and Marketing Artistically and Commercially Successful Songs*. 3rd ed. Cincinnati: Writer's Digest Books, 2006.

Bridges-Johns, Cheryl. "Epiphanies of Fire: Paramodernist Preaching in a Postmodern World." Paper delivered at the annual meeting of the Academy of Homiletics, Santa Fe, NM, December 1996.

Brueggemann, Walter. *Cadences of Home: Preaching among Exiles*. Louisville: Westminster John Knox, 1997.

———. *Finally Comes the Poet: Daring Speech for Proclamation*. Minneapolis: Augsburg Fortress, 1989.

———. "Voices of the Night—Against Injustice." In *To Act Justly, Love Tenderly, Walk Humbly: An Agenda for Ministers*, edited by Walter Brueggeman, Sharon Parks, and Thomas Groome, 5–28. New York: Paulist Press, 1986.

Burhman, Steve. "Finding God in Momo's Music Scene: Theological Conversation and the Prospect of Authentic, Transformative Community in Post-Christian Society." Paper presented toward the completion of the Master of Theology degree (M.Th.), University of Oxford, Hilary, 2008.

Burke, Kenneth. *A Rhetoric of Motives*. Berkeley: University of California Press, 1969.

Buttrick, David. *Homiletic: Moves and Structures*. Philadelphia: Fortress, 1987.

Buxton, David. "Rock Music, the Star System, and the Rise of Consumerism." In *On Record: Rock, Pop, and the Written Word*, edited by Simon Frith and Andrew Goodwin, 427–40. New York: Routledge, 1990.

Callahan, Kate. "Some Thoughts on Voice and Modes of Listening." http://www.sysx.org/soundsite/texts/02/VOICE.html. Accessed September 29, 2009.

Calvin, John. *Institutes of the Christian Religion*. Edited by John T. McNeill. Louisville: Westminster John Knox, 1960.

Campbell, Charles L. *Preaching Jesus: New Directions for Homiletics in Hans Frei's Postliberal Theology*. Grand Rapids, Mich.: Eerdmans, 1997.

———. "Principalities, Powers, and Fools: Does Preaching Make an Ethical Difference." *Homiletic* 33 (2008): 1–10.

———. *The Word before the Powers: An Ethic of Preaching*. Louisville: Westminster John Knox, 2002.

Campbell, Charles L., and Stanley P. Saunders. *The Word on the Street: Performing the Scriptures in the Urban Context*. Grand Rapids, Mich.: Eerdmans, 2000.

Carey, James W. "A Cultural Approach to Communication." *Communication* 2, no. 2 (1975): 1–25.

———. *Communication as Culture: Essays on Media and Society*. Boston: Unwin Hyman, 1989.

Carter, Michael. "*Stasis* and *Kairos*: Principles of Social Construction in Classical Rhetoric." *Rhetoric Review* 7 (1988): 97–112.

Certeau, Michel de. *The Practice of Everyday Life*. Berkeley: University of California Press, 1984.

Chantler, Abigail. *E. T. A. Hoffmann's Musical Aesthetics*. London: Ashgate, 2006.

Chauncey, Sarah. "Songwriters on Songwriting." *Canadian Musician* 20 (1998): 42–48.

Chun, Rene. "Fleeing Cold Perfection for Lovable Lo-Fi Sound." *The New York Times*, January 8, 1993, 33.

Cobb, John. *Process Theology: An Introductory Exposition*. Philadelphia: Westminster John Knox, 1976.

Cobb, Kelton. *The Blackwell Guide to Theology and Popular Culture*. Malden, Mass.: Blackwell, 2005.

Cohen, Nicole S. "The Valorization of Surveillance: Towards a Political Economy of Facebook." *Democratic Communiqué* 22 (2008): 5–22.

Collins, Peter. *How Not to Speak of God*. Brewster, Mass.: Paraclete Press, 2006.

Conley, Katharine. "Radio and the Mediation of the Everyday." In *Robert Desnos, Surrealism, and the Marvelous in Everyday Life*, 87–120. Lincoln: University of Nebraska Press, 2004.

Connor, Steven. *Postmodernist Culture: An Introduction to Theories of the Contemporary*. 2nd ed. London: Blackwell, 1997.

Cooper, Burton Z., and John S. McClure. *Claiming Theology in the Pulpit*. Louisville: Westminster John Knox, 2003.

Cooren, François. "Toward Another Ideal Speech Situation: A Critique of Habermas' Interpretation of Speech Act Theory." *Quarterly Journal of Speech* 86, no. 3 (2000): 295–317.

Corbin, Alain. *Village Bells: Sound and Meaning in the Nineteenth-Century French Countryside.* Translated by Martin Thom. New York: Columbia University Press, 1998.

Cornell, Drucilla. *Moral Images of Freedom: A Future for Critical Theory.* New York: Rowman & Littlefield, 2008.

Couldry, Nick. "The Hidden Injuries of Media Power." *Journal of Consumer Culture* 1 (2001): 155–77.

Cox, Christoph and Daniel Warner, eds. *Audio Culture: Readings in Modern Music.* New York: Continuum, 2008.

Crossan, John Dominic. *The Dark Interval: Towards a Theology of Story.* Sonoma, Calif.: Eagle Books, 1988.

Crowther, Paul. *Critical Aesthetics and Postmodernism.* Oxford: Clarendon, 1993.

Csepregi, Gabor. "On Sound Atmospheres." In *Aural Cultures*, edited by Jim Drobnick, 169–78. Toronto: YYZ Books, 2004.

Davis, Gerald L. *I Got the Word in Me and I Can Sing It, You Know: A Study of the Performed African-American Sermon.* Philadelphia: University of Pennsylvania Press, 1985.

Deconinck-Brossard, Françoise. "The Art of Preaching." In *Preaching, Sermon and Cultural Change in the Long Eighteenth Century*, edited by Joris van Eijnatten, 95–109. London: Brill, 2009.

Denisoff, R. Serge, and William L. Schurk. *Tarnished Gold: The Record Industry Revisited.* New Brunswick, N.J.: Transaction Publishers, 1997.

DeNora, Tia. *Music in Everyday Life.* New York: Cambridge University Press, 2000.

Derrida, Jacques. *Of Grammatology.* Translated by Gayatri Chakravorty Spivak. Baltimore: The Johns Hopkins University Press, 1974.

Deuze, Mark. "Toward an Ethics of the Sociable Web: A Conversation between Trebor Scholz and Mark Deuze." http://mailman.thing.net/pipermail/idc/2007-July/002652.html. Accessed September 30, 2009.

DeVoss, Dànielle Nicole, and James E. Porter. "Why Napster Matters to Writing: File-Sharing as a New Ethic of Digital Delivery." *Computers and Composition* 23, no. 2 (2006): 178–210.

Dimitriadis, Greg. *Performing Identity/Performing Culture: Hip Hop as Text, Pedagogy, and Lived Practice.* New York: Peter Lang, 2008.

Dolar, Mladen. *A Voice and Nothing More.* Cambridge, Mass.: MIT Press, 2006.

Dunsby, Jonathan. "Roland Barthes and the Grain of Panzéra's Voice." *Journal of the Royal Musical Association* 134, no. 1 (2009): 113–32.

Dykstra, Craig. "D. Min. Seminars and the Analysis of 'Style.'" Ms., D. Min. Office, Louisville Presbyterian Theological Seminary.

Eliot, T. S. "The Metaphysical Poets," *Times Literary Supplement* 20, October 1921.

Erikson, Erik. *Childhood and Society*. 2nd ed. New York: W. W. Norton, 1963.

Farley, Edward. *Good and Evil: Interpreting a Human Condition*. Minneapolis: Fortress, 1990.

Farley, Wendy. *Eros for the Other: Retaining Truth in a Pluralistic World*. University Park: Pennsylvania State University Press, 1996.

———. "Evil, Violence, and the Practice of Theodicy." In *Telling the Truth: Preaching about Sexual and Domestic Violence*, edited by John S. McClure and Nancy J. Ramsay, 11–20. Cleveland: United Church Press, 1998.

———. *Tragic Vision and Divine Compassion: A Contemporary Theodicy*. Louisville: Westminster John Knox, 1990.

———. *The Wounding and Healing of Desire*. Louisville, Westminster John Knox, 2005.

Fish, Stanley. *Is There a Text in This Class?* Cambridge, Mass.: Harvard University Press, 1980.

Flavell, John A., and Patricia T. Botkin. *The Development of Role-Taking and Communication Skills in Children*. New York: John Wiley & Sons, 1968.

Florence, Anna Carter. *Preaching as Testimony*. Louisville: Westminster John Knox, 2007.

Fortune, Marie. *Love Does No Harm: Sexual Ethics for the Rest of Us*. New York: Continuum, 2006.

Foster, Hal, ed. *Postmodern Culture*. London: Pluto Press, 1985.

Fox, Darrin. "Paul Westerberg's Schizoid Craftiness." *Guitar Player*, March 2004, 20.

Frank, Thomas. *The Conquest of Cool: Business Culture, Counterculture, and the Rise of Hip Consumerism*. Chicago: University of Chicago Press, 1997.

Frederick, Marla F. *Between Sundays: Black Women and Everyday Struggles of Faith*. Berkeley: University of California Press, 2003.

Frisby, David, and Mike Featherstone, eds. *Simmel on Culture*. London: Sage, 2000.

Friskics-Warren, Bill. *I'll Take You There: Pop Music and the Urge for Transcendence*. New York: Continuum, 2005.

Frith, Simon, and Andrew Goodwin, eds. *On Record: Rock, Pop, and the Written Word.* New York: Routledge, 1990.

Fulkerson, Mary McClintock. *Places of Redemption: Theology for a Worldly Church.* New York: Oxford University Press, 2007.

Gadamer, Hans-Georg. "Aesthetics and Hermeneutics." In *Philosophical Hermeneutics,* translated and edited by David E. Linge, 95–104. Berkeley: University of California Press, 1977.

———. *Philosophical Hermeneutics.* Translated and edited by David E. Linge. Berkeley: University of California Press, 1977.

———. *Truth and Method.* New York: Continuum, 2004.

Geertz, Clifford. *The Interpretation of Culture.* New York: Basic Books, 1973.

Gelbart, Matthew. *The Invention of "Folk Music" and "Art Music": Emerging Categories from Ossian to Wagner.* New Perspectives in Music History and Criticism 16. Cambridge: Cambridge University Press, 2007.

Gilmour, Michael J. *Call Me Seeker: Listening to Religion in Popular Music.* New York: Continuum, 2005.

Glanvill, Joseph. *Essay Concerning Preaching: Written for the Direction of a Young Divine; and Useful Also for the People, in order to Profitable Hearing.* London, 1678.

Godowa, Brian. *Hollywood Worldviews: Watching Films with Wisdom and Discernment.* Downers Grove, Ill.: InterVarsity, 2002.

Goodwin, Andrew. "Sample and Hold: Pop Music in the Digital Age of Reproduction." In *On Record: Rock, Pop and the Written Word,* edited by Simon Frith and Andrew Goodwin, 258–74. London: Routledge, 1990.

Gray, Jonathan, Cornel Sandvoss, and C. Lee Harrington, eds. *Fandom: Identities and Communities in a Mediated World.* New York: New York University Press, 2007.

Grossberg, Lawrence. "Is There a Fan in the House? The Affective Sensibility of Fandom." In *The Adoring Audience: Fan Culture and Popular Media,* edited by Lisa A. Lewis, 50–68. New York: Routledge, 1992.

Gumbrecht, Hans Ulrich, and Michael Marrinan, eds. *Mapping Benjamin: The Work of Art in the Digital Age.* Stanford: Stanford University Press, 2003.

Habermas, Jürgen. *The Theory of Communicative Action.* Translated by Thomas McCarthy. 2 vols. Boston: Beacon Press, 1984–87.

Hall, Russell. "Mary Gauthier—the Philosophy of Songwriting and Starting Late." *Goldmine* 31, no. 16 (2005): 12.

Hardt, Hanno. *Myths for the Masses.* London: Blackwell, 2004.

Hauerwas, Stanley. "The Democratic Policing of Christianity." *Pro Ecclesia* 3 (1994): 227–29.

———. "Reinhold Niebuhr's Natural Theology." In *With the Grain of the Universe: The Church's Witness and Natural Theology*. Grand Rapids: Brazos Press, 2001.

Hauerwas, Stanley, and William H. Willimon. *Resident Aliens: Life in the Christian Colony*. Nashville: Abingdon, 1989.

Hennion, Antoine. "The Production of Success: An Antimusicology of the Pop Song." In *On Record: Rock, Pop, and the Written Word*, edited by Simon Frith and Andrew Goodwin, 185–206. London: Routledge, 1990.

Hermes, Joke. "Media Figures in Identity Construction." In *Rethinking the Media Audience: The New Agenda*, edited by Pertti Alasuutari, 69–85. London: Sage, 1999.

Henry, Paget. *Caliban's Reason: Introducing Afro-Caribbean Philosophy*. New York: Routledge, 2000.

Hertig, Young Lee. *Cultural Tug of War: Korean Immigrant Family and Church in Transition*. Nashville: Abingdon Press, 2002.

Hilkert, Mary Catherine. *Naming Grace: Preaching and the Sacramental Imagination*. New York: Continuum, 2006.

Hill, Warren. "Writing: Methods and Inspiration for Songwriting." *Canadian Musician* 22 (2000): 59.

Hills, Matt. *Fan Cultures*. New York: Routledge, 2002.

———. "Fandom between Cult and Culture." In *Fan Cultures*, 117–30.

Hirschkind, Charles. *The Ethical Soundscape: Cassette Sermons and Islamic Counter-Publics*. New York: Columbia University Press, 2006.

hooks, bell. *Talking Back*. Boston: South End Press, 1989.

Hoover, Stewart. "Audiences." In *Key Words in Religion, Media, and Culture*, edited by David Morgan. New York: Routledge, 2008.

Hopewell, James F. *Congregation: Stories and Structures*. Philadelphia: Fortress, 1987.

Howard, Jay R., and John M. Streck. *Apostles of Rock: The Splintered World of Contemporary Christian Music*. Lexington: University of Kentucky Press, 1999.

Howard, Rebecca Moore. "Collaborative Pedagogy." In *A Guide to Composition Pedagogies*, edited by Gary Tate, Amy Rupiper, and Kurt Schick, 54–70. Oxford: Oxford University Press, 2000.

Howe, Jeff. "The Rise of Crowdsourcing." *Wired*, June 2006.

Hullot-Kentor, Robert. "What Is Mechanical Reproduction?" In *Mapping Benjamin: The Work of Art in the Digital Age*, edited by Hans Ulrich Gumbrecht and Michael Marrinon, 158–70. Stanford: Stanford University Press, 2003.

Hursthouse, Rosiland. *On Virtue Ethics*. Oxford: Oxford University Press, 1999.

Ihde, Don. "Auditory Imagination." In *The Auditory Culture Reader*, edited by Michael Bull and Les Back, 61–66. Oxford: Berg, 2003.

Jaynes, Julian. *The Origin of Consciousness in the Breakdown of the Bicameral Mind*. Boston: Houghton Mifflin, 1976.

Jeffries, Stuart. "A Rare Interview with Jurgen Habermas." *Financial Times*, April 30, 2010. http://www.ft.com/cms/s/0/eda3bcd8 -5327-11df-813e-00144feab49a.html. Accessed September 22, 2010.

Johns, Daniel. "Writing, Inspired by Disasters." *Canadian Musician* 25 (2003): 58.

Johnson, Randal. Introduction to Pierre Bourdieu, *The Field of Cultural Production: Essays on Art and Literature*, 1–25. New York: Columbia University Press, 1993.

Jones, W. Paul. *Theological Worlds: Understanding the Alternative Rhythms of Christian Belief*. Nashville: Abingdon, 1989.

Julian of Norwich. *Showings*. Translated by Edmund Colledge and James Walsh. New York: Paulist Press, 1978.

Kalinich, Lila J. "The Logos in Lacan." *St. Vladimir's Theological Quarterly* 32 (1988): 367–83.

Kärkkäinen, Veli-Matti. *The Trinity: Global Perspectives*. Louisville: Westminster John Knox, 2007.

Kearney, Richard. *The God Who May Be: A Hermeneutics of Religion*. Bloomington: Indiana University Press, 2001.

Kermode, Frank. *Romantic Image*. London: Routledge & Kegan Paul, 1957.

Kilde, Jeanne Halgren. *When Church Became Theatre: The Transformation of Evangelical Architecture and Worship in Nineteenth-Century America*. New York: Oxford University Press, 2002.

Kimball, Dan. *The Emerging Church: Vintage Christianity for New Generations*. Grand Rapids, Mich.: Zondervan, 2003.

Kinneavy, James L., and Catherine R. Eskin. "*Kairos* in Aristotle's Rhetoric." *Written Communication* 11 (1994): 131–42.

Knudsen, Robert. "The Transcendental Perspective of Westminster's Apologetic." *Westminster Theological Journal* 48 (1986): 223–39.

Kreitzer, Larry. *Gospel Images in Fiction and Film: On Reversing the Hermeneutical Flow*. London: Continuum, 2002.

———. *The New Testament in Fiction and Film: On Reversing the Hermeneutical Flow*. Sheffield: Sheffield Academic, 1993.

———. *The Old Testament in Fiction and Film: On Reversing the Hermeneutical Flow*. London: Continuum, 1994.

Kristeva, Julia. "Word, Dialogue and Novel." In *The Kristeva Reader*, edited by Toril Moi, 34–61. London: Blackwell, 1986.

Lakoff, George, and Mark Johnson, *Metaphors We Live By*. Chicago: University of Chicago Press, 1980.

Larkin, Colin, ed. *The Encyclopedia of Popular Music*. 5th ed. London: Muze UK, 2007.

Lauer, Janice M. *Invention in Rhetoric and Composition*. West Lafayette, Ind.: Parlor Press, 2004.

Lawson, John. *Lectures Concerning Oratory*. Trinity College, Dublin. Printed by George Faulkner in Essex Street, 1759.

Leary, Chris. "When We Remix . . . We Remake!!! Reflections on Collaborative Ethnography, the New Digital Ethic, and Test Prep." *Journal of Basic Writing* 26, no. 1 (2007): 88–104.

Leiter, Richard. "Good News for Bad Lyric Writers: K. A. Parker Gives up the Secrets to Writing Great Lyrics." *Keyboard*, November 2001, 126, 128.

Levinas, Emmanuel. *Otherwise than Being*. Translated by Alphonso Lingis. The Hague: Martinus Nijoff, 1981.

Levine, Lawrence. "Slave Songs and Slave Consciousness." In *American Negro Slavery*, edited by Alan Weinstein and Frank Gatell, 153–69. New York: Oxford University Press, 1973.

Lewis, Lisa, ed. *The Adoring Audience: Fan Culture and Popular Media*. New York: Routledge, 1992.

Littler, Jo. "Making Fame Ordinary: Intimacy, Reflexivity, and 'Keeping It Real." *Mediactive* 2 (2004): 8–25.

Loder, James E. *The Transforming Moment: Understanding Convictional Experiences*. San Francisco: Harper & Row, 1981.

Lonergan, Bernard. *Insight: A Study of Human Understanding*. Edited by Frederick E. Crowe and Robert M. Doran. Toronto: University of Toronto Press, 1957.

Lowry, Eugene. *The Homiletical Plot: The Sermon as Narrative Art Form*. Atlanta: John Knox, 1980.

Lyden, J. *Film as Religion: Myths, Morals, and Rituals*. New York: New York University Press, 2003.

Lynch, Gordon. *Understanding Theology and Popular Culture*. New York: Blackwell, 2005.

Lyon, David. *Jesus in Disneyland: Religion in Postmodern Times*. Cambridge: Polity Press, 2000.

MacIntyre, Alastair C. *After Virtue: A Study in Moral Theory*. 3rd rev. ed. London: Gerald Duckworth, 2007.

Magill, Frank N., ed. *Masterpieces of World Philosophy*. New York: Harper & Row, 1961.

Marcus, Greil. *Mystery Train: Images of America in Rock 'n' Roll Music*. 5th ed. New York: Plume, 2008.

McCarthy, John, and Peter Wright. *Technology as Experience*. Cambridge, Mass.: MIT Press, 2004.

McCartney, Andra. "Soundscape Works, Listening, and the Touch of Sound." In *Aural Cultures*, edited by Jim Drobnick, 179–88. Toronto: YYZ Books, 2004.

McClure, John S. "Collaborative Preaching from the Margins." *Journal for Preachers* 22 (Pentecost 1996): 37–42.

———. *The Four Codes of Preaching: Rhetorical Strategies*. Minneapolis: Fortress, 1991. Repr., Louisville: Westminster John Knox, 2003.

———. "In Pursuit of Good Theological Judgment: Newman and the Preacher as Theologian." In *Loving God with Our Minds: The Pastor as Theologian*, edited by Michael Welker and Cynthia A. Jarvis, 202–19. Grand Rapids, Mich.: Eerdmans, 2004.

———. "The Other Side of Sermon Illustration." *Journal for Preachers* 12 (Lent 1989): 2–4.

———. *Other-Wise Preaching: A Postmodern Ethic for Homiletics*. St. Louis: Chalice Press, 2001.

———. *The Roundtable Pulpit: Where Leadership and Preaching Meet*. Nashville: Abingdon, 1995.

McClure, John S., Ronald J. Allen, L. Susan Bond, Dan P. Moseley, and Lee G. Ramsey Jr. *Listening to Listeners: Homiletical Case Studies*. St. Louis: Chalice Press, 2004.

McClure, John S., and Nancy J. Ramsay, eds. *Telling the Truth: Preaching about Sexual and Domestic Violence*. Cleveland: United Church Press, 1998.

McLaren, Brian. *A Generous Orthodoxy*. Grand Rapids, Mich.: Zondervan, 2004.

McLuhan, Marshall. *The Gutenberg Galaxy: The Making of Typographic Man*. Toronto: University of Toronto Press, 1967.

McNally, David. *Bodies of Meaning: Studies on Language, Labor, and Liberation*. Albany: State University of New York Press, 2001.

Meyer, Birgit, and Annelies Moors, eds. *Religion, Media, and the Public Sphere*. Bloomington: Indiana University Press, 2006.

Meyer, Birgit, and Jojada Verrips. "Aesthetics." In *Key Words in Religion, Media, and Culture*, edited by David Morgan, 20–29. New York: Routledge, 2008.

Miller, Carolyn R. "*Kairos* in the Rhetoric of Science." In *A Rhetoric of Doing: Essays on Written Discourse in Honor of James Kinneavy*, edited by Stephen Witte, Neil Nakadate, and Roger Cherry, 310–27. Carbondale: Southern Illinois University Press, 1992.

Miller, Keith D., and Elizabeth A. Vander Lei. "Collaboration, Collaborative Communities, and Black Folk Culture." In *The Right to Literacy*, edited by Andrea A. Lunsford, Helene Moglen, and James Slevin, 50–60. New York: Modern Language Association of America, 1990.

Miller, Perry. *The American Puritans: Their Prose and Poetry*. New York: Doubleday Anchor Books, 1956.

Miller, Vincent J. *Consuming Religion: Christian Faith and Practice in a Consumer Culture*. New York: Continuum, 2004.

Milner, Greg. *Perfecting Sound Forever: An Aural History of Recorded Music*. London: Faber & Faber, 2009.

Minock, Mary. "Toward a Postmodern Pedagogy of Imitation." *Journal of Composition Theory* 15 (1995): 489–510.

Moltmann, Jürgen. *The Trinity and the Kingdom*. San Francisco: Harper & Row, 1981.

Morgan, David, ed. *Key Words in Religion, Media, and Culture*. New York: Routledge, 2008.

Moore, Laurence R. *Selling God: American Religion in the Marketplace of Culture*. New York: Oxford University Press, 1994.

Morone, James A. *Hellfire Nation: The Politics of Sin in American History*. New Haven: Yale University Press, 2003.

Mouw, Richard. *Consulting the Faithful: What Christian Intellectuals Can Learn from Popular Religion*. Grand Rapids, Mich.: Eerdmans, 1994.

Muers, Rachel. *Keeping God's Silence: Towards a Theological Ethics of Communication*. London: Blackwell, 2004.

Mulligan, Mary Alice, and Ronald J. Allen. *Make the Word Come Alive*. St. Louis: Chalice Press, 2005.

Mulligan, Mary Alice, Diane Turner-Sharazz, Dawn Ottoni Wilhelm, and Ronald J. Allen. *Believing in Preaching: What Listeners Hear in Sermons*. St. Louis: Chalice Press, 2005.

Muuss, Rolf E. *Theories of Adolescence*. 3rd ed. New York: Random House, 1975.

Negus, Keith. *Popular Music in Theory: An Introduction*. Middletown: Wesleyan University Press, 1996.

Nelson, Willie, with Bud Shrake. *Willie: An Autobiography*. New York: Pocket Books, 1989.

Neumann, Erich. *The Origins and History of Consciousness*. Translated by R. F. C. Hull. Princeton: Princeton University Press, 1995.

Newbigin, Lesslie. *Foolishness to the Greeks: The Gospel and Western Culture*. London: SPCK, 1986.

————. *The Other Side of 1984: Questions for the Churches*. Geneva, WCC Press, 1983.

Newman, John Henry. *An Essay in Aid of a Grammar of Assent*. London: Burns, Oates, 1870.

Niebuhr, H. Richard. *Christ and Culture*. San Francisco: Harper-SanFrancisco, 1956.

Nielsen, Greg M. *The Norms of Answerability: Social Theory between Bakhtin and Habermas*. Albany: State University of New York Press, 2002.

Ong, Walter. *Orality and Literacy: The Technologizing of the Word*. New York: Routledge, 1982.

————. *The Presence of the Word: Some Prolegomena for Cultural and Religious History*. New Haven: Yale University Press, 1967.

Ostwalt, Conrad. *Secular Steeples: Popular Culture and the Religious Imagination*. Harrisburg, Pa.: Trinity Press, 2003.

Otto, Rudolf. *The Idea of the Holy: An Inquiry into the Non-rational Factor in the Divine*. Translated by John W. Harvey. Whitefish, Mont.: Kessinger, 2004.

Pecknold, Diane. *The Selling Sound: The Rise of the Country Music Industry*. Durham: Duke University Press, 2007.

Perkins, David. "Hell Yeah! Pairing Southern Religion and Punk/ Postmodern Aesthetics in the Construction of Southern Gothic Music." Paper presented at the Forum on Music and Christian Scholarship, Yale University, March 9, 2007; revised version presented to the Popular Music and Religious Identity class at Vanderbilt Divinity School, September 16, 2008.

Pinn, Anthony. *Noise and Spirit: The Religious and Spiritual Sensibilities of Rap Music*. New York: New York University Press, 2003.

Pohl, Christine. *Making Room: Recovering Hospitality as a Christian Tradition*. Grand Rapids, Mich.: Eerdmans, 1999.

Porter, James E. "Intertextuality and the Discourse Community." *Rhetoric Review* 5 (1986): 34–47.

Powell, Mark Allan. *Encyclopedia of Contemporary Christian Music*. Peabody, Mass.: Hendrickson, 2002.

Pro Tools Reference Guide: Version 5.1 for Macintosh and Windows. Palo Alto, Calif.: Digidesign, 2001. http://akarchive.digidesign .com/support/docs/PT_51_Reference_Guide.pdf. Accessed September 8, 2009.

Redmond, Sean. "Intimate Fame Everywhere." In *Framing Celebrity: New Directions in Celebrity Culture*, edited by Sean Su Holmes and Sean Redmond, 27–43. London: Routledge, 2006.

Reid, David H. C. "Organizing Material." In *Best Advice for Preaching*, edited by John S. McClure, 65–84. Minneapolis: Fortress, 1998.

Rice, Jeff. "The 1963 Hip-Hop Machine: Hip-Hop Pedagogy as Composition." *College Composition and Communication* 54 (2003): 453–71.

Richardson, Derek. "The Soul of the Song." *Acoustic Guitar*, December 2006, 55.

Rodgers, Jeffrey Pepper. "Ring Some Changes." *Acoustic Guitar*, May 2006, 74.

Rosenberg, Bruce A. *The Art of the American Folk Preacher*. New York: Oxford University Press, 1970.

Russell, Letty M. *Just Hospitality: God's Welcome in a World of Difference*. Edited by J. Shannon Clarkson and Kate M. Ott. Louisville: Westminster John Knox, 2009.

Russell, Tom, and Sylvia Tyson, eds. *And Then I Wrote: The Songwriter Speaks*. Vancouver, Canada: Arsenal Pulp Press, 1995.

Sadler, Rodney S., Jr. "Can the Cushite Change His Skin? Cushites, 'Radical Othering,' and the Hebrew Bible." *Interpretation* 60 (2006): 386–403.

Safranski, Rüdiger, and Ewald Osers. *Schopenhauer and the Wild Years of Philosophy*. Cambridge, Mass.: Harvard University Press, 1991.

Salzburg, Steve. "Carole King." In *Off the Record: Songwriters on Songwriting*, by Graham Nash, 137 (Kansas City, Mo.: Manuscript Originals, 2002).

Sandywell, Barry, and David Beer. "Stylistic Morphing: Notes on the Digitisation of Contemporary Music Culture." *Convergence* 11, no. 4 (2005): 106–21.

Saussure, Ferdinand de. *Course in General Linguistics*. Edited by Charles Bally and Albert Sechehaye. Translated by W. Baskin. London: Peter Owen, 1974.

Scaggs, Austin. "Q & A: John Mellencamp." *Rolling Stone*, February 8, 2007, 28.

Schmidt, Leigh Eric. *Hearing Things: Religion, Illusion, and the American Enlightenment*. Cambridge, Mass.: Harvard University Press, 2000.

Schmidt, Siegfried J. "From Aura-Loss to Cyberspace: Further Thoughts on Walter Benjamin." In *Mapping Benjamin: The Work of Art in the Digital Age*, edited by Hans Ulrich Gumbrecht and Michael Marrinan, 79–82. Stanford: Stanford University Press, 2003.

Schulz, Dorothea E. "Soundscape." In *Key Words in Religion, Media, and Culture*, edited by David Morgan, 172–86. New York: Routledge, 2008.

Schwartz, Hillel. "The Indefensible Ear: A History." In *The Auditory Culture Reader*, edited by Michael Bull and Les Back, 487–501. Oxford: Berg, 2003.

Sennett, Richard, and Jonathan Cobb. *The Hidden Injuries of Class*. Cambridge: Cambridge University Press, 1972.

Serna, Adrianne. "Letting It Rip: Patty Griffin." *Acoustic Guitar*, September 2007, 58–65.

Shafer, R. Murray. *The Tuning of the World*. New York: Random House, 1977.

Sharp, Ken. "Smokey Robinson: More Love." *Goldmine* 34 (May 23, 2008): 42–44, 46–47.

Sheff, David. "All We Are Saying: The Last Major Interview with John Lennon and Yoko Ono." *Playboy*, January 1981. http://www.john-lennon.com/playboyinterviewwithjohnlennon andyokoono.htm. Accessed October 6, 2009.

Shiga, John. "Copy-and-Persist: The Logic of Mash-up Culture." *Critical Studies in Media Communication* 24 (2007): 93–114.

Silverstone, Roger. *Media and Morality: On the Rise of the Mediapolis*. Cambridge: Polity Press, 2006.

Simos, Mark. "The New Weird America: Songwriting In and Out of a Tradition." *Sing Out!* 46 (2002): 86–87.

Slater, Don. *Consumer Culture and Modernity*. Cambridge: Polity Press, 2005.

Smith, James K. A. *Who's Afraid of Postmodernism? Taking Derrida, Lyotard, and Foucault to Church*. Grand Rapids, Mich.: Baker Academic, 2006.

Smith, Ted A. *The New Measures: A Theological History of Democratic Practice*. New York: Cambridge University Press, 2007.

Smithers, Chris. "The King of California (Dave Alvin)." *Acoustic Guitar*, May 2007, 59, 61–65.

Smitherman, Geneva. *Talkin and Testifyin: The Language of Black America*. Detroit: Wayne State University Press; Boston: Houghton Mifflin, 1977.

Šoštarić, Sanja. *Coleridge and Emerson: A Complex Affinity*. Boca Raton, Fla.: Universal, 2003.

Stackhouse, John Gordon. *Making the Best of It: Following Christ in the Real World*. Oxford: Oxford University Press, 2008.

Steiner, George. *In Bluebeard's Castle: Some Notes towards the Redefinition of Culture*. New Haven: Yale University Press, 1974.

Stern, Richard, Clayton Jefford, and Guerric Debona. *Savior on the Silver Screen*. Mahwah, N.J.: Paulist Press, 1999.

Stewart, Charles, ed. *Creolization: History, Ethnography, Theory*. Walnut Creek, Calif.: Left Coast Press, 2007.

Stillman, Peter R. *Introduction to Myth*. 2nd ed. Upper Montclair, N.J.: Boynton/Cook, 1985.

Stolow, Jeremy. "Technology." In *Key Words in Religion, Media, and Culture*, edited by David Morgan, 187–97. New York: Routledge, 2008.

Suchocki, Marjorie. *God, Christ, Church*. New rev. ed. New York: Crossroads, 1989.

———. *The Whispered Word: A Theology of Preaching*. St. Louis: Chalice Press, 1999.

Swenson, Kyle. "Sarah McLachlan: Tale of the Mastery Builder." *Keyboard* 23 (1997): 36–39, 41, 43.

Sylvan, Robin. *Traces of the Spirit: The Religious Dimensions of Popular Music*. New York: New York University Press, 2002.

Székely, David. "Gesture, Pulsion, Grain: Barthes' Musical Semiology." *Contemporary Aesthetics* (December 18, 2006). http://www .contempaesthetics.org/newvolume/pages/article.php?articleID =409. Accessed September 29, 2009.

Tankel, Jonathan David. "The Practice of Recording Music: Remixing as Recoding." *Journal of Communication* 40 (1990): 34–46.

Taylor, Charles. *The Ethics of Authenticity*. Cambridge, Mass.: Harvard University Press, 1991.

Thompson, Clive. "Live in the Moment: As a New Generation of Search Engines Mine the Signals of the Here and Now, Google Remains Stuck in the Past." *Wired*, October 2009, 46.

Tichi, Cecelia, ed. *Reading Country Music: Steel Guitars, Opry Stars, and Honky-Tonk Bars*. Durham: Duke University Press, 1998.

Tilley, Terrence W. "Toward a Theology of the Practice of Communicative Action." In *Postmodern Theologies: The Challenge of Religious Diversity*, edited by Terrence W. Tilley, 5–16. Maryknoll, N.Y.: Orbis Books, 1995.

Tillich, Paul. *The Courage to Be*. New Haven: Yale University Press, 1952.

———. *The Dynamics of Faith*. New York: Harper & Row, 1956.

———. *Systematic Theology*. Vol. 1. Chicago: University of Chicago Press, 1967.

Tomlinson, Dave. *The Post Evangelical*. Grand Rapids, Mich.: Zondervan, 2003.

Toulmin, Stephen. *The Uses of Argument*. Cambridge: Cambridge University Press, 1958.

Tulloch, John, and Henry Jenkins. *Science Fiction Audiences: Watching "Dr. Who" and "Star Trek."* London: Routledge, 1995.

Turino, Thomas. *Music as Social Self: The Politics of Participation*. Chicago: University of Chicago Press, 2008.

Ulmer, Gregory L. *Heuretics: The Logic of Invention*. Baltimore: The Johns Hopkins University Press, 1994.

Unwin, Timothy A., ed. *The Cambridge Companion to Flaubert*. Cambridge: Cambridge University Press, 2004.

Vande Berg, Leah R. "Living Room Pilgrimages: Television's Cyclical Commemoration of the Assassination Anniversary of John F. Kennedy." *Communication Monographs* 62 (1995): 47–64.

Vanhoozer, Kevin J., Charles A. Anderson, and Michael J. Sleasman, eds. *Everyday Theology: How to Read Cultural Texts and Interpret Trends*. Grand Rapids, Mich.: Baker Academic, 2007.

Vattimo, Gianni. *After Christianity*. Translated by Luca D'Isanto. New York: Columbia University Press, 2002.

Vicentino, Nicola. *Ancient Music Adapted to Modern Practice*. Edited by Claude V. Palisca. Translated by Maria Rika Maniates. New Haven: Yale University Press, 1996.

Vitanza, Victor J. "From Heuristic to Aleatory Procedures: Or Toward 'Writing the Accident.'" In *Inventing a Discipline: Rhetoric Scholarship in Honor of Richard E. Young*, edited by Maureen Daly Goggin, 185–206. Urbana, Ill.: National Council of Teachers of English, 2000.

Volosinov, V. N. *Marxism and the Philosophy of Language*. Translated by Ladislav Matejka and J. R. Titunik. Cambridge, Mass.: Harvard University Press, 1929.

Wagner, R. "Bewitching the Box Office: Harry Potter and Religious Controversy." *Journal of Religion and Film* 7, no. 2. http://www.unomaha.edu/jrf/Vol7No2/bewitching.htm 7/17/09.

Ward, Pete. *Growing up Evangelical: Youthwork and the Making of a Subculture*. London: SPCK, 1996.

_____. *Liquid Church*. Peabody, Mass.: Hendrickson, 2002.

_____. *Mass Culture: Eucharist and Mission in a Post-Modern World*. London: Bible Reading Fellowship, 1999.

_____. *Selling Worship: How What We Sing Has Changed the Church*. Bletchley: Paternoster Press, 2005.

Waters, Lindsay. "The Cameraman and Machine Are Now One: Walter Benjamin's Frankenstein." In *Mapping Benjamin: The Work of Art in the Digital Age*, edited by Hans Ulrich Gumbrecht and Michael Merrinan, 133–41. Stanford: Stanford University Press, 2003.

Webb, Jimmy. *Tunesmith: Inside the Art of Songwriting*. New York: Hyperion Books, 1998.

Welsch, Wolfgang. *Undoing Aesthetics*. Translated by Andrew Inkpin. London: Sage, 1997.

Whitehead, Alfred North. *The Aims of Education*. New York: Free Press, 1967.

Whorf, Benjamin Lee. "A Linguistic Consideration of Thinking in Primitive Communities." In *Language, Thought, and Reality: Selected Writings of Benjamin Lee Whorf*, edited by John B. Carroll, 65–86. Cambridge, Mass.: MIT Press, 1973.

Wilder, Eliot. *DJ Shadow's Endtroducing*. New York: Continuum, 2008.

Willimon, William H. *The Intrusive Word: Preaching to the Unbaptized*. Grand Rapids, Mich.: Eerdmans, 1994.

———. *Peculiar Speech: Preaching to the Baptized*. Grand Rapids, Mich.: Eerdmans, 1992.

Wilson, Charles Reagan. *Judgment and Grace in Dixie: Southern Faiths from Faulkner to Elvis*. Athens: University of Georgia Press, 1995.

Wilson, Tom. "We're Talking about Communication, We're Not Talking about Self-Indulgence, Part II." *Canadian Musician* 24 (2002): 58.

Wink, Walter. "The Myth of Redemptive Violence: Exposing the Roots of 'Might Makes Right.'" *Sojourners* 21 (1992): 18–21, 35.

Winquist, Charles E. *Epiphanies of Darkness: Deconstruction in Theology*. Philadelphia: Fortress, 1986.

Wittgenstein, Ludwig. *Philosophical Investigations*. Translated by G. E. M. Anscombe. New York: Macmillan, 1973.

Wordsworth, William. *The Poems of William Wordsworth*. Edited by Nowell Charles Smith. New York: Methuen, 1908.

Yoder, John Howard. "How H. Richard Niebuhr Reasoned: A Critique of *Christ and Culture*." In *Authentic Transformation: A New Vision of Christ and Culture*, edited by Glenn H. Stassen, D. M. Yeager, and John Howard Yoder, 31–89. Nashville: Abingdon, 1996.

Yong, Amos. *Hospitality and the Other: Pentecost, Christian Practices, and the Neighbor*. Maryknoll, N.Y.: Orbis Press, 2008.

Zollo, Paul. *Songwriters on Songwriting*. Expanded 4th ed. Cambridge, Mass.: Da Capo, 2003.

INDEX OF SONGWRITERS, COMPOSERS, MUSICIANS, AND BANDS

INDEX OF NAMES

INDEX OF TOPICS